HARVARD STUDIES IN MONOPOLY AND COMPETITION

1. CORPORATE SIZE AND EARNING POWER
William Leonard Crum

2. THE CONTROL OF COMPETITION IN CANADA
Lloyd G. Reynolds

HARVARD STUDIES IN
MONOPOLY AND COMPETITION

LONDON : HUMPHREY MILFORD
OXFORD UNIVERSITY PRESS

THE CONTROL OF COMPETITION IN CANADA

BY

LLOYD G. REYNOLDS

ASSOCIATE IN POLITICAL ECONOMY IN JOHNS HOPKINS UNIVERSITY

CAMBRIDGE, MASSACHUSETTS
HARVARD UNIVERSITY PRESS
1940

PRINTED AT THE HARVARD UNIVERSITY PRESS
CAMBRIDGE, MASSACHUSETTS, U.S.A.

To

MY MOTHER AND FATHER

EDITOR'S NOTE

THIS IS THE SECOND of a series of monographs on selected aspects of the general problem of monopoly and competition, reporting specific studies in the research program of a special committee of the Harvard Department of Economics. The investigation leading to the present monograph was financed in part by a grant from the A. W. Shaw Fund and the Harvard Committee on Research in the Social Sciences.

A third volume, by John P. Miller, entitled "Unfair Competition" will appear shortly.

EDWARD S. MASON

PREFACE

THE PROBLEMS DISCUSSED HEREIN arise in similar form in all industrial countries. The root of these problems is the domination of many industries by a small number of producers, who endeavor to regulate prices and production in their own interest. Their interest, however, is ordinarily different from the interest of consumers, and their operations are therefore unlikely to achieve maximum efficiency in the sense of the greatest possible contribution to economic welfare. It is not possible with the imperfect data now available to measure the amount by which a given industry falls short of perfect efficiency. It should be possible, however, to discover the main types of inefficiency which exist in any economic system, and to say something about their relative importance. The main requisite for this task is some norm from which divergences can be detected, some standard of what constitutes desirable performance for a particular industry or an economic system. The first half of this study attempts to appraise the efficiency of Canadian industry by the use of norms developed in recent years by economic theorists.

When the sources of industrial inefficiency have been explored, there remains the practical problem of how to deal with them. To what extent can they be reduced by government action, and what sort of action is indicated? The policies adopted by European and American governments in this field fall into a few general patterns: control of natural monopolies, preservation of competition, regulation of trade practices, publicly-supervised price and production agreements, public ownership and operation of industry. While these may be viewed as alternative lines of action, they are also to a considerable extent supplementary to each other. Any effective program for economic efficiency must probably make simultaneous use of several of these policies. But what sort of results may each be expected to produce, and within what limits? How decide which industries should be treated in one way, which in another? The last half of the study endeavors to throw some light on these questions by examining Canadian experience in industrial regulation.

The object of the study has not been to describe uniquely Canadian phenomena, but rather to inquire what light Canadian experience sheds on the general problems outlined above. An effort has been made throughout to frame hypotheses which may prove useful to students of industrial organization in other countries. It is hoped that the results obtained may prove particularly useful to students of these problems in the United States because of the very similar industrial structure of the two countries. In many Canadian industries, indeed, the leading producers are owned by or affiliated with United States concerns. This is true of automobiles, tires, gasoline, tobacco, rayon, aluminum and a long list of other products. The problem of controlled prices is somewhat more acute in Canada, because the relative smallness of the Canadian market makes it easier for a few large firms to acquire a dominant position, and because Canada has been even more tolerant of price agreement than has the United States. In both countries, however, price agreement is commoner than is ordinarily supposed, and gives rise to similar problems.

The legislation designed to deal with these problems also presents many similarities. The Combines Investigation Act is comparable to the Sherman Act both in its intent and in its application by the courts. The achievements and failures of the Combines Act provide a good indication of the results which may be expected from simple prohibition of price control. Again, the provincial milk control acts, resale price maintenance acts, and others laws restricting competition are very similar to state legislation in this country. The movement for government-supervised price-fixing schemes in Canada has drawn much of its inspiration from the similar movement in the United States. The enactment of the National Industrial Recovery Act, in particular, greatly stimulated the demand for similar legislation in Canada. While this movement proved abortive on a national scale, several provinces now have codes of fair competition for selected industries. Another severe decline in business activity might be expected to produce a renewed demand in both countries for price-fixing on a national scale.

These considerations are sufficient to explain the structure of the book. The first five chapters describe the techniques used by business groups to control prices and production, and explore some of the economic consequences of this control. The last half of the volume is concerned with Canadian legislation bearing on competition. When the statutes are set side by side, their contradictory character at once becomes apparent. There has been no consistent Canadian policy toward competition, nor has there been any determined and informed attempt to meet the problems discussed in the first five chapters. In general, Canadian governments have tended to foster private enterprise by giving business men what they want. Since business men usually want to restrict competition, the trend of the legislation has been in this direction, and this trend has been greatly intensified during the past decade. The title of the book is intended to suggest that much more effort — public and private — has been spent in curbing competition than in preventing combination.

The attempt to make each group of producers rich at the expense of the rest is not a policy likely to promote the general welfare. It seems a simple matter to demonstrate this and to draft counter-proposals designed to curb particular groups in the public interest. The general interest, however, is nobody's interest, and such proposals are slow to find political support.

The legislative reforms suggested in the final chapter are included, not because the writer has any expectation of their enactment in the near future, but because it is hoped that discussion of them may serve an educational purpose.

In an attempt to keep the volume concise and readable, the treatment of each topic has been abbreviated as much as possible. The impressionistic picture thus created is sufficiently accurate for most purposes. The careful student, however, will wish to read the original sources, which consist mainly of the hearings and reports of Royal Commissions and similar investigatory bodies. Technical language has been avoided because of a belief that the central problems of economics can be stated simply, and that unless they are so stated the subject will fall increasingly into disrepute. Except for small portions of Chapters III and IV, the general reader should encounter no difficulties, while the student can readily translate the arguments presented into theoretical terms.

The list of those in the Dominion and Provincial services who furnished information for the study is too long to be enumerated here. Mr. F. A. McGregor, Commissioner of the Combines Investigation Act, and the members of his staff were particularly helpful. Dr. J. M. Cassels of the Institute for Consumer Education first suggested the study, collaborated with me in its early stages, and criticized the final product. Professors E. S. Mason and D. H. Wallace of Harvard University and Professor V. W. Bladen of the University of Toronto read the entire manuscript and made many valuable suggestions. Professor F. R. Scott of McGill University made helpful comments on Chapters VI and IX. I am happy to express my indebtedness and gratitude to these and to the many others who contributed in some measure to the volume.

L. G. R.

Cambridge, Massachusetts
August, 1939

CONTENTS

THE CONTROL OF COMPETITION IN CANADA

We command that no one may presume to exercise a monopoly of any kind of clothing, or of fish, or of any other thing serving for food, or for any other use . . . nor may any persons combine or agree in unlawful meetings, that different kinds of merchandise may not be sold at a less price than they have agreed upon among themselves. Workmen and contractors for buildings, and all who practice other professions, and contractors for baths, are entirely prohibited from agreeing together . . . and if any one shall presume to practice a monopoly, let his property be forfeited and himself condemned to perpetual exile.

Edict issued by the Emperor Zeno to the Praetorian Prefect of Constantinople, A.D. 483. Translation of A. H. Marsh, Q.C., in 8 *Canadian Law Times* 299.

People of the same trade seldom meet together, even for merriment and diversion, but the conversation ends in a conspiracy against the public, or in some contrivance to raise prices. It is impossible indeed to prevent such meetings, by any law which either could be executed, or would be consistent with liberty and justice. But though the law cannot hinder people of the same trade from sometimes assembling together, it ought to do nothing to facilitate such assemblies, much less to render them necessary.

Adam Smith, *The Wealth of Nations*, Book I, Chapter X.

I

PRIVATE CONTROL OF COMPETITION: MANUFACTURING

MOST DEFENSES OF PRIVATE ENTERPRISE assume that the existing system is competitive, and that competition leads necessarily to efficiency. The first part of this book is essentially an inquiry into the adequacy of these assumptions. This is evidently a matter of the highest importance, for if either assumption should prove unsound the efficiency of the system is open to serious question.

Concerning the existence of competition there is at present a wide divergence of opinion. Some writers appear to regard Canadian industry as predominantly competitive, while others assert with equal force that most industries are ruled by monopolies. This difference of opinion is due partly to the secrecy of business operations, partly to the lack of organized inquiry into the subject. During the past decade, however, information accumulated by governmental investigations has been steadily clarifying the structure of the Canadian economy. The time has now come when one can appeal to the facts with some hope of an answer.

The issue has been confused, too, by a loose use of words. In popular speech, "competition" commonly refers to any sort of rivalry among producers. This usage is unfortunate, for the economic effects of rivalry in price may be quite different from the effects of rivalry in advertising, delivery, or other services. The classical economists seem to have had in mind primarily rivalry in price, and this usage will be followed here. In an unplanned economy, prices are the main regulators of economic action, and the extent to which they are free or controlled is of decisive importance. The presence or absence of competition in any industry, then, will be determined by the following test: does each producer decide independently on his selling price, or is the price set by some type of agreement among producers?

"Monopoly" will also be used in the strict sense of control by a single seller of the entire supply of a product for which close substitutes are not available. It is apparent at once that many manufacturing industries cannot be classified as either monopolistic or competitive. In many industries there are several producers who attempt to win business from each other by advertising and other methods, but who agree to observe a fixed price. This must be recognized as a third distinct case, probably more common in practice than either monopoly or competition.[1]

The most striking fact about Canadian manufacturing is the fewness of producers in most fields. In most industries there are not more than ten important producers, and in many there are only three or four [Table 1]. Several factors help to account for this high concentration of output. With a population smaller than that of New York state, Canada offers a relatively small domestic market. In industries which can operate efficiently only on a large scale, a few plants are sufficient to supply the country's needs.[2] This limited market, moreover, is divided by

[1] Industries may also be classified on the basis of the standardized or differentiated character of the product, and according to the number of producers. The common — almost universal — situation in Canadian industry is that of a few producers selling a differentiated product. In Chamberlinian terms, the general situation is one of monopolistic competition with few sellers. See E. H. Chamberlin, *Theory of Monopolistic Competition*, Cambridge, 1933. The important *practical* distinction, then, appears to be between those industries in which the few producers agree on prices and those in which they do not.

[2] In some cases the Canadian market is so small that it does not pay to produce the article at all. The iron and steel companies, for example, have decided against the production of many specialized products on this ground.

TABLE 1

CONTROL OF OUTPUT IN SELECTED MANUFACTURING INDUSTRIES *

Industry	Cumulative percentage of output controlled by:				
	1 Firm	2 Firms	3 Firms	4 Firms	5 Firms
Automobiles	40	65	89	..	..
Ammunition, explosives, ammonia, chlorine	100	..	..	..	..
Agricultural implements	..	..	..	75	..
Brewing (Ontario and Quebec)	..	60	..	..	..
Cement	90	..	..	..	..
Copper	53	..	..	93	..
Canning (fruit and vegetable)	67	83	..	..	..
Cotton yarn and cloth	48	..	79	..	..
Electrical equipment (heavy)	..	..	100	..	..
Fertilizer	..	..	70	..	..
Lead	91	..	..	..	..
Meat Packing	59	85	..	..	..
Milling	..	..	..	..	73
Nickel	71	..	..	..	..
Oil	55	..	..	..	..
Pulp and paper	..	..	..	..	90
Rubber footwear	39	50	61	72	..
Silks (real)	23	42	61	..	..
Silk (artificial)	66	100	..	..	..
Sugar	..	..	..	..	100
Tires	..	..	..	..	65
Tobacco	70	90	..	..	..
Zinc	74	..	..	..	..

* The material for this Table was obtained from evidence before the Price Spreads Commission, from the Report of the Commission, from investigations under the Combines Act, from financial journals, and from *Social Planning for Canada*, Toronto, Thomas Nelson and Sons, 1935. The figures refer to volume of output or of sales in a given year. Most of the figures relate to 1933, though a few relate to 1934 or 1935. The Table may thus be taken as a cross-section of the situation in the middle thirties.

topographical barriers into four distinct regions: the Pacific coast, the prairies, central Canada, and the maritime provinces.

See Advisory Board on Tariff and Taxation, Hearing of December 3–11, 1929, pp. 22, 36.

Even though an article is produced in Canada by ten or fifteen companies, it may be sold in a particular region by only one or two companies. The chemical, iron and steel, gasoline and brewing industries provide particularly good illustrations.

The fact that certain types of ore occur in only a few areas has helped to limit the number of metal producers. The most striking example is the complete concentration of nickel mining in the Sudbury district. Copper production is also concentrated in Ontario, lead and zinc mining in British Columbia, asbestos mining in Quebec.

The number of firms in each industry has been further reduced through consolidations. The great majority of these took place during the years 1909–12 and 1925–30.[3] The years 1909–12 were marked particularly by mergers in the heavy industries. Canada Cement, Amalgamated Asbestos, Canadian Car and Foundry, Dominion Steel Corporation, and Steel Company of Canada date from this period. Important textile, tobacco, brewing, milling, and paper combinations were also formed, however, and nearly every industry in the country was affected. During the late twenties important consolidations took place in the pulp and paper, milling, baking, brewing and distilling, packing, canning, chemical and dairy industries. Once more nearly every important industry of the country was affected, and still larger combinations were being planned when the depression brought the movement to an end. Evidence is presented below that the dominant motives in these consolidations were the desire for price control and for promoters' profits.

The extension of many large United States producers into Canada, finally, has operated as a check on competition. Perhaps the most notable examples are Imperial Oil (formed in

[3] Out of a total of 374 consolidations between 1900 and 1933, 58 occurred during 1909–12 and 231 during 1925–30. Report of the Royal Commission on Price Spreads, 1935 (referred to hereafter as the Price Spreads Report), p. 28.

1880 as a Standard Oil subsidiary) and Imperial Tobacco (incorporated in 1895 as the American Tobacco Company of Canada). While the parent concerns were being prosecuted and dissolved under the Sherman Act, their Canadian offspring led an untroubled life and still dominate their respective industries. Canadian Celanese, Canadian Westinghouse, Canadian General Electric, Aluminium Limited, International Harvester, the "big three" automobile companies and the "big four" tire producers occupy the same dominant position in Canada that their parent companies enjoy in the United States.

Concentration of output in a few hands is often regarded as synonymous with price control. It is true that where producers are few agreement on prices is to be expected. Under certain conditions, however, three or four producers may compete vigorously for many years. The presence or absence of competition in an industry can be determined only by a careful examination of the available evidence. This evidence is often so fragmentary and unreliable that it is difficult to determine in which class a given industry belongs. The classification of industries presented below [Table 2], while based on the best information now available, may contain some errors. Moreover, since the situation in each industry is subject to change, the classification will already be out of date when this book appears. Information is not available concerning some industries, notably automobile production, but the classification does account for about four-fifths of the net value-product of Canadian manufacturing.

MONOPOLY

The situation in most of these industries is so well known as to require no comment. Courtauld's (Canada) Ltd. is the sole producer of rayon (viscose) yarns, while cellulose acetate yarns are produced only by Canadian Celanese. Canada Cement produces nearly all of the cement output. Canadian

Industries Limited produces all of the ammunition and explosives. The refining and manufacturing of aluminum is confined

TABLE 2

CLASSIFICATION OF CANADIAN MANUFACTURING INDUSTRIES

	Price agreement	
Monopoly	Informal	Formal
Aluminum	Agricultural Implements	Fertilizers
Cement	Brewing	Leather
Electrical equipment, heavy	Copper	Rubber footwear
Explosives	Cotton cloth, yarn and thread	Tobacco products
Lead	Gasoline	Most paper products (except newsprint)
Nickel	Sugar	Most plumbing and heating equipment
Rayon yarn	Some iron and steel products	Many hardware products
Steel rails	Some textile products	
Some chemicals	Some canned foods	
Some iron and steel products		
Some non-ferrous metal products		

Competition	
Few producers	Many producers
Flour	Bread
Meat packing	Boots and shoes
Newsprint	Clothing
Silk cloth	Furniture
Silk hosiery	Jam
Tires	
Woolen and worsted yarn and cloth	

to Aluminium Limited. All of the nickel used in Canada is refined by the International Nickel Company. Falconbridge Nickel, formed in 1930, sells only in the European market, where it has obtained a foothold by shading International Nickel's prices.[4] Sales of lead and zinc are controlled by Consolidated Mining and Smelting.

[4] Nickel prices on this continent have never been competitive except

In the chemical industry, because of specialization by products and regions, monopoly is more extensive than appears on the surface. Twelve companies produce acids, alkalies and salts. Canadian Industries Limited, however, is the only producer in Eastern Canada of ammonia, chlorine, hydrochloric acid, sodium sulphate, and caustic soda. Shawinigan Chemicals has a monopoly of calcium carbide, American Cyanamide produces all the calcium cyanamide and sodium cyanide, and so on.[5] The production of heavy electrical equipment is similarly divided among the five leading firms in the industry. Bell Telephone and its affiliate, Northern Electric, produce all of the telephone equipment, the Marconi Company has a monopoly of equipment for wireless telegraphy, while power generating equipment is produced by General Electric and Westinghouse. Anaconda American Brass is the only producer in Canada of brass, copper and nickel silver in bars, rods, sheets, slates and tubing.

The multiplicity of iron and steel products makes it impossible to classify this industry under any one head. Most of the major products would probably fall either under "monopoly" or under "price agreement," but to draw the dividing line correctly would require a careful study of individual products.[6] The three producers of primary products are Dominion Steel and Coal at Sydney, Steel Company of Canada at Hamilton,

---

during the years 1918–20 in which Mond Nickel was invading the American market. Harmony was restored during the twenties, however, and in 1928 Mond sold out to International Nickel. Falconbridge Nickel, the only other producer in Canada, has never sold on this continent. W. Y. Elliott, ed. *International Control in the Non-Ferrous Metals*, New York, 1937, pp. 145–150.

[5] Dominion Bureau of Statistics, Mining, Metallurgical and Chemical Branch: Chemicals and Allied Products in Canada, 1933, p. 55.

[6] See Advisory Board on Tariff and Taxation, Record of Public Sittings, Reference No. 2 (Iron and Steel Industry), 1929. These hearings are a valuable source as regards both the structure of the industry and the history of public policy.

and Algoma Steel at Sault Ste. Marie. Dominion Steel produces for sale coal, pig iron, ingots, billets, rods, bars, wire nails and staples, and rails (most of which are exported). Steel of Canada ordinarily uses all of its limited pig iron production and turns out a wide variety of finished steel products. Algoma sells pig iron, ingots, billets and rails. Algoma's location gives it a preferential position in the area between the Soo and the Rocky Mountains, while Dominion Steel enjoys a similar position from Sydney to Montreal. In Ontario the situation appears to be one of price agreement among the three producers, with a certain amount of competition for large orders.

It is likely that many finished steel products are monopolized. Evidence is available, however, only in the case of rails (Algoma), tubes (Page-Hersey Tubes), and automobile parts. Several automobile parts makers, including Kelsey Wheel (wheels, hubs and drums) and Holmes Foundry (cylinder blocks), have no competitors in Canada. There do not appear to be more than ten makers of any automobile part, and the usual number is three or four.[7] Ford and General Motors follow the policy of buying from different parts makers whenever possible, and the number of supply sources for each company is thus still further restricted. A study of bargaining between parts makers and auto companies, and between steel companies and the railroads, would shed considerable light on the operation of bilateral monopoly.

Hundreds of miscellaneous articles are produced by only one company in Canada. These are overlooked in most discussions of monopoly because of their smallness or because, being producers' goods, their origin is of interest only to the purchasing agents of other companies.

[7] Tariff Board of Canada, Report on the Automotive Industry, 1935.

PRICE AGREEMENT

It has already been pointed out that most manufactured goods are produced by only a few companies. Where this is the case the actions of each producer are closely watched by its rivals. Each firm knows that a price cut will be matched very quickly by other producers, and that it can gain only a temporary advantage in this way. The futility of price cutting and the advantages of price stability thus become apparent to all. This will not lead necessarily to a formal price agreement. Prices may be supported quite as effectively by an unwritten law against price cutting. In many industries the relations between producers are similar to those between friendly nations. There is a strong desire to avoid doing anything which might be interpreted by other companies as a "hostile" act, or which might disturb existing market relations. Courtesy requires that other producers be notified in advance of important changes of policy and that policies which offend other concerns be withdrawn or modified.[8] While there is a legal distinction between mere friendliness and a written price agreement, the economic effects of the two may be precisely the same.

Anyone who reads through the investigations of the past decade must be impressed with the extent to which competition has been attenuated throughout Canadian industry. Price agreements have been formed at one time or another in nearly every industry listed in Table 2. The chief difference between the "price agreement" and "competition" groups is that in the former the agreements have been well observed, while in the lat-

[8] See, for example, the Exhibits presented to the Royal Commission on Textiles, 1936. These Exhibits are filled with letters of the following type: "Dear Tom: Here are our price lists for the spring season on such-and-such items. What do you think of them, and what are you planning to do? Best wishes, Joe." Tom then writes back, "Dear Joe: Your prices look about right to us, and we are planning to announce the same." This, surely, is the language of colleagues rather than of competitors.

ter they have broken down. The reasons for the failure of certain industries to achieve control of prices are considered in the next section.

The price-agreement group divides itself readily into two sub-groups. Where the firms involved are few, large and responsible, little control machinery is needed and agreements are extremely informal. In some cases there is tacit agreement to follow the prices of a single (usually the largest) producer. In other cases simple exchange of price lists and occasional letters or conversations prove sufficient. Where producers are smaller, more numerous and more difficult to control, the trade association form of organization has commonly been used. This usually involves paid officers, regular reports and conferences, a rather elaborate written agreement, and prescribed penalties for breach of the agreement. It will be convenient to consider first the informal agreements, which cover the more important products, and then to describe the methods of the trade associations.

The Imperial Oil Company for many years refined nearly all of the gasoline sold in Canada. Its percentage of the total output has declined in recent years, falling from 79 per cent in 1921 to 55 per cent in 1932, but its tank-wagon price is still accepted by the other oil companies.[9] In addition, the compa-

[9] Clear evidence of this was obtained in 1932 by the Standing Committee on Banking and Commerce of the House of Commons. Mr. Victor Ross, Vice-President of Imperial Oil, testified as follows: "*Q.* Why is it that all the oil companies throughout the Dominion charge exactly the same price from place to place? *A.* Well, they cannot very profitably sell under our prices. They cannot get business by selling over our prices.

"*Q.* They fix their prices on yours? *A.* Generally. They are getting much bigger. . . . I have not the slightest doubt some day the time will arrive when some of those other companies will be doing the price fixing." Minutes of Proceedings and Evidence, p. 23.

A special investigator appointed by the Province of Ontario in 1925 came to the same conclusion: "It was frankly stated by officers of the other companies that, inasmuch as the Imperial Oil Company Ltd. holds a

nies endeavor to protect the tank-wagon price by maintaining a fixed retail price. Two main control techniques are used: (1) Dealers are given a special discount if they will contract to buy gasoline from only one company, and the great majority have now become "100 per cent accounts." The contract between the company and the dealer usually provides that the company may set the retail price and that supplies may be withheld from the dealer if he sells below this price.[10] (2) "Independent" dealers are controlled by a tacit agreement among the companies to withhold supplies from price cutters. There is evidence that executives of the larger companies meet fairly regularly to discuss prices and methods of "cleaning up the market" in areas where price cutting has developed.[11]

The Imperial Tobacco Company, which produces about three-quarters of all tobacco products, controls prices in that industry. While cigarette prices in the United States vary considerably, some ninety-five per cent of Canadian cigarettes

---

predominant position in the trade in Canada, it has been and is their custom to follow prices set by it from time to time. Such a course was upheld by them on the ground that it is a common trade practice for the largest producer in any line of business to set prices and other dealers to follow him." Report of G. T. Clarkson to the Government of Ontario, January 11, 1926. Quoted in Evidence of the 1932 investigation at p. 37 *et seq.*

[10] British Columbia, Report of the Royal Commission on Coal and Petroleum Products, 1936, p. 74.

[11] Mr. C. E. Thompson, manager of the Independent Gasoline Company, a Vancouver wholesaler, testified as follows: "The meeting was called to maintain the price, that we would agree to sell at the posted price of 30 cents and . . . if any distributor sold to a station operator and that station operator cut the price, the supplier was to discontinue the supply and other companies were not to supply during the time that he was being disciplined. *Q.* By what method were the other companies to know that he was being disciplined? *A.* They were to inform the Retail Merchants Association, who in turn would notify the other companies." Mr. Thompson testified further that he was reluctant to enter the agreement, but "Our suppliers told us in Seattle that they had been approached to discontinue our supply . . . if we did not conform to the regulations here." *Ibid.*, p. 75.

are sold at a standard price of twenty cents per package of twenty. Prices are maintained through an agreement between Imperial and the wholesalers of tobacco, and through additional agreements among the wholesalers themselves. Wholesalers are obliged to promise that they will not cut the wholesale price of any product of Imperial *or of any other tobacco company*, and that they will not sell to any price-cutting retailer. Imperial has frequently cut off supplies not only from price cutters but also from coöperative wholesale houses.[12] Dealers are unwilling to risk incurring this penalty, which amounts to exclusion from the trade, and price cutting is therefore rare and short-lived. There is some evidence that independent manufacturers would like to reduce prices but are not sufficiently strong to break away from Imperial's control.[13]

Canadian Canners appears to be accepted as price leader for certain sorts of canned goods, notably tomatoes.[14] The largest

[12] Merco Wholesale Limited, an Edmonton wholesale grocery house owned by some fifty Alberta retailers, has been unable to secure tobacco since 1936. An order sent directly to Imperial Tobacco in Montreal, accompanied by a certified cheque for $1,150, was returned with the reply that "we have no account with you and are unable to accede to your request at this time." Efforts to secure supplies through Alberta jobbers have also been unsuccessful. Department of Labor: Report of Investigation into an Alleged Combine in the Distribution of Tobacco Products, 1938, pp. 12–13. Refusal to sell to coöperatives is fairly common among Canadian manufacturers; the agricultural implement makers, for example, follow a common policy on this point.

[13] In the summer of 1935, for example, the second-largest producer, W. C. Macdonald, Inc., began to sell cigarettes in Ontario and Quebec at 24 for 20 cents. "The Imperial Tobacco Company advised the trade that if it had to meet this competition it would reduce the profit margins of wholesalers and retailers, and a delegation of wholesalers from Western Canada and elsewhere met in Montreal in August and . . . objected to the company's price reductions." Department of Labor, Report of Investigation into an Alleged Combine . . . , p. 30. The Macdonald Company was eventually obliged to conform to Imperial's prices.

[14] Mr. W. Rankin, of King and Rankin, testified before the Price Spreads Commission as follows: "*Q.* Whose quotation is it that seems to govern the market? Is there any one firm? *A.* All seem to wait for the Canadian

producer of bath tubs, lavatories, sinks, etc. is the Standard Sanitary Manufacturing Company, and its prices are followed by the two other companies in the industry.

Where no one firm acts as price leader, informal agreement is more difficult to detect. Several cases, however, seem to be well established. The sugar refining industry, which requires a heavy investment in equipment, has for more than fifty years been dominated by a small number of firms. The Select Committee appointed in 1888 to enquire into trade combinations in Canada reported a price agreement in this industry.[15] Nearly thirty years later the war-time Cost-of-Living Commissioner reported: "It appears that the relations between the refineries and the wholesale grocery trade constitute resale price-fixing arrangements made by way of tacit agreement." [16]

The Textile Commission secured evidence of stable price agreements among producers of cotton yarn,[17] cotton underwear,[18] and carpets.[19] The fertilizer companies in each region sell at uniform prices, and retailers selling below the agreed price are unable to obtain supplies.[20] There is clear if indirect evidence of agreement among the copper producers. Although 90 per cent of Canadian copper is exported, the price in Canada

---

Canners to come out with their list. *Q*. And their list price seems to establish the market, does it? *A*. Pretty well." Evidence, p. 3310.

[15] Report of the Select Committee, May 16, 1888, pp. 7–9.

[16] *Labour Gazette*, June, 1917, pp. 482–487.

[17] J. G. Dodd, sales manager of Dominion Textiles, testified as follows before the Royal Commission on Textiles, 1936: "*Q*. It is a uniform price to all customers? *A*. Yes. *Q*. Among these four mills? *A*. Right." Mr. Dodd also stated that this agreement was in existence when he joined Dominion Textiles in 1909. Evidence, p. 11,164.

[18] Textile Commission Exhibit 1237 contains a schedule of underwear prices dated August 1, 1919.

[19] Textile Commission Exhibit 1239 (Correspondence of Guelph Carpet and Worsted Company).

[20] Evidence before the Price Spreads Commission, pp. 2034–2035 and 2108–2138 (evidence of Mr. Grubb, Fertilizer Division of Canadian Industries, Ltd.).

usually exceeds the London price by almost the total of freight from London to Montreal plus the import duty on copper.[21] Agreement among manufacturers of farm implements, while it has never been admitted by the companies, has been strongly suspected by others.[22] The fact that price changes are made in unison, and the remarkable stability of implement prices during the depression years both point in this direction. Agreement seems to be common also in inter-manufacturer sales of all sorts. Most railway supplies, for example, are sold by only a few companies, and the suppliers frequently agree to present identical tenders.[23]

Trade association activity in Canada has centered upon price control since its beginning. The Select Committee of

[21] "It appears that Canadian purchasers of Canadian produced and refined copper, zinc, and lead are paying the London price, c.i.f. British port, plus a portion of the duty and the freight from British port to Canada. The amount charged over and above the London price appears to vary according to 'what the traffic will bear'; it changes from purchaser to purchaser and from order to order." Tariff Board of Canada, Report on Reference no. 40, Brass, Copper and Nickel Silver Commodities, p. 13.

[22] "The Committee is of the opinion . . . that there is competition in the matter of securing sales but little or no effective competition in the matter of prices as between companies. . . . The companies insist that no understanding existed between them in the matter of the January, 1936, increase and that the increases resulted from the same conditions arising in each company. It is extremely difficult for the Committee to understand the remarkable coincidence of the increase occurring in the same month of the same year and, generally speaking, on the same implements and to the same extent." Report of the Special Committee on Farm Implement Prices, House of Commons, 1937, p. 1264.

[23] There are only two large producers of blue serge suitable for uniforms. "It was the custom of Mr. Dodd [of Patons] to get in touch with Mr. Barrett or Mr. Cooke of Dominion Woolen and Worsteds . . . and they would arrange between themselves what price would be quoted independently by each and the price would be the same." Brief of Mr. J. C. McRuer for the Textile Commission, pp. 333–334. The explanation given by the manufacturers was: "We'll have to quote the same price in the end anyway, so we might as well do it in the beginning." Textile Commission Evidence, pp. 10, 878–879. It is almost certain that the three railway car companies and the two locomotive companies have similar arrangements.

1888 reported associations of oatmeal millers, binder-twine manufacturers, iron founders, biscuit and confectionery makers, coal dealers, coffin-makers and undertakers. Early combinations seem also to have existed in the oil, salt and leather industries.[24] Most of these were simple price agreements, but the oatmeal millers had a fully developed cartel. They closed up ten mills, pensioned the owners, and allotted the annual output among the remaining mills, imposing a fine for excess production and paying a bonus for under-production.

Several hardware associations were formed during the nineties, and a considerable number of paper products were brought under control soon after 1900. It has been estimated that between 40 and 70 combinations had their headquarters in Toronto in 1905.[25] Some of these have since been dissolved but others have been formed, particularly in the textile and building supplies industries. It is safe to say that at least fifty price-fixing trade associations are operating in Canada today, and the number may be considerably higher. One gains the impression, too, that these organizations have grown in solidar-

[24] O. D. Skelton, *General Economic History of the Dominion, 1867–1912*, Toronto, 1913 (Publisher's Association of Canada), pp. 122–123, 187–191.

[25] In 1905 the plumbers and sellers of building supplies in Toronto were brought to trial for combining to restrain competition. As a result of disclosures during the trial, the offices of Jenkins and Hardy (Toronto accountants and professional trade association secretaries) were raided, and certain of their papers seized and examined. The seized documents gave evidence of price agreements covering (among other things) axles, churns, cordage, harness, handles, wheels, edged implements, springs, lanterns, stamped metal ware, saws, trunks, tacks, wringers, washing machines, wooden-ware, oatmeal, canned goods, lead pipe, soil pipe, plate glass, screws, bolts and wire nails. *Labour Gazette*, January, 1906, p. 778. It is surprising, and perhaps significant, that no trials resulted from these disclosures. One combination (the Canadian Tack Manufacturers' Association) was indeed given preliminary investigation before a magistrate and the officers of the firms involved were committed for trial, but no further trace of the case appears in the records.

ity as well as in numbers. The firm which breaks or withdraws from an agreement suffers severer criticism and more effective retaliation today than would have been the case a decade ago.

The simplest sort of agreement, covering merely list prices and terms of sale, is most commonly found in industries — such as baking, milling, and textiles — which are in the early and experimental stages of organization. Agreement on prices alone usually proves to be unsatisfactory, for producers are likely to turn out more than can be sold at the agreed price and are then tempted to dispose of the surplus by secret price cutting. Mature trade associations, therefore, usually make some provision for control of production. The common practice is to assign a certain percentage of the annual output to each firm, with a fine for production in excess of the quota and a bonus for under-production. Agreement on prices and output leads naturally to agreement on other points and to techniques for disciplining recalcitrant members. The result is a complex written agreement which, aside from the fact that it has no legal sanctions, looks very much like the post-war German cartel. Most of these highly developed agreements are to be found in industries — such as hardware and paper products — where trade associations have existed for several decades, and most of them are administered by four professional trade association secretaries. They therefore tend to be very similar in form, and many are identical.

The content of these agreements may best be described by presenting two typical instances. Manufacturers of rubber footwear have agreed informally on prices since at least 1924. In January, 1932, the agreement was put in writing and given stronger sanctions. The eight firms in the industry bound themselves for a period of three years to observe uniform list prices, discounts, and terms of sale. Rivalry in quality was much reduced by provisions for standardization of the product. Indirect price concessions were checked by limiting the sale of footwear as "obsolete" or "imperfect." A percentage of total footwear sales was allotted to each member on the basis of previous production. A firm selling more than its quota in any month was required to pay 25 per cent of the value of its excess sales to the association, while firms selling less than their share were given a corresponding bonus. A firm exceeding its quota for an entire year was to have its quota for the next year increased by 25 per cent of the excess, and *vice versa*. All of the companies posted cash bonds, varying in amount from $10,000 to $75,000, with the secretary of the association. The secretary was empowered to examine the books of any member company at any time, and to impose as a fine for breach of the agreement any sum from $100 up to the full amount of the offender's deposit.[26]

A slightly different form of agreement involves the creation of a single selling company. In December, 1930, the manufacturers of cardboard boxes, who had already coöperated for some years through a trade association, secured the incorporation of Container Materials, Limited. The head office of this company was established in the offices of Messrs. Hardy and Badden, a Toronto firm of trade association executives. A board of directors was elected, composed of one member from each of the sixteen participating companies, and H. J. Badden was made President and Secretary Treasurer. Each company then signed two agreements with Container Materials, Limited: one binding it not to manufacture for or sell to anyone except Container Materials, the other permitting it to sell its product as agent for Container Materials, at prices set by the latter. There is no evidence that Container Materials was intended to handle any goods or perform any marketing functions. The contracts were simply an indirect and apparently very effective method of maintaining prices.

[26] Price Spreads Report, pp. 73–75. See also Evidence before the Price Spreads Commission, pp. 2200–2212.

In other respects the organization conformed quite closely to that of the rubber manufacturers. A uniform method of calculating prices was developed. The quality of boxes was carefully regulated. Quantity discounts, credit terms, and charges for printing and other services were standardized. A system of delivered prices was established. Each firm was given a percentage of total production, and any firm exceeding its quota was taxed a part of the value of its excess sales — originally set at 5 per cent, but gradually raised to 30 per cent — while firms falling below their quotas received a corresponding bonus. In addition, each company consented to a deduction of 1 per cent of the value of its sales, to be left on deposit with Container Materials. On December 31, 1937, these deposits totalled $254,232.[27] This arrangement not only provided the combination with large financial resources, but also gave it a strong hold over its members. The secretary was given the usual power to examine the records of members and to impose penalties. Fines were fairly frequent in the first years of the combination, but decreased in frequency as its authority became established.

Prices were maintained at a highly profitable level. A net loss for the group in 1931 was transformed into a profit of 16.7 per cent on invested capital in 1937.[28] During the years 1934–37, no losses were incurred by any paper box manufacturer. A natural consequence was the entrance of five new producers to the industry between 1931 and 1938. The combination was able, however, to induce all of these new arrivals either to observe the fixed prices or to refrain from production. These operations were in some cases rather costly. The O. and S. Corrugated Products Company, formed in 1935 with a plant investment of only $28,120, received $69,690 from Container

[27] Department of Labour, Report of Investigation into an Alleged Combine in the Manufacture of Paperboard Shipping Containers, 1939, p. 17.

[28] *Ibid.*, p. 47.

Materials during the next two years for *not* producing. The equipment of two other concerns was bought by Container Materials at a cost of more than $80,000, and subsequently sold at auction for $5,655.[29] The members of the combination seem to have considered these payments as insurance premiums against the risk of competition.

It is noteworthy that the Canadian associations perform scarcely any of the service functions which characterize trade associations in the United States. General statistical services, institutional advertising, coöperative research, and the like are very rare. The activities of the Canadian association center upon the maintenance of "fair prices" and it is judged largely by its success or failure in this field. One trade association secretary, indeed, remarked that "manufacturers up here wouldn't be bothered with an association that couldn't control prices."

COMPETITION

The industries which have not been subjected to price control may also be divided into two groups. In several important industries, competition has persisted under apparently unfavorable conditions. Plants are large and the number of important producers is small: five in flour, two in meats, three in newsprint, six in tires, three in silk cloth. In most of these industries, too, price agreements have been formed from time to time, but have been broken so often as to be ineffective. The main reasons for the failure of price control in these cases will appear from a survey of the principal control schemes.

The manufacturers of silk hosiery formed an open-price association in 1928 and adopted a formal price agreement in 1932. To avoid the appearance of collusion, the firms involved wrote identical letters to the secretary of the association, saying in effect: "Just for your information, these are our minimum

[29] *Ibid.*, pp. 53–61.

prices. We don't mind if you let other manufacturers know about them." The minimum prices, of course, were identical, having been previously arranged by a committee. Manufacturers were to notify the secretary immediately of any price change, and in March, 1933, a fifteen-day waiting period was introduced. In July, 1934, the agreement was made more elaborate, possibly in imitation of N.R.A. code provisions. The companies now agreed to give no bonuses, rebates, premiums, or subsidies of any kind and no advertising allowances. Discontinued lines were to be labelled as such and a permit obtained from the secretary before they could be offered for sale at a lower price. Provision was also made for laying charges of infringement and for inspection of the accounts of alleged offenders by the secretary. In spite of these elaborate provisions, the agreement was never fully effective because of a controversy between producers of branded and unbranded goods. Firms making branded goods insisted on a uniform price for branded and unbranded hosiery, while firms selling unbranded goods insisted with equal force on a price differential. An attempt was made to impose a uniform price, with the result that one firm selling low-priced goods was never a party to the agreement, while other unbranded producers felt obliged to make secret cuts in order to obtain sales.[30] In 1935 the principal producer of branded goods withdrew and the agreement collapsed.

A similar agreement was made by the woollen and worsted

[30] "Had the agreement taken place at any time, a 100 per cent agreement on price, it would have resulted in probably five or six of the mills securing 90 per cent of the business and the remaining mills would have closed up. . . . The mills making merchandise that was sold on a price appeal basis . . . felt the better mills should hold the umbrella over them . . . that those mills making quality merchandise should maintain their prices but give the others an opportunity to undersell in order to dispose of their production." Evidence of Mr. Thompson, President of Canadian Silk Products, before the Textile Commission, pp. 11,265 and 11,279.

manufacturers in June, 1933, covering standardized products such as serges and piece dyes. Minimum prices and uniform credit terms were established, and provision was made for punishment of price cutters. Hield Brothers, however, insisted from the outset that prices had been set too high and finally withdrew from the agreement late in 1934. The explanation seems to be that Hield's costs were the lowest in the industry and that they preferred to cut prices and expand their sales. Attempts to win them back were unsuccessful,[31] and the agreement broke up.

An agreement covering wool yarn was formed in 1931, and worsted machine yarn was included in 1935. This agreement, like that in silk hosiery, seems to have broken down because of the attempt to set a uniform price. Producers of the less widely-known brands, finding their sales greatly reduced, made secret concessions which led to a renewal of open price competition.[32]

There are three principal producers of newsprint paper. Consolidated Paper (formerly Canada Power and Paper) and Abitibi Power and Paper, Canadian concerns with mills in Ontario and Quebec, have daily capacities of about 2,000 tons

[31] One such attempt in January, 1935, is reported in a letter from Mr. R. H. Hield to the home office in England: "Dodd of Patons got in touch with me last week and wanted me to go up to a meeting in Toronto for Friday to discuss a minimum price basis. . . . He said that Patons, Barrymores and Duponts had deliberately allowed Dominion Woolens and ourselves to book the serge business, but that they were not prepared to go on allowing this a free field and that unless some form of minimum basis was arrived at they would also start competing for the business. I said that is perfectly obvious and quite logical, but . . . we would not bind ourselves in any way to any minimum price; and he ended by saying that this was perfectly definite and that 'the gloves were now off' or words to that effect." Royal Commission on Textiles, Exhibit 757.

[32] Report of the Royal Commission on Textiles, pp. 138–144. One man was secretary of all the textile agreements. There is a well-established division of labor in this field. Most of the paper products agreements are administered by one man, the building supplies agreements by another man, and most of the hardware agreements by a partnership.

each. International Paper and Power, a United States firm, has a daily capacity in Canada and Newfoundland of some 2,500 tons. The remaining capacity, some 6,000 tons daily, is controlled by about a dozen smaller producers. Sales are made to large buyers of newsprint, principally in the United States, under contracts which usually run for one year. These contracts are negotiated in the fall, and the price for the following year is determined at that time. The problem of the paper producers, then, is to agree on a price in advance of the fall season and to prevent mills from breaking the price.

As productive capacity began to outrun consumption in the late twenties, Abitibi and Canada Power and Paper took steps to check production and regulate prices. These companies and their associates bought controlling interests in a large number of independent producers, including Thunder Bay, Bathurst, Quebec Pulp and Paper, Ste. Anne, Murray Bay, Manitoba and Donnacona, in an attempt to prevent the construction of new plants. In May, 1927, the Canadian Newsprint Company was set up to allocate production among its constituent firms, determine prices, and act as a joint selling agency. International Paper and a considerable number of independents, however, did not join the cartel. With only about 50 per cent of capacity under its control, Canadian Newsprint was ineffective and dissolved in 1928.

In 1928 the provincial governments of Ontario and Quebec intervened and encouraged the formation of the Newsprint Institute, which included almost everyone except International Paper and controlled 70 per cent of production capacity. A slight increase was secured in 1929 prices. In the fall of 1929, however, International Paper refused to follow a proposed increase for 1930. When the provincial premiers threatened the company with increased stumpage dues on timber cut from crown lands, International countered with the plea that its adherence to any price agreement would constitute a breach of the Sherman Act! The proposed increase was not made. In 1930 the Institute failed even to maintain existing prices. Declining business put heavy pressure on mills to increase their volume by shading prices. Secret price cutting set in and the Institute collapsed completely at the end of August. Prices fell from $55 per ton f.o.b. mill in 1929 to $40 delivered in New York in 1933, and remained at this level through 1935.[33]

Newsprint mills located in Canada appear to have drawn closer together in recent years, but their ability to increase prices has been limited by the policy of the Great Northern Paper Company, a Maine producer with large timber reserves and relatively low costs. In spite of the expressed desire of Canadian producers for higher prices, Great Northern announced a price of $41.00 for 1936 and $42.50 for 1937. Early in 1937 Canadian producers, encouraged by rising demand, took the initiative in announcing a price of $50.00 for 1938. In the fall of 1937, Great Northern and other firms in the eastern states announced a price of $48.00, and for the first time in many years there were two price levels in the industry. The sales of Canadian producers fell by about a million tons in 1938, and while part of this can be traced to inventory accumulation in 1937 and to the 1937–38 recession, part of the decline must also be attributed to the fact that they were undersold by United States and European producers.

[33] The above account was obtained largely from the files of the *Financial Post*. See particularly the issues of May 13, 1927; Dec. 21, 1928; Dec. 12, 1929; Feb. 6 and Oct. 2, 1930; Oct. 1, 1932; Oct. 14 and Dec. 15, 1933; Dec. 8, 1934; Oct. 19, 1935; Aug. 8, 1936. See also, H. Marshall, F. A. Southard and K. W. Taylor, *Canadian-American Industry*, New Haven, 1936, pp. 47–52.

The price of $40 meant large losses for most producers, but in view of the extreme over-expansion of the industry this was to be expected. It is possible that had competition been completely unrestricted the price would have fallen still lower. It is likely, however, that the price was not much above the competitive level in 1932–33, and still less in 1934–37, during which time costs increased considerably faster than prices.

Price control in this industry has been difficult for several reasons. The capacity of Canadian paper mills doubled between 1925 and 1930, while consumption of newsprint in the United States increased by only twenty per cent. As a consequence the industry was by 1930 operating at only two-thirds of capacity, and all firms were making intensive efforts to secure volume. Large newsprint buyers in the United States made the most of the situation. International cut its prices in 1929 in order to secure a large Hearst contract. In 1930 Canada Power and Paper offered the Hearst interests a bonus of common stock in order to secure a contract, and this was an important factor in the breakdown of the Newsprint Institute. The failure of attempts to raise prices between 1934 and 1937 can also be traced to negotiations between independent paper producers and the Hearst and Scripps-Howard interests. International Paper, finally, is a low cost producer. Three-quarters of its capacity has been installed since 1924, as compared with half of Consolidated Paper's and only one-quarter of Abitibi's. With modern, efficient equipment [34] and relatively low costs it is natural that International should prefer to cut its prices and expand its sales rather than to accept the quota allotted to it by a cartel. The political influence of the newspaper publishers and the possibility of prosecution under the Sherman Act may also have exerted a restraining influence on International Paper.

The Canadian National Millers' Association, formed in 1920, issues "domestic regulations" which are concerned mainly with flour prices. All brands of flour produced in Canada are classified into several grades, and the price differentials between these

[34] One authority in 1934 rated 70 per cent of the American-owned capacity (which means very largely the mills of International Paper) as "efficient," while only 35 per cent of Canadian-owned capacity was rated as "efficient." See C. P. Fell, "The Newsprint Industry," *The Canadian Economy and Its Problems*, Toronto, 1934, p. 51.

grades are stated as percentages of the "basic price." Once the basic price has been established, the price of a particular brand can be computed very quickly. The regulations also provide for uniformity of discounts, credit terms, allowances for cartage and for returned bags, etc. These regulations are not invariably observed in practice. The milling industry has operated at only about 50 per cent of capacity since 1917–18,[35] and the temptation to secure increased sales by shading the official price is very great. On the other hand, the persistence of extensive unused capacity over so long a period would seem to indicate that prices are not entirely free.

In most cities the larger bakers have for many years had agreements on bread prices. Before any change is made in the established price, all of the leading producers must agree on the wisdom of the change.[36] These agreements are frequently broken, however, and severe price wars occasionally develop. Excess capacity, the large number of small independent producers, and the activities of chain stores are responsible for the failure of price control. Most of the chains, instead of baking their own bread, purchase it on six or twelve month contracts from one of the large bakeries. By shopping about from one baker to another, they are able to buy bread at little more than its direct cost. They then retail this bread on a small margin

[35] Price Spreads Report, p. 89. "Capacity" is not used here in any exact sense. The difficulties involved in an exact definition of "capacity" and "excess capacity" are discussed in Chapter IV.

[36] Mr. James Dempster, a Toronto baker, testified as follows: "*Q.* Is there any general understanding among bakeries as to maintaining a uniform price? *A.* There is always a preliminary discussion regarding the fairness or necessity of lowering or raising a price. . . . Before the price was shifted upwards, every firm must feel it is absolutely necessary or there is no move. . . . There must be acquiescence in the necessity of the move. *Q.* By all the bakers? *A.* By a complete — by the bakers, yes. *Q.* In how large an area? *A.* Quite locally. That works all through the province in localities." Evidence before the Price Spreads Commission, pp. 1387–1388.

in competition with the bread sold by the baker from his own wagons. In order to retain his business, the baker must keep his price within one or two cents of the chain price. Only a very strong combination of bakers, prepared to fix prices to the chains as well as to consumers, could prevent the chains from exerting a downward influence on the retail price structure.

The persistence of competition in these industries can be traced to one or more of the following conditions: (1) Differences of interest among producers. Producers whose costs are relatively low because of greater efficiency or because they sell an unadvertised "price line" are often unwilling to remain in a price agreement. (2) Excess capacity, which makes it profitable for producers to accept new orders at less than average total cost. (3) The pressure of large buyers. Producers who present an unbroken front to small buyers may be tempted by a large order to make secret price concessions. In some industries, such as newsprint, all three of these factors operate together and make price control particularly difficult. It must be admitted, however, that this is not a conclusive explanation, since these same conditions exist in some industries in which price control has been established. The personalities involved, the customs of the trade, the amount and kind of trade association experience and many other factors help to determine whether prices in a particular industry will be free or controlled. For this reason it cannot be assumed that all of these industries will remain competitive. Some of them may very well pass over into the "price agreement" column as conditions become more favorable and as the technique of control is learned by failure and renewed experiment.

The last column of Table 2 includes a group of industries which seem to have remained competitive because entrance to them is easy and the average scale of plant is small.[37] In the

[37] It has been estimated by a member of the industry that a hosiery firm could begin business with $60,000, that a woollen mill could start up

boot and shoe, clothing and furniture industries, for example, the number of producers is so large that it would be very difficult to enforce a price agreement. Even if an agreement could be established, its existence would be threatened continually by the entrance of new producers. The competitive character of these industries, however, is at present being undermined from another source. A large part of their annual output is bought by a few chain and department stores.[38] The numerous, small, unorganized manufacturers are at a great disadvantage in bargaining and the buyer is able within limits to dictate the price, specifications, delivery dates and other terms of the bargain. There exists, indeed, a strong tendency for manufacturers in these industries to become merely contractors making goods to order for large retailers.

Canadian experience, then, supports the view that competition is self-annihilating rather than self-perpetuating. Where producers are few and large the pressure for price control is very strong and the obstacles can usually be surmounted over a period of time. Where producers are many and small, competition seems to result in domination of the manufacturer by the merchant. It occasionally happens, of course, that an industry which has been controlled by agreement reverts to competition, but cases of this sort are much too rare to offset the tendency toward agreement. It is therefore reasonable to assume that the major part of Canadian manufacturing output will continue to be sold at controlled prices.

Such a conclusion has important implications for economic

---

on $40,000 and a knitting mill on $3,000. The average capital possessed by 750 makers of women's garments in Canada at the time of commencing business was $4,000 (survey made for the Price Spreads Commission — see Evidence, p. 4325), while $10,000 would certainly be sufficient for a canning plant and still less for a bakery.

[38] In 1930, department stores alone sold 42 per cent of the women's clothing, 46 per cent of the furniture, 32 per cent of the shoes, and 27 per cent of the men's clothing. Price Spreads Report, p. 206.

study. It is clear that theories which assume the general prevalence of competition cannot describe at all adequately the operation of the Canadian economy. It would be at least equally reasonable to assume that the system is completely monopolistic. But this assumption would also be of little use, for an industry in which producers agree on prices while "competing" in other ways will yield results quite different from those of monopoly and possibly even less desirable. The efficiency of private capitalism clearly needs to be reassessed in the light of the actual operations of industry.

II

PRIVATE CONTROL OF COMPETITION: EXTRACTIVE INDUSTRIES; TRADE

THE PROBLEM OF PRICE CONTROL is usually discussed almost entirely in terms of manufacturing. The price of a finished good to consumers, however, does not depend merely upon the manufacturer's price policy, but upon a succession of price determinations made in a series of markets running from the farmer or miner at one end of the chain to the retail storekeeper at the other. Monopoly elements in any one of these markets will have an effect on the final price. It is therefore necessary to examine the conditions under which primary products are sold to manufacturers, and also the extent of competition in wholesale and retail trade.

AGRICULTURE

Canadian economists and public officials have probably written more pages about agricultural marketing than about any other topic. These discussions, however, deal almost entirely with technical problems of assembling, grading, handling and merchandising, and with the possibility of raising farmers' incomes by increased marketing efficiency. Much less attention has been given to the question of price determination. It is known that there are few buyers for some agricultural products, and farmers frequently complain of collusion among these buyers to depress prices. How accurate are these complaints? The fragmentary evidence now available can do little more than indicate the areas in which more information is necessary. It will be convenient to consider first those products which are sold under competitive conditions, and to leave until the end those whose prices are closely controlled.

The Winnipeg Grain Exchange is commonly regarded as the prototype of a perfectly competitive market. There are many buyers and sellers, attempts to manipulate the market are rare, and market information is more plentiful than for most commodities. Moreover, since most of the Canadian wheat crop is exported, wheat prices at Winnipeg follow Liverpool prices fairly closely. In only four post-war years, however, — 1920, 1921, 1922, and 1937 — has the market been free from some measure of control. The Alberta Wheat Pool was organized in 1923. Similar pools were set up in Saskatchewan and Manitoba in 1924, and a central selling agency, Canadian Coöperative Wheat Producers, Limited, was incorporated. This agency handled about fifty per cent of the Canadian wheat crop from 1924 to 1929. The greater part of this wheat was sold directly to Canadian millers, foreign millers and importers, but sales were also made on the Winnipeg market. The volume and timing of pool sales seems to have influenced at least the short-term fluctuations of wheat prices. In the fall of 1929, to cite the most spectacular example, the pool held off the market in the hope of a price increase, with the result that Winnipeg prices were for some time about 25 cents above prices in Liverpool.

After the collapse of the pool during the winter of 1929–30, the Dominion government stepped in to support the market by large-scale purchases. These purchases continued until the fall of 1935, at which time the stabilization agency had on hand some 205 million bushels of wheat. The Canadian Wheat Board, established in 1935, succeeded in disposing of the accumulated surplus during 1936 and 1937 at a profit of more than nine million dollars. The other main activity of the Board was to set a minimum price for wheat by undertaking to buy wheat from any producer at 87½ cents per bushel. The Board was obliged to take delivery of some 90 million bushels of the 1935 crop, which was sold at a loss of about 12 million dollars. During the last half of 1936 and all of 1937 the market price never fell below 90 cents per bushel and the Board's minimum was ineffective. Prices fell sharply during the first half of 1938, however, and the Board once more intervened to set a minimum price of 80 cents per bushel.[1]

Dairy farmers ordinarily receive competitive prices because of the fact that milk may be turned to several uses. A dairy farmer in Ontario or Quebec usually has the alternative of selling his milk to a fluid-milk distributor, a butter factory, a cheese factory or (in some areas) a condensery. An increase in the price of one dairy product is transmitted to other products through a diversion of milk into the product whose price has risen.[2] Competition among buyers, however, is by no means universal. In the prairie provinces, for example, fluid-milk markets are few and small, cheese factories are rare, and the principal market is the local creamery. Since creameries are usually from 20 to 40 miles apart, each creamery can within limits set the price in its own territory. Some creameries discriminate between different parts of their territory, paying a higher price for cream in districts where they are obliged to compete with another creamery for the available supply. There are also instances of agreement between creameries on buying prices. These practices have undoubtedly stimulated the growth of coöperative creameries and cheese factories, which ensure that the farmer will receive the full market value of his produce.

Butter and cheese are sold in organized competitive markets. Wholesale trade in cheese centers in Montreal. Since Great Britain is the principal export market, Montreal cheese prices follow British prices closely. Toronto and Montreal are the

[1] For a fuller account of the marketing of wheat during the past twenty years see the Report of the Royal Grain Inquiry Commission, 1938. For a good general discussion of the grain market, see D. A. MacGibbon, *The Canadian Grain Trade*, Toronto, 1932.

[2] For a discussion of the determination of milk prices under competitive conditions, see J. M. Cassels, *A Study of Fluid Milk Prices*, Cambridge, Mass., 1937.

market centers for creamery butter. The creameries sell through brokers to wholesalers, who package the butter and sell it to retailers. The wholesale trade is highly competitive and is conducted on a margin of not much more than one cent per pound. Prices in other centers correspond closely with those in Toronto and Montreal.

About one-half of the cattle and hogs consumed in Canada pass through meat packing plants,[3] the remainder being killed and dressed by farmers and local butchers. The packers buy most of their supplies at the stockyards, whose carefully framed trading rules are intended to bring about a competitive price. In recent years there have been frequent complaints that the two largest buyers [4] are in agreement and that this has operated to depress the price of livestock. There is considerable evidence of agreement between Swift's and Canada Packers both as to buying prices and as to the proportion of the available supply which each shall buy.[5] There are other buyers in the market, however, particularly wholesale butchers, exporters, feeders

[3] Estimate of W. B. Somerset, Ontario Commissioner of Marketing, for the Price Spreads Commission. Evidence, p. 4947.

[4] Canada Packers handles about 60 per cent of all meat packed in Canada, the Swift Canadian Company about 25 per cent.

[5] See in this connection the testimony of Mr. A. Mackenzie, formerly chief buyer for Canada Packers in the Toronto market, concerning the informal understanding which [he claimed] existed in that market. Each morning all the Canada Packers buyers met to determine their price policy for the day. Mackenzie then telephoned to Swift's, asked what they intended to do, and reached an understanding on prices. It was also understood that Swift's was to buy 32 per cent of the supply in the market, while Canada Packers was to buy the remainder. If either got ahead of its quota, its buyers would slacken their purchases until the other company caught up. Occasionally, a slight amount of "cross buying" (the offering by one company of a price in excess of the agreed price) occurred on certain grades of cattle, but this was always smoothed over. The agreement was on the whole well observed. Mackenzie estimated that if this practice of consultation on prices had not prevailed, producers would have received from fifty cents to one dollar more per hundred pounds for their cattle. Evidence before the Price Spreads Commission, pp. 1079–1083.

and speculators. There are also in some areas rival packers of considerable size. P. Burns and Company does a large business in Alberta, while in Quebec the Coöperative Fédérée has a plant with an annual capacity of 20,000 cattle. In pork packing, which does not require such a large plant as beef packing, small firms are still numerous and important. It does not seem likely, therefore, that the large packers are able to control the general trend of livestock prices, or to keep prices consistently below the level which would be reached under pure competition. They are able, however, to depress prices temporarily by taking full advantage of (or even creating) an overstocked market. The "savings" made in this way during a year probably amount to a considerable sum.

The structure of the market is being rapidly altered through the increased shipment of livestock by truck.[6] The trucker is more anxious to dispose of his load quickly than to obtain the highest price for the farmer, and finds it convenient to deliver the animals directly to the packing plant. The packer is also glad to buy at the plant gate and save handling charges. Two complaints are brought against the new method of marketing: (1) it is claimed that packers buy livestock from truckers at less than the stockyards price. A check made by investigators for the Price Spreads Commission during the month of March, 1934, seems to support this contention.[7] The packer has complete freedom of grading when buying direct. In addition, direct purchases are made on an off-car basis, while in the stockyards animals are fed and watered before being sold; this may make a difference of 75 pounds in the weight of a 1,000 pound cow. The farmer saves the commission merchant's fee, the stockyard

[6] One-half of all hogs delivered at stockyards in 1936 arrived by truck, while one-third of the cattle came by truck. Department of Agriculture, Livestock Branch, Seventeenth Annual Market Review, 1936, p. 16. If truck shipments delivered direct to packing plants were included, the percentage of the total shipped in this way would be considerably increased.

[7] Average cost of cattle, calves, sheep and lambs per 100 lbs. dressed

charges, and part of the freight which he would otherwise have had to pay. In spite of these savings, it is probable that he obtains a smaller net return from direct sales than could be obtained from selling at the yards. This uneconomic behavior, where it exists, is due to the farmer's imperfect knowledge of market conditions and the failure of the trucker to inform him adequately. (2) It is argued that the weakening of the stockyards system by direct sales is detrimental to the producer. This seems a reasonable argument. Elimination of the central competitive market would probably put producers at a considerable disadvantage in selling to the two large buyers.

There are in each province a few large buyers of eggs and poultry,[8] who obtain supplies through country storekeepers and their own buying agents. Surpluses above local needs are disposed of through brokers in Toronto and Montreal. The basic price for eggs and poultry is established on the Toronto and Montreal markets. The accuracy with which this price is reflected in prices paid to producers, however, depends on the extent of buying competition. Outside of such thickly-settled

---

weight, Swift's Toronto Plant, two weeks ended March 31, 1934.

	Purchased on Stockyards	Purchased Direct	Difference
Cattle	$ 8.16	$ 6.30	$1.86
Calves	10.21	9.13	1.08
Sheep	7.66	5.71	1.95
Lambs	15.88	12.53	3.35

Average cost of hogs per 100 lbs. dressed weight, Canada Packers' Plants, month ended March 31, 1934.

	Purchased on Stockyards	Purchased Direct	Difference
Toronto	$12.25	$11.85	$0.40
Montreal	12.73	12.10	0.63
Winnipeg	12.00	11.51	0.49

Evidence, pp. 2325–2327, 2369–2370.

[8] These are usually meat packers, creameries, feed companies, etc., though there are a few firms which specialize in the poultry business.

areas as southwestern Ontario, buying competition is probably insufficient to ensure a competitive price to producers. In many districts there is a single buyer or a few buyers who agree on prices. In these areas, advances in the Toronto price are reflected only slowly and partially while declines are passed back to the farmer at once. The growth of trucking and the development of coöperatives, however, are placing the producer in a more advantageous position. It is also possible that the central grading stations now being established by the Dominion government will attract enough buyers and sellers to develop into competitive produce exchanges.

The structure of the fruit and vegetable market differs in different producing areas. A large part of the British Columbia output is shipped to the prairie provinces, where it is protected from competition by the rigorous prairie climate, the distance of the prairies from other producing areas, and the tariff imposed on United States produce. The situation is thus highly favorable to price control. As early as 1923, British Columbia apple growers undertook to maintain a fixed price in the prairie market by allotting sales quotas to shippers and by selling the surplus on the British market at a competitive price. Shippers outside of the coöperative, however, were able to secure the benefits of this policy without incurring the expense of membership, and membership fell off year by year. By 1926 the coöperative controlled only 60 per cent of the total tonnage, and an unusually large crop in that year led to the complete breakdown of price control. The growers next appealed to the provincial government, and in March, 1927, a marketing act was passed. Under this act the "Interior Tree-Fruit and Vegetable Committee of Direction" was established, with power to license all shippers, to set prices and to regulate shipments. The Committee followed a moderate price-policy and operated successfully until February, 1931, when the British Columbia marketing act was held by the Supreme Court of Canada to be beyond the powers of the province. The apple crops of 1932 and 1933 were marketed with fair success under a voluntary agreement. Owing partly to pressure from British Columbia, a Dominion marketing act was passed in 1934. British Columbia growers hastened to take advantage of the Act and marketing schemes were established for almost every important fruit and vegetable product. When this act was also declared invalid in 1936, British Columbia passed a new provincial law and the marketing boards continued to operate. This law was upheld by the Privy Council in 1938. Nearly all important products are now controlled and there is every prospect that this control will continue.[9]

Most of the fruits and vegetables produced in Ontario are sold within the province under competitive conditions. In the smaller towns and cities, farmers usually sell directly to retailers and consumers at public markets. In Toronto, most produce still passes through the hands of commission merchants and wholesalers, but even here the increase of trucking is tending to shorten the marketing chain. Keen competition appears to exist, though abuses have been pointed out from time to time.[10] The situation has been altered recently by the Farm Products

[9] The operation of the Natural Products Marketing Act of 1934 and of the provincial acts now in force will be discussed in Chapter VIII, below. For a fuller account of the development of market control in British Columbia, see Department of Agriculture, Economics Branch, *The Economic Annalist*, February–March, 1931, and June, 1933.

[10] See, for example, Department of Labour, Investigation into an alleged combine in the distribution of fruits and vegetables produced in Ontario, 1926. No price-combinations among dealers were discovered. It was found, however, that Toronto commission merchants charged a uniform commission of 12½ per cent, plus a cartage fee averaging 1.25 per cent whether any cartage service was performed or not. These rates were considered exorbitant by the Commissioner. Inaccurate returns to growers were also found to be common, with underpayments considerably exceeding overpayments. In some cases commission merchants had even "sold" produce to themselves at their own price and paying themselves the regular commission; such transactions are clearly illegal.

Control Act of 1937, which may lead in time to selling monopolies of many products.

The situation in Ontario differs from that in British Columbia in that a large proportion of the fruit and vegetable output is sold to canning factories on contract. Canadian Canners, which has much the largest chain of factories, appears to set the contract price to growers.[11] This price varies from one district to the next, though it is not clear that any systematic policy of discrimination is followed. More important than the nominal price is the grading and dockage of the crop. It is alleged that in years of large crops the companies grade very severely and dock heavily. In years of shortage, on the other hand, companies sometimes compete for supplies by more lenient grading and dockage policies. The net effect of the system is not clear, but there is some reason to think that farmers receive less on the average for their cannery sales than for sales on the fresh fruit and vegetable market. If this is so, why do they continue to sell so much to the canneries? Part of the answer lies in inertia and ignorance of market conditions; part no doubt lies in the greater security of sales on contract. Products intended for the cannery usually require less care than products sold on the fresh market. It must be remembered, too, that the farmer is bound to the canning company in several ways. He usually buys his young plants from the company, and pressure may be put on him at this time. He usually needs a bank loan to carry him over the growing season, and many banks are willing to

[11] Mr. F. McIntosh of Associated Quality Canners testified as follows: "*Q*. Perhaps you could tell us who it is that fixes the price for the crop paid to the farmer? *A*. Am I compelled to answer that? *Q*. I think so. *A*. . . . There is a dominating factor in it. *Q*. What is the dominating factor? *A*. The large company. *Q*. The large company, that is, Canadian Canners? *A*. Yes, sir. . . . *Q*. By and large the situation is that the price paid by Canadian Canners is the ruling price for tomatoes? *A*. Yes. *Q*. And the price varies somewhat in districts? *A*. Yes." Evidence before the Price Spreads Commission, pp. 3422–3423.

make loans only with a cannery contract as security. One can say at least that competition for produce between the canning factories and the fresh market is very imperfect, and that studies in this field should bring interesting results.

The maritime provinces are large producers of apples (Nova Scotia) and potatoes (New Brunswick). Two-thirds of the apple crop is normally exported to Great Britain, where it is sold in a competitive market. Although most of the export trade is in the hands of a few firms, buying competition is provided by coöperatives which handle about one-third of the crop.[12] The New Brunswick potato growers are in a less fortunate position. No recent investigation has been made, but a 1925 inquiry disclosed that the export trade in potatoes was in the hands of two groups of shippers, who agreed to buy at the same price. Changes in the buying price were made by the leading exporter, Mr. Guy Porter, from whose office word was passed around rapidly to other buyers. Most of the farmers, lacking frost-proof cellars for winter storage and being usually in immediate need of money, were forced to sell their crop before the freeze-up at the shippers' price. These shippers who coöperated so well in dealing with the farmers, however, continued to engage in fierce selling competition on the Cuban market, leading at intervals to drastic price reductions. The agreement on buying prices made it possible to pass these reductions back to the farmers, who were thus forced to provide Cuban consumers with potatoes at very low prices.[13] There is no evidence that conditions have changed appreciably since 1925. The exporters have recently attempted to coöperate in selling on certain markets, particularly the Argentine, but this will not necessarily bring higher prices to producers.

[12] See W. V. Longley, "The Nova Scotia Apple Industry," N. S. Department of Agriculture, Bulletin 113, 1931.

[13] Department of Labour, Investigation into an alleged combine in the marketing of New Brunswick potatoes, 1925.

The sale of fluid milk is now regulated by all of the provinces. During the twenties the price paid to farmers in each market was usually determined by negotiation between the organized distributors and the farmers' representatives, while the price of milk to consumers was determined by agreement among the distributors. During the depression, however, this arrangement tended to break down. The price of milk for butter and cheese, which depends on the world price of these products, fell faster than the price of milk for fluid use. Farmers grew increasingly eager to enter the fluid milk field, and many set up as producer-distributors. The situation also enabled existing distributors to buy milk at less than the agreed price and to reduce their selling prices accordingly. Price cutting grew more and more severe. Under pressure from farmers and distributors, one province after another adopted legislation designed to stabilize milk prices. This means in most cases that the farmer-distributor agreements now include prices to consumers as well as to producers and are given legal sanction.[14]

Most of the leaf tobacco grown in Canada is produced in a few counties of southwestern Ontario. The Imperial Tobacco Company is much the largest purchaser of tobacco, and for many years set the price paid to growers.[15] It was thus in the

[14] Provincial legislation in this field is discussed in Chapter VIII. See also H. A. Innis and others, *The Dairy Industry in Canada*, pp. 168–188.

[15] Purchasing was done by negotiation between the company buyer and the individual farmer during the months of October and November. It was the invariable custom for Imperial Tobacco to "open the market," *i.e.*, no buyer from the smaller companies entered the tobacco area until the day on which Imperial began to buy. It was also an unwritten rule that no one might offer a price above the top price set by Imperial. There seems even to have been some sort of division of customers, for a farmer who refused an offer from one buyer was usually not visited by another. The knowledge that he must accept the buyer's offer or not sell his tobacco at all placed the farmer in a very weak position, and undoubtedly induced him to sell for less than he would have demanded had there been competition among buyers. See Department of Labour, Report of an alleged combine of tobacco manufacturers, 1933.

unusual position of being able to control both the price of its raw material and the price of the finished product. During the depression, however, growers became increasingly dissatisfied with their treatment by the Company. In 1933, they organized three coöperative sales agencies and in 1934 secured a marketing board under the Natural Products Marketing Act. The manufacturers, who had recently been investigated by the Price Spreads Commission and by the Combines Investigation office, were in a conciliatory frame of mind, and agreed to deal with the Board. The price of the crop is now negotiated by a joint committee of three growers and three buyers. Buyers are free to buy from whatever members of the growers' association they select, and at any price they choose. If at the end of the season, however, the average price paid by any buyer is less than the agreed price, he must remit the difference to the Board. Since the invalidation of the Natural Products Marketing Act the system has been continued on a voluntary basis, the manufacturers apparently considering that the additional amount paid for tobacco is justified as a public relations measure.

It is apparent from the above survey that a considerable part of Canada's agricultural output is still sold under competitive conditions. The prices of an increasing number of products, however, are controlled by buyers or sellers or by an agreement between them. It is often forgotten that the concentration of manufacturing means few buyers of raw materials as well as few sellers of finished goods. Even where the number of manufacturers is large, as in butter production or canning, the bulk and perishability of agricultural produce may confine the farmer to a local market. There is thus a strong natural tendency for agricultural markets to be dominated by the buyers.

The desire of farmers to escape from buyer control has been a major factor in the development of marketing coöperatives. The coöperatives have provided desirable competition for private buyers and have in some cases eliminated the private buyer entirely. It is noteworthy, however, that they have scarcely ever been able to achieve a monopoly position without government support. The large number of producers, their traditional independence, and the attempt of individual farmers to reap the benefits without incurring the costs of membership, make it almost impossible for a voluntary association to obtain complete control of supply.

The inability of voluntary coöperatives to control supply has led to a demand for government regulation of agricultural marketing, and this demand has grown considerably stronger since 1929. Several products are now marketed through central selling agencies which control supplies and prices.[16] This type of control has thus far been applied mainly to perishable products such as milk, fruit and vegetables, the production of which is highly concentrated and which are sold to relatively few buyers. There is a tendency under these plans to fix not only the price paid to farmers but the price charged to consumers. Processors and distributors argue that they can guarantee a fixed price to the farmer only if their own returns are guaranteed, and for this reason are usually able to secure farmer support for their proposals. There is thus a marked tendency toward complete cartelization of the food industries, with prices fixed at every stage from the grower to the final consumer.[17]

[16] These control plans are described in Chapter VIII.

[17] This survey has been concerned almost entirely with products which reach central markets in the larger cities. This is admittedly only a part of the total picture. A large percentage of farm production is consumed on the farm. What determines the amounts thus consumed? To what extent do the amounts consumed on the farm vary with variations in the prices of the products? A considerable part of the total, too, passes from farmers to consumers either directly or by means of small-town retailers. Competition doubtless eixsts in these markets, but how perfect is it? and how closely do the prices in local markets correspond with each other and with central market prices? Much more light is needed on these questions before we can deal adequately with the determination of agricultural prices.

OTHER EXTRACTIVE INDUSTRIES

Many of the primary metal products are not marketed and have no market price. The metal is mined, smelted, refined, rolled and sometimes fabricated by a single integrated concern, whose operations may extend over several countries. Nickel, for example, is mined at Sudbury and smelted at Coniston or Copper Cliff, Ontario. It may be refined either at Port Colborne, Ontario, or Clydoch, Wales. The pure nickel is rolled at Huntington, West Virginia, or Birmingham, England, and part of it re-enters Canada as sheets, bars, rods of nickel or some nickel alloy. The product has advanced several stages toward completion, it has appeared in Canadian trade figures as both an export and an import, yet there has been no problem of pricing. If any price is attached to the semi-finished products, this is done merely as a matter of accounting convenience by the International Nickel Company. Similar illustrations could be given for copper, aluminum, and other metals.

Forestry operations present somewhat the same picture. In British Columbia there is a separate logging industry and the logs are sold to lumbermen in a competitive market. In eastern Canada, however, most lumber companies cut their own logs. The larger paper companies, too, have their own timber limits, cut their own logs and prepare their own wood-pulp. A considerable amount of wood-pulp, however, is sold in the open market to paper mills which have inadequate pulping facilities, and some is exported to the highly competitive United States market.

The market for coal differs from one region to another. More than 80 per cent of the British Columbia output is produced by Canadian Collieries and the Crow's Nest Pass Coal Company. The price which these companies may charge is limited by the price of fuel oil and of Alberta coal. The British

Columbia Royal Commission, however, concluded that this was insufficient protection to domestic consumers, and in 1937 a Coal and Petroleum Products Control Board was given wide regulatory powers over the industry. On the prairies regulation has been adopted for opposite reasons. Most of the prairie coal supply comes from some 300 mines in the province of Alberta. The capacity of these mines is much in excess of their present output [18] and price cutting has been a natural consequence. Price agreements among the larger companies have all broken down after short periods.[19] Producers finally appealed to the provincial government, a Royal Commission investigated the situation, and provincial control was provided for in 1935. This legislation and the similar legislation in Saskatchewan are discussed in Chapter VIII.

Less than ten per cent of the coal used in Ontario and Quebec is produced in Canada. Bituminous coal is imported from the United States at prices which will cease to be competitive if

[18] The Mines Branch of the Alberta government estimated the annual capacity in 1934 as 10.25 million tons, on a basis of 275 days' operation for bituminous mines and 150 days for sub-bituminous and lignite mines. The actual output in the peak year 1928 was 7.34 million tons, while 1934 production was only 4.75 million tons. Report of the Royal Commission on the Alberta Coal Industry, 1935, p. 9.

[19] In 1934, for example, the sixteen principal mines in the Drumheller Valley formed a central selling agency. A production quota was allotted to each mine on the basis of its average production in the years 1930–33. Mines exceeding their quotas were fined and mines falling short of their quota were compensated. All coal was sold through the agency, Drumheller Coal Operators, Limited, at a fixed price of $3.60 per ton. The agreement worked reasonably well during 1934–35 and several large contracts were handled "successfully." When negotiations were opened in 1935 with a view to renewal of the agreement for another year, however, dissension arose because of the demand of some producers for larger quotas. "85% of the operators, it is stated, were prepared to accept the percentages of the previous year; others representing 15% were discontented and claimed larger allowances." It proves impossible to reach an agreement, and prices were "seriously disorganized" during 1935–36. *Ibid.*, pp. 83–84.

the powers of the Bituminous Coal Commission are upheld in the courts. Anthracite comes principally from the United States, Great Britain, and Germany, with smaller imports from Russia, Belgium, and Indo-China. In each of these countries the price is controlled either by the government or by a cartel, but there is vigorous competition among them in the Canadian market.

The Dominion Steel and Coal Company has a monopoly of coal production in Nova Scotia and sells nearly all of the bituminous coal used in the maritime provinces. There are considerable imports of anthracite, however,[20] and the possibility of importing sets an upper limit to the prices which Dominion Steel may charge. Within this limit, the company appears to follow the ordinary rules of price-discrimination, charging highest prices in those areas where competition is least likely.

The deep sea fishing industry of Nova Scotia is dominated by a few large buyers. There are only six buyers of salt fish, four in Lunenburg and two in Halifax. The Lunenburg companies own all of the desirable sites on the small harbor and refuse to allow newcomers to enter the business.[21] These companies outfit the fisherman for his voyage and sell groceries to his family on credit during his absence. When he returns after from one

[20] In 1935, 28.4 per cent of the coal used in Halifax and 29.5 per cent of the coal used in Saint John was imported anthracite. Report of the Royal Commission on Anthracite Coal, 1937, p. 15.

[21] "*A*. . . . in Lunenburg, we haven't any more sites, the waterfront is all used up . . . we had another firm there 10 years ago, and the minute that firm died out the other firms bought the site up to keep somebody else from stepping in . . . it is a small harbour. *Q*. Then these sites become very valuable? *A*. They become so valuable that they cannot be bought at any figure at all. I will give you an instance: about three years ago we [*i.e.*, the fishermen] started to organize, we were going to build a cold storage, and we went to one firm and asked them for a site which they were not using and they said they would not consider selling it at all, that they would keep it." Evidence before the Price Spreads Commission, IV, 42.

to three months, his catch is turned over to the company and the proceeds credited against his indebtedness. The individual fisherman is evidently in a very weak bargaining position,[22] particularly since the companies can recoup any increase in fish prices by charging higher prices for groceries and clothing. There are four important buyers of fresh fish, who furnish fishermen with ice, bait and other supplies and buy the catch at prices agreed on among themselves. The largest buyer also owns three steam trawlers, and the fish obtained in this way are used as a weapon in bargaining with the fishermen. As in the New Brunswick potato case, companies which coöperate in buying have been unable to maintain selling agreements. There is vigorous price competition in the sale of fish in Quebec and Ontario markets, and the burden of this competition falls largely on the fisherman.

WHOLESALE AND RETAIL TRADE

The prices received by primary producers and by manufacturers have now been discussed. It remains to examine the pricing of the finished goods as they proceed on their way to the consumer. Although the wholesaler plays a decreasing part in the distributive process, more than half of the groceries, food products, dry goods, hardware, lumber and paper products sold in Canada still pass through wholesale markets.[23] Wholesale trade is usually thought of as highly competitive. During the

[22] "*Q*. Is there any bargaining at all between the fisherman . . . and the storekeeper? *A*. Bargain, but here is the situation: they say, if you do not want us to take them, you will just have to leave them remain there. . . . *Q*. You get the same price from all? *A*. Yes. For instance, if the merchants [in Halifax] want to make the price of fish four dollars per quintal, there would be the same thing in Lunenburg." *Ibid.*, p. 4.

[23] Dominion Bureau of Statistics: Wholesale Trade in Canada, 1936, pp. 24–44. Only 20.8 per cent of all sales by manufacturers in 1930 were made to wholesalers, however. Dominion Bureau of Statistics, Distribution of Sales by Manufacturing Plants in Canada, 1934.

past fifty years, however, more agreements have been discovered among wholesalers than among manufacturers. This may merely indicate that competition among wholesalers is so active that formal agreement is necessary to eliminate it, while in manufacturing informal methods are sufficient. The available evidence, however, casts grave doubt on the assumption that competition prevails.

Agreements among wholesalers have usually had two objects: protection of the wholesalers' margin, and "preservation of the channels of trade," *i.e.*, prevention of direct sales by manufacturers to retailers and consumers. The threat of boycott is held over the heads of manufacturers to ensure their "coöperation." The Dominion Wholesale Grocers' Guild, formed in 1903, provides an excellent illustration of these methods. The object of this organization was to conclude agreements with manufacturers, binding the latter to (1) set a list price to the retail trade, (2) set a standard wholesalers' discount from this list price, (3) route all sales to retailers through wholesale houses, and (4) refuse to sell to any wholesaler breaking the list price, or to any coöperative wholesale house. Manufacturers who refused to accept these terms were boycotted by Guild members. The Guild was unsuccessfully prosecuted by the Province of Ontario in 1910,[24] and flourished so well that it was again brought to trial in 1923. A long list of manufacturers with whom agreements had been concluded was presented at the 1923 trial. The structure of the Guild had not changed greatly since the beginning, except that it was more difficult to enter the organization in 1923 than in 1910. An applicant for membership could be admitted only with the approval of the member nearest him. He was obliged, moreover, to make a lengthy declaration, swearing among other things that he was a "legitimate" wholesaler (not a coöperative buying agency in disguise!), and that he would abide by the established list prices.

[24] *Rex v. Becket et al.*, 20 O.L.R., 410–432.

The association was again acquitted,[25] apparently because of a technical flaw in the indictment, and there is no evidence that it has been dissolved.

Association among jobbers of building supplies dates back at least forty years. The Toronto jobbers around 1900 formed an agreement with the Toronto master plumbers' association, whereby members of each association bound themselves to deal only with members of the other. The prices to be charged by the jobbers to the plumbers and by the plumbers to consumers were fixed. Since manufacturers' prices were already fixed in most cases, the result was to freeze all the elements entering into the price of a plumbing installation. Members of the combination were prosecuted in 1907 and fines totalling $10,000 were imposed.[26] The idea lived on, however, and reappeared during the twenties in the Amalgamated Builders' Council, which operated over the area between Toronto and Windsor. In some cities the price of plumbing installations was increased by more than 50 per cent during the lifetime of this organization. In addition, direct sales of plumbing supplies to consumers were prohibited, manufacturers were forced to deal only with members of the combine under penalty of boycott, and jobbers who ventured to sell below the prices set by the combine were forced out of business by cutting off their supplies. The Amalgamated Builders' Council was investigated under the Combines Act, prosecuted and broken up.[27] The plumbing contractors do not appear to have entered into any agreements since this investigation. Coöperation among jobbers and manufac-

[25] *Attorney-General of Ontario v. Canadian Wholesale Grocers Association et al.*, 53 O.L.R., 627–665.

[26] *Rex v. Master Plumbers' Association and Central Supply Association*, 14 O.L.R., 295–321.

[27] *Rex v. Singer et al.*, 1931 O.L.R., 202–221; *Rex v. White et al.*, Ontario Supreme Court, April 1, 1932 (unreported). See also, Department of Labour, Report of Investigation into the Amalgamated Builders' Council, 1930.

turers continues through the Plumbing and Heating Institute, but the extent to which the Institute has been used for price control is uncertain.[28]

The tobacco wholesalers are organized in thirteen local associations, all of which appear to operate in exactly the same way. The agreement of the Northern Alberta Tobacco Jobbers' Association, for example, binds its members to charge fixed wholesale prices, to withhold supplies from price-cutting retailers, and to observe standard credit terms and freight charges. If investigation reveals that any member has broken the agreement, the Association recommends to Imperial Tobacco that the offender be sold tobacco only at the jobbers' selling price or that he be cut off the list entirely for a stated period. The mere threat of this penalty is sufficient to produce close observance of the agreement. Imperial also promises not to recognize (*i.e.*, sell tobacco to) any new wholesaler without the approval of the Association, and the jobbers are thus enabled to prevent additions to their numbers.[29] Imperial seems to have taken the lead in organizing the local associations and in promoting price maintenance agreements. The jobbers, however, have fallen in very willingly with these suggestions and have become an effective police force for the industry.

Agreement seems also to have been common in the coal trade. An investigation under the Combines Act in 1933 revealed a highly effective combination among importers and distributors of British anthracite coal. By a series of written agreements, the first of which was signed in 1929, the Canadian Import Company and three other companies secured the exclusive right

[28] Manufacturers' price agreements, where these exist, appear to be administered independently of the Institute. The Institute probably does make some attempt, however, to stabilize the prices charged by jobbers in the same competitive area. It also carries on institutional advertising and provides statistical services.

[29] Department of Labour, Report of investigation into an alleged combine in the distribution of tobacco products, 1938, pp. 10–23.

to buy coal from the leading British sellers. These companies, through a gentlemen's agreement, succeeded in maintaining the price of Scotch and Welsh anthracite at a level highly profitable to themselves. A second investigation in 1937 revealed that control of the British anthracite trade had been tightened still further through the secret purchase by Senator L. C. Webster, owner of the Canadian Import Company, of controlling interests in his competitors. Anthracite is now being imported from Belgium, Germany and other countries, however, in sufficient quantities to assure effective competition.[30]

The Alberta Royal Commission of 1935 reported approvingly that the two leading coal wholesalers in Edmonton are on friendly terms.[31] In Vancouver and Victoria, Canadian Collieries for many years sold its coal through a small number of "approved" dealers, who were easily able to control prices. The prices charged by these dealers, indeed, led to considerable importations of Alberta coal and caused Canadian Collieries to insert in its contracts a clause preventing the dealer from selling its coal *above* a specified price.[32]

Agreements in other lines of trade have been reported from time to time. The British Columbia fruit investigation of 1924 reported agreement among fruit and vegetable jobbers in several prairie cities.[33] The Board of Commerce in 1919 discov-

[30] Department of Labour, Report of investigation into an alleged combine in British anthracite coal, 1933. Report of the Royal Commission on Anthracite Coal, 1937.

[31] "Edmonton is fortunate in that two of the principal wholesalers in the city are friendly and act rather on lines of coöperation than of cutthroat competition. . . . The two wholesalers in question have a friendly arrangement as to areas canvassed, and so avoid unnecessary overlapping." Report of the Commission, pp. 84–85.

[32] Report of the B. C. Royal Commission on Coal and Petroleum Products, 1936, pp. 41–42, 61.

[33] Department of Labour, Report on investigation into an alleged combine in the distribution of fruits and vegetables, 1925. Since that time, while the number of jobbers has decreased, competition among them ap-

ered two extensive combinations of hardware jobbers, one in British Columbia and one in eastern Canada. The eastern group, composed of 14 dealers in Ontario and Quebec, submitted to the Board a seven-page price list covering most of the staple hardware items. It should be remembered, too, that most of the manufacturers' agreements discussed in the previous chapter guarantee the wholesaler a fixed margin by fixing both the list price to retailers and the discounts to wholesalers.

The total number of wholesalers in Canada is very large, and this has undoubtedly contributed to the belief that wholesale trade is competitive. The number of wholesalers of a particular article in a particular area, however, is usually small, and the incentive to agreement is strong. It seems likely from existing evidence that agreement is the rule and competition the exception in wholesale trade, but fuller information is necessary before a definite conclusion can be reached.

The economic characteristics of retail trade are discussed in Chapter V. It is sufficient here to remind ourselves that competition in retail markets is highly imperfect. Consumers are notoriously poor judges of quality, while many retailers are only a little better informed. Buyers are usually ignorant of the prices charged by different sellers, and even when they have this knowledge they frequently prefer for one reason or another to pay a higher rather than a lower price. Even standardized articles may usually be bought at several different prices within a single shopping area. Many merchants fail each year, but their places are taken by newcomers, a large proportion of whom have no experience of retailing and no qualifications except optimism. Small, poorly located units change hands frequently but there is no evidence that they tend to be eliminated. There is reason to think that retail stores are too numerous and too small, and that the cost of retailing is considerably higher

pears to be more active, due largely to the price policies of the Safeway chain-store system which operates a number of jobbing houses.

than it need be if the industry were organized in the most efficient way.

SUMMARY

The foregoing is far from being a complete account of price control in the Canadian economy. The labor and capital market have not been discussed, and nothing has been said about the transportation, power, building and service industries. Discussion has centered upon the pricing of manufactured goods at various stages between the primary producer and the final consumer. Even within this limited field large areas are conjectural or entirely unknown. The areas which have been explored do not lend themselves to simple generalizations. To conclude that Canadian industry is "competitive" or "monopolistic" would have little meaning. Actually, the markets discussed above form a mosaic of different types of price determination, which can at best be reduced to some sort of order by classification.

There is ample evidence that the pressure for price control is strong and persistent in all parts of the economy. To the business man, "coöperation" is the normal state of affairs and competition is a destructive element which must be controlled or eliminated. Competition tends nevertheless to persist where sellers are so numerous as to make organization difficult, where the pressure of a divergent interest (as, for example, extensive unused capacity or particularly low production costs) pulls individual sellers away from the group, and where a few powerful buyers are able to break down the united front of sellers. Even where free price determination remains, however, there is no approach to the "pure competition" of economic theory except in the marketing of a few agricultural products. The commonest situation is one in which a few large buyers or sellers compete in a markedly imperfect market.

A few products are able to pass from primary producer to

retailer without encountering price control at any stage of the journey — butter, cheese, some woollen and silk products, and a small number of less important articles. At the opposite extreme are cigarettes, bathtubs, and other articles which are controlled from the cradle to the grave. Most products occupy an intermediate position, passing through one or more free markets and one or more controlled markets on their way to the consumer. Many illustrations can be constructed from the material presented above. At the end of the journey, all consumer goods are passed through a highly imperfect retail market.

III

THE PROBLEM OF INEFFICIENCY: MONOPOLY

BEFORE questions of public policy can be discussed with any assurance, it is necessary to go beyond mere description of the existing system to an evaluation of its operation. But evaluation implies a criterion of excellence. It is not possible to judge the performance of an economic system or a particular industry without having in mind some standard of efficiency. It is necessary at the outset, then, to erect a standard of efficiency, however rough, which can command general understanding and assent.

A perfectly efficient economic system would satisfy the wants of its members to the fullest extent permitted by existing technical knowledge and natural resources. The attainment of this goal involves at least four things. The productive resources of the community must be fully used; there must be no involuntary unemployment of either labor or equipment. These resources must be employed in producing the goods most desired by consumers by the most efficient methods. (This implies that consumers are free to choose what they will buy, and that they have adequate knowledge concerning the satisfactions yielded by different goods.) Individuals must be able to make a free and informed choice among alternative occupations. Finally, there must be no marked inequality of incomes.[1] It will be observed that these conditions are very general. They might conceivably be realized under either private or public owner-

[1] Economists will see at once that this is a very incomplete presentation. It is not possible, however, to elaborate and qualify it here, nor is it necessary, since the requisites for economic efficiency have been discussed at length by many writers. See particularly A. C. Pigou, *The Economics of Welfare*, London, 1929 (Third Edition).

ship of the means of production. Acceptance of these criteria of economic efficiency does not commit us in advance to any one type of economic organization.

The group of problems with which we are concerned here, usually summarized as "the monopoly problem," turn around the second of the above conditions.[2] This condition — that the goods most desired by consumers must be produced at minimum cost — may be broken down into still simpler elements. It requires, in the first place, that each good shall be produced in plants of the most efficient size, that these plants shall be operated at capacity, and that the best available techniques shall be used. Second, more of any good should be produced so long as consumers are willing to pay enough to cover the additional cost of production. Third, over a period of years the price of a good should no more than cover the costs of a producer of average efficiency (including in cost interest on the invested capital).

Are costs of production in Canadian industry as low as they might be? Do the prices of goods tend to equal the cost of producing them? It is curious that these questions have not been raised more frequently in the past. The explanation is partly that the general prevalence of competition has been taken for granted. Economic theorists have shown, moreover, that under conditions of "pure competition" an economic system will tend to reach a high level of efficiency.[3] If, then, competi-

[2] The discussion contained in the next three chapters thus constitutes only a partial evaluation of the efficiency of the Canadian economy. A complete evaluation would require discussion of unemployment, inequality of incomes, social stratification and other subjects. It is not possible, of course, completely to isolate the "monopoly problem" from these other matters. The interrelation between this problem and the problem of unemployment, in particular, will appear at several points in the subsequent discussion.

[3] By "pure competition" is meant a situation in which a standardized product is dealt in by a large number of buyers and sellers. Wheat and a few other agricultural products perhaps come closest to realizing the conditions of pure competition. It can be shown that under these conditions

tion leads to efficiency, and if competition already exists, its preservation should be the main object of public policy. Government should aim to prevent fraud and coercion, to check the growth of monopolies, to provide information, and the system may then safely be left to run itself. Most of those who have thought about the "monopoly problem" during the past fifty years seem to have conceived of it in this way.

It has been possible to take this view only by assuming that monopoly is rare, that it is unnatural, and that non-monopolized industries are purely competitive. But these assumptions are entirely unjustified. Monopoly is extensive, it is based on geographical and technical conditions, and must in most cases be accepted as permanent. Many non-monopolized industries are dominated by a few producers controlling prices and output by agreement. Even where price rivalry does exist, the conditions are very different from the "pure competition" of economic theory. There is no reason to assume that these industries serve the public better than the monopolies, or that the system as a whole operates with anything like maximum efficiency. The policy of fighting monopoly has been ineffective, not merely because it has never been thoroughly applied, but also because it was based on an inadequate analysis of the situation. We are faced, not simply with a monopoly problem, but with a much more complex and far-reaching problem of economic inefficiency.

The next two chapters attempt to appraise the relative efficiency of monopoly, price agreement and competition, and an additional chapter is devoted to the structure of retail trade. This analysis is valuable in itself, and is indispensable as a background for any discussion of Canadian policy toward competition.

---

unit cost tends to be reduced to a minimium and the price tends to equal the unit cost. See, for example, J. E. Meade and C. F. Hitch, *Economic Analysis and Policy*, New York, 1938, pp. 101–125.

THE LEVEL OF MONOPOLY PRICES

A monopolist guided solely by economic considerations would charge a price high enough to yield him the greatest possible profit. In practice, however, it is doubtful whether many monopolists charge all that the traffic will bear. In the case of basic raw materials, many of which are monopolized in Canada, this price would be relatively high and profits would be very large. To set prices at this level, however, would bring protests from customers and might lead to a public investigation. Political strategy thus dictates a price high enough to yield substantial profits but not so high as to draw down public censure. Methods of concealing profits are well enough developed, however, and Parliament is tolerant enough to permit profits of 15 or 20 per cent to be earned with complete respectability.

Scattered data concerning the earnings of monopolists appear in the Price Spreads Report and in other public documents. During the five years 1929–33, the Imperial Tobacco Company averaged more than 13 per cent on its capital stock and surplus after paying all taxes, setting up liberal depreciation allowances and reserves, and paying generous bonuses to the executives of the company.[4] Canadian Celanese averaged 9.4 per cent on capital and surplus over the seven years 1929–35, while Courtauld's averaged 10 per cent from 1926–35.[5] The pre-war profits of International Nickel were very large, rising in some years to 100 per cent. Profits have been smaller since 1917–18 but are still very substantial.[6] The Dominion Textile Company's no par common, which replaced $100 par common on a three-to-one basis in 1923, has paid dividends of $5 in every year except 1933 ($4.75) and 1934

[4] Price Spreads Report, p. 52.
[5] Textile Commission, Report, p. 120.
[6] Elliott, *op. cit.*, pp. 130–165.

($4.00).[7] The average return on stockholders' investment during the relatively poor years 1933–35 was 18.2 per cent.[8]

Isolated examples, however, cannot prove a general tendency. In an effort to establish the general tendency, the published statements of Canadian monopolies were studied over the period 1928–37. The record, unfortunately, is far from complete. Many companies do not publish earnings statements, and in other cases the continuity of the series is broken by corporate reorganizations. Even where net profits are made public, the meaning of the profits figure is doubtful and there is a strong tendency toward understatement of earnings. It is pointed out in Chapter VII that the capitalization of most of these companies has been inflated by writing-up assets and inserting values for "goodwill" and other intangibles. This makes the profit ratio seem less than it actually is. Profits, moreover, may be concealed by charging unduly large amounts to depreciation, by charging new investment to operations, by setting up needlessly large contingency reserves, and by other methods.[9]

It was considered worthwhile, however, to present the apparent earnings of ten companies for which data are available. While the sample is small, it includes several of the largest

[7] Textile Commission, Report, p. 122.

[8] Textile Commission, brief of J. C. McRuer, p. 199. Goodwill was excluded in making this computation.

[9] Evidence of the widespread use of these methods appeared in the hearings of the Textile Commission. Counsel for the Commission calculated that the Dominion Textile Company over-depreciated its plant by $15,179,238 between 1920 and 1936. This estimate seems to me somewhat high, but there can be no doubt that there was extensive concealment of profits in this way. The Company had no consistent depreciation policy. In general, it seems that small charges were made to depreciation when profits were low and much larger charges when profits were high. In addition, the company concealed profits by under-valuing inventories and by charging large sums to operations for improvements and new equipment. Much the same sort of evidence was presented with regard to Canadian Cottons, Ltd., and Montreal Cottons, Ltd. Textile Commission, Brief of J. C. McRuer, pp. 177–194.

Canadian monopolies, and the years included cover a complete business cycle. Table 3 compares the earnings of these com-

TABLE 3

EARNINGS OF SELECTED CANADIAN AND U. S. COMPANIES, 1927–37. (NET EARNINGS AFTER CHARGES AS A PERCENTAGE OF COMMON AND PREFERRED STOCK, SURPLUS AND RESERVES.)

Year	Monopolies Canada *	All Manufacturing Canada †	All Manufacturing United States ‡
1927	...	6.2%	8.4%
1928	13.0%	6.3	9.8
1929	19.7	6.9	13.4
1930	16.6	4.7	7.1
1931	9.7	3.3	3.3
1932	6.0	1.9	0.3
1933	3.4	1.5	3.1
1934	9.6	2.5	4.3
1935	10.8	2.7	6.7
1936	14.3	..	..
1937	19.1	..	..
Average	12.2%	4.0%	6.3%

* Canada Cement, Canadian Westinghouse, Canadian General Electric, Canadian Celanese, Canadian Industries Limited, International Nickel, Consolidated Mining and Smelting, Imperial Tobacco, Canadian Brewing Corporation, and National Breweries.

† C. R. Coughlin, *Earnings Record and Financial Policies of a Selected Group of Canadian Companies*, B. Comm. Thesis, Queen's University, Kingston, 1937 (unpublished). Coughlin's data were obtained, as were my own, from balance sheets published in Houston's *Annual Financial Review*. Of his 50 companies, 13 were public utilities, 5 pulp and paper, 5 iron and steel, 6 textiles, 5 milling and baking, and the remaining 16 miscellaneous manufacturing.

‡ National City Bank series, which includes 615 manufacturing companies in the United States.

panies with the general level of manufacturing profits in Canada and the United States. The result is so striking that imperfections in the comparison may perhaps be overlooked. The Canadian monopolies earned 12.2 per cent annually on stockholders' investment over the ten years 1928–37. Over the comparable period 1927–35, manufacturing companies generally were able to earn only 4.0 per cent in Canada and 6.3 per cent in the United States. It is clear that large monopoly profits exist, though it is impossible to measure them exactly because of the bookkeeping methods of the monopolists and the lack of any sure measure of "normal" profits.

This situation has two main results. Those who continue to buy the product in spite of its high price are forced to pay a tax to the monopolist. The amount of this tax is indicated to some extent by the surplus profits of the monopolist, but may be either more or less than this amount.[10] There is thus a transfer of income from consumers to managers, promoters, and stockholders. Since the income of these groups may be presumed to be above the general average, inequality of incomes is accentuated. Moreover, the principle that income should correspond to economic services rendered is offended, for much of the income diverted to promoters and officials comes to them merely because of the strategic positions which they occupy. The second result is that the output of the good is too small, since some would-be users are deterred from buying it by its high price.

The important practical question is whether these evils would be corrected by breaking up the monopoly into several separate firms. The situation which would result is sometimes called "oligopoly" (="few sellers") and it will be convenient to adopt this terminology here. Would the output of the good, then, be greater and its price be lower under oligopoly than under monopoly? No general answer can be given to this question. The result will depend on many factors, including the following: (1) The size of the market. (2) The importance of the economies of large-scale production. (3) The susceptibility of the

[10] The tax is equal to the difference between the monopoly price and the price (*i.e.*, the cost) which would prevail under conditions of competition. The tax will be greater than the monopolist's profits if his unit cost is higher than the cost under competition, and *vice versa*.

product to trade-marking and advertising, and the extent to which selling costs may increase under oligopoly. (4) The extent of price agreement among the oligopolists. (5) The conditions of entrance to the industry. (6) The shape of the demand curve. (7) The rate of change of demand. Any combination of these conditions may be set up and an appropriate result obtained.

Investment in the industry will usually be greater under oligopoly than under monopoly. If entrance to the industry is free, new firms may be expected to enter until profits are reduced to normal. If entrance is restricted the oligopolists themselves may expand their investment beyond the most profitable point because of failure to consider the long-run effects of their actions or ignorance of each other's plans. Even where there is a concerted effort to restrict total investment in the industry to the most profitable level, this goal may not be achieved. If demand is increasing at an uncertain rate there is room both for optimistic error and for attempts to capture a larger share of the market by expanding more rapidly than other producers.[11] In addition, oligopoly may involve a considerable expansion of facilities for sales promotion. Much of this investment will be in subsidiary industries such as printing and advertising, but it must still be attributed to the product whose sale is being promoted.

It does not follow, however, that price will be lower and output greater under oligopoly. Where the product is such as to invite large selling expenditures, or where the market is so small that one one firm can operate efficiently, the oligopoly price may easily be above the monopoly price.

Since most Canadian monopolies make producers' goods which give little scope for advertising, the problem of selling expenditures scarcely arises. The smallness of the market for

[11] This point is well argued in D. H. Wallace, *Market Control in the Aluminum Industry*, Cambridge, 1937, pp. 338–343.

many products is a more serious obstacle. In those cases where production is carried on in a single plant because of a restricted market or a limited source of raw materials, it would not be practicable to break up the monopoly. Where the article is produced in a chain of plants, however, as in the case of cement, gasoline, tobacco, rayon cotton yarn and thread, chemicals and explosives, each of these plants could probably be operated by a separate company with little change in production costs. The new situation would in many cases be one of regional monopoly because of the scattered location of the plants and the long freight hauls between regions. Where oligopoly resulted, as might occur in Central Canada for some products, there would probably be tacit agreement among the oligopolists on matters of industrial policy. If new investment were prevented, as would probably be the case, prices and output might show very little change from the period of monopoly.

Oligopoly may still be preferable to monopoly. There is always a chance that price competition may break out, particularly during depression periods. There may also be more rapid technical progress, and a somewhat better chance for new producers to gain a foothold. A careful survey of the alternatives, however, removes any hope that great gains may be achieved by the trust-busting method.

THE STRUCTURE OF PRICES

Information about the prices charged by monopolies in different areas and to different buyers is naturally very difficult to obtain. Discrimination among customers, however, seems to be common. In aluminum, "discrimination between different groups of consumers seems to take the form of charging lower prices to those groups, such as the automobile and electric industries, whose demand is more elastic, and higher prices to groups whose resort to other materials is less likely." [12] Again,

[12] D. H. Wallace in Elliott, *op. cit.*, at p. 270.

"most of the nickel produced was sold under long-term contracts at rates differing with the position and strength of the consumer. The armament syndicate in Europe was able to secure long-term contracts at a low price by threatening to produce its own nickel . . . the published prices of nickel were not the prices at which most of the nickel was sold."[13] It is common knowledge that a similar situation exists in the sale of heavy iron and steel products.

Geographical price discrimination is also common. The fertilizer association, for example, maintains one price list for western Ontario and another list for eastern Ontario and Quebec. Manufacturers located in western Ontario do not ship into Quebec, and vice versa.[14] The Quebec price is considerably below the Ontario price, possibly because of the influence of the Coöperative Fédérée, a large farmers' buying organization which is represented at the price-fixing meetings of the Quebec group. It was pointed out in Chapter I that many other price-fixing trade associations maintain basing point systems.

The technique of price discrimination is well illustrated by the practices of the petroleum industry. While there are several producers of petroleum, and it is thus technically incorrect to include the industry in a chapter on monopoly, the price policies of the industry are determined by the Imperial Oil Company.[15] Imperial Oil has discriminated between gasoline and fuel oil buyers, between wholesalers and retailers, between different regions of Canada and even between localities within the same region. The situation in British Columbia is now particularly well known as a result of recent investigations,[16]

[13] A. Skelton in Elliott, *op. cit.*, at p. 136.

[14] Price Spreads Report, pp. 76–78.

[15] See above, pp. 12–13.

[16] See particularly British Columbia, Royal Commission on Coal and Petroleum Products, Report, Vol. 1, 1936, and Tariff Board of Canada, Report on Reference 84 (Petroleum Products).

and most of the illustrative material presented below is drawn from that province. It is highly probable, however, that the situation is substantially the same in most other parts of Canada.

British Columbia is almost a perfect setting for a monopolist. Competition from other parts of Canada is barred by the long freight haul to the coast. The nearest domestic refinery is at Coutts, Alberta, on the other side of the Rockies. Competition from the United States is hindered by the tariff and, more effectively, by arrangements between Imperial Oil and its affiliates in the United States. The fact that the province is broken up by mountain ranges and that large towns are usually separated by a considerable distance facilitates price discrimination among localities.

The Imperial Oil refinery near Vancouver has more than half the refining capacity of the province, and produces an even larger proportion of the gasoline output [Table 4]. A considerable part of its output is sold to smaller refiners at very favorable prices in order to secure their coöperation in price-fixing and to discourage them from operating or expanding their own refineries. The Union Oil Company, for example, has not operated its refinery since 1926 because of an agreement

TABLE 4

PRODUCTION AND SALES OF PETROLEUM PRODUCTS, BRITISH COLUMBIA, 1934 *

(million gallons)

	GASOLINE		FUEL OIL	
Refiner	Production	Sales to dealers and consumers	Production	Sales to dealers and consumers
Imperial Oil	28.5	13.0	91.6	38.1
Shell Oil	10.3	10.5	20.0	1.1
Home Oil	4.8	9.5	5.6	7.2
Union Oil	...	5.6	...	72.7

* British Columbia, Royal Commission on Coal and Petroleum Products, Report, Vol. 1, pp. 5–6.

with Imperial which allows it to buy gasoline and fuel oil at very low prices.

The refiners' tank-wagon price for gasoline bears no direct relation to its cost of production. The companies have admitted more than once at public inquiries that they do not know their cost of production, and that price is set entirely on the basis of "competition," *i.e.*, on the basis of what the traffic will bear. Indeed, the bookkeeping arrangements of the companies are such that price is allowed to determine cost. Refining costs are allocated among gasoline, fuel oil and other products on the basis of the price at which the product can be sold. Gasoline, which sells at a much higher price than fuel oil, is thus said to cost more, and the higher the price the greater the cost. Costs derived in this way have been used successfully by the companies to justify the existing price structure and to demonstrate the need for higher tariffs, and few government investigators seem to have noticed the circular character of the reasoning.

The United States mid-continent field is used as a basing point for Canadian prices. The tank-wagon price at any Canadian point is obtained by converting the mid-continent price to Imperial gallons and adding rail freight to destination, customs duties, sales tax and handling charges. Hamilton, Ontario, which is nearest to the basing point, has the lowest tank-wagon price in Canada, while western Canadian points have the highest prices.[17] Rail freight from the basing point to Vancouver is 12.25 cents per gallon, and a mid-continent price of 6 cents per Imperial gallon is thus converted into a Vancouver price of 22 or 23 cents. In practice, however, it is crude oil which is shipped from the mid-continent field. This oil moves by water at a rate

[17] The tank-wagon price at leading Canadian cities in December, 1931, was as follows: Hamilton 17.6¢, Toronto 19.0¢, Montreal 18.9¢, Halifax 20.0¢, Winnipeg 20.3¢, Regina 23.5¢, Calgary 22.1¢, Vancouver 22.7¢. House of Commons, Banking and Commerce Committee, 1932, Gasoline inquiry, Exhibit 228.

of 0.31 cents per gallon and, moreover, enters Canada duty free. The Vancouver price thus includes a very large "mythical freight" and a smaller "mythical duty." There can be no doubt that this price structure yields a very large refinery profit to the companies operating in British Columbia.[18] Not only is the British Columbia consumer overcharged, but he is overcharged more severely than the Ontario or Quebec consumer. The Vancouver price should be considerably lower than the Ontario price because of the advantage of low water rates on the crude oil, yet in practice it is several cents higher. There is a similar discrimination against consumers in the prairie provinces, and to a lesser extent in the maritime provinces.

There is discrimination within British Columbia against cities and towns remote from Vancouver. The price-structure in September, 1935, is shown in Table 5. The price to consumers in the interior is increased in two ways: by charging a

[18] There seems no reason why the cost of refining at Vancouver should be much higher than the cost in the mid-continent field. The Imperial Oil plant, at least, is large enough for economic operation. Moreover, it is a "skimming plant," which does not require such expensive equipment as the "cracking plants" now used by the larger United States companies. The British Columbia Commission contended on these grounds that the tank-wagon price in Vancouver should not be higher than the mid-continent price plus freight and handling charges on the crude oil, plus a wholesaling margin of 2 cents. Such a computation would in 1934 have given a tank-wagon price of not more than 10 cents, whereas the price actually charged to Vancouver retailers was 18 cents. British Columbia, Commission on Coal and Petroleum Products, Report, Vol. 1, pp. 29 *et seq.*

The Tariff Board said in this regard: "The Vancouver price of gasoline appears to be totally out of line with prices on the Pacific Coast . . . there appears to be no reason why the price of gasoline in Vancouver should be higher than in Seattle. It is contended that the price of gasoline is approximately five cents higher in Vancouver than it should be under conditions of perfect competition. . . . These contentions were not successfully refuted by the oil companies. . . . The [tank-wagon] price does not represent cost plus profit at the refinery door, but it is the price which the traffic will bear." Tariff Board of Canada, Report on reference 84, pp. 132–134.

The retail price at Vancouver is usually 5 or 5½ cents higher than the price in Seattle, a short distance away.

TABLE 5

ANALYSIS OF THE GASOLINE PRICE STRUCTURE IN BRITISH COLUMBIA, SEPTEMBER 15, 1935 *

(cents per gallon)

Town or City	(1) Whole-sale price	(2) Freight from Imp. Oil Refinery	(3) Retail price	(4) Retailers margin	(5) "Added" whole-sale margin	(6) "Added" retail margin	(7) Total discrimi-nation
Vancouver	23.5	...	27.5	4.0	....	0.0	0.0
Victoria	24.5	.7	28.5	4.0	+0.3	0.0	+0.3
Fernie	27.5	8.3	33.0	5.5	−4.3	+1.5	−2.8
Cranbrook	28.5	8.1	35.0	6.5	−3.1	+2.5	−0.6
Nelson	30.5	6.5	37.0	6.5	+0.5	+2.5	+3.0
Trail	30.5	6.5	37.0	6.5	+0.5	+2.5	+3.0
Penticton	30.5	4.8	37.0	6.5	+2.2	+2.5	+4.7
Kelowna	30.5	5.2	37.0	6.5	+1.8	+2.5	+4.3
Vernon	30.5	5.2	37.5	7.0	+1.8	+3.0	+4.8
Kamloops	29.5	4.2	36.5	7.0	+1.8	+3.0	+4.8
Merritt	29.5	3.8	36.5	7.0	+2.2	+3.0	+5.2
Princeton	29.5	4.0	37.0	7.5	+2.0	+3.5	+5.5
Prince George	32.5	7.4	39.0	6.5	+1.6	+2.5	+4.1
Smithers	31.5	5.2	40.0	8.5	+2.8	+4.5	+7.3
Prince Rupert	26.5	1.2	32.5	6.0	+1.8	+2.0	+3.8

* British Columbia, Royal Commission on Coal and Petroleum Products, Report, Vol. 1, p. 43. Column 5 is the excess of the wholesale price over the Vancouver wholesale price plus freight. Column 4 is the excess of the retailers' margin over the Vancouver retail margin of 4 cents.

wholesale price more than sufficient to cover freight from the refinery, and by allowing a larger margin to retailers. The companies argue that larger wholesale and retail margins are necessary in order to cover higher distributive costs per unit in the smaller centers, but this means merely that distributive facilities in these areas are seriously overbuilt. The causal sequence seems to be as follows: the isolation of these districts from other sources of supply, the effective leadership of Imperial Oil, and the inelastic demand for gasoline have made possible the fixing of a price high enough to afford large distributive margins. These margins have encouraged building of service stations and bulk storage stations much in excess of actual needs. The companies then use these costs to justify high prices, and the circle is complete. In Fernie and Cranbrook, where there is competition from the independent refinery at Coutts, Alberta, prices are relatively low.

Discrimination is practiced between different types of dealer as well as between localities. The gasoline sales of the Imperial Oil Company in 1934, for example, were as follows:

Sold to	Amount sold (000 gallons)	Average price (cents per gallon)
Union Oil Company	7,670	10.38
Home Oil Company and other jobbers	7,234	12.62
Retailers and Consumers	13,634	22.26

[British Columbia, Royal Commission on Coal and Petroleum Products, Report, Vol. 1, pp. 23–24.]

The Union Oil Company receives the lowest price as an inducement to keep its own refinery closed. If the estimates of refinery costs noted above are correct, however, even this low price is profitable to Imperial Oil. On its sales to retailers, then, Imperial was obtaining a wholesale margin of at least 12 cents, and other refiners and jobbers were obtaining almost as much. The wholesale margin in the United States is rarely more than 2 cents per gallon.[19] A large part of the margin obtained by the British Columbia companies apparently goes to make up heavy operating losses on company-owned service stations, and to build new stations. Consumers are being taxed to provide funds for the building and subsidizing of superfluous retail outlets. The retailing operations of the companies are described in the following chapter.

There is discrimination, finally, between gasoline and fuel oil. These products emerge from the refining process in relatively stable proportions, and from a purely physical standpoint

[19] W. Hamilton and associates, *op. cit.*, p. 145.

might be said to have the same unit cost. Differences in demand conditions, however, make price discrimination profitable. Fuel oil competes with coal for heating and motive power, and the demand for it is therefore quite elastic. Gasoline, which is not subject to the competition of substitutes and which forms only a minor part of the cost of operating a car, has a markedly inelastic demand. The refiners thus obtain the greatest return by charging a relatively high price for gasoline, while setting the price of fuel oil sufficiently low to move the entire output. In 1934 Imperial Oil sold fuel oil at the refinery door for 2.5 cents per gallon, while the price of gasoline to jobbers was more than four times as great.[20]

The British Columbia Commissioner criticized this policy as injurious both to coal producers and gasoline consumers, and proposed that fuel oil prices should be raised and gasoline prices reduced. This proposal seems to be based on a misunderstanding of the situation. The reduced price of gasoline would tend to increase the output of fuel oil by increasing the consumption of gasoline. The higher price of fuel oil would reduce oil sales and a large unsold surplus would quickly accumulate. It would seem necessary, then, to reduce *both* the price of gasoline and the price of fuel oil. Such a policy would work some injury to coal producers, but this injury would probably be slight. The demand for gasoline is probably so inelastic that a reduction of several cents in the price would produce only a small increase in sales. The increase in the output of fuel oil would therefore be small, and could be moved by a slight reduction in price.

The price policy of Imperial Oil has been that which one would expect from an intelligent monopolist. Prices have been set high enough to yield large profits, yet not so high that they could not be defended with some show of reason before investigating committees. Consumers in peripheral regions of Canada

[20] British Columbia, Report of the Commission on Coal and Petroleum Products, Vol. 1, pp. 20–24.

and in the smaller cities and towns have been charged highest prices. The price structure has been so arranged that jobbers and small refiners are willing to coöperate with the leader. Only in the dissipation of profits through service-station competition has the behavior of the industry been something less than rational.

These policies have worked a double injury to consumers. The high level of prices has had the undesirable effects noted in the preceding section. The net effect of the discriminatory price structure would also seem to have been injurious. The large profits of Imperial Oil have not been levied impartially on all consumers, but have weighed heaviest on those remote from centers of population who were probably least able to bear the burden. In addition, the large margins allowed to jobbers and to some retailers have encouraged the wasteful multiplication of distributive facilities.

PRICE RIGIDITY AND ECONOMIC STABILITY

Recent studies of price behavior indicate that the prices of some articles fall very little during periods of depression while other prices fall a great deal.[21] It does not follow, however, that the prices which fall little are controlled while those which fall greatly are competitively determined. The price of an article sold under competitive conditions might fall very little during

[21] Means, studying the behavior of 747 items from United States Bureau of Labor Statistics wholesale price index over the period 1926–33, found that 191 items had changed less than once every ten months, while at the other extreme 181 items had changed at least three times every four months. It was also found that the prices which changed most frequently fell farthest during the depression, while prices which changed rarely fell relatively little. G. Means, *Industrial Prices and their Relative Inflexibility*, Senate Document 13, 74th Congress, 1st Session. A similar analysis of 499 items from the Dominion Bureau of Statistics wholesale price index yielded strikingly similar results for Canada. J. L. McDougall and A. F. W. Plumptre, "The Inflexibility of Canadian Wholesale Prices," *Canadian Journal of Economic and Political Science*, November, 1938.

depression if the trend of demand for the article were sharply upward, while the price of a monopolized article might fall greatly if production costs were being rapidly reduced. The alleged rigidity of controlled prices can be established only by a direct comparison of the movement of controlled and competitive prices during the cycle.

With this object, thirty-seven important manufactured articles were divided into the three classes set up in Chapter I. A price index was then computed for each group over the period 1927–38 [Table 6 and Figure 1].[22] Between 1929 and 1933 the prices of the monopolized goods fell by about 10 per cent, while under price agreement the decline was about 13 per cent. Agreements thus seem to be able to resist downward pressure on prices almost as effectively as monopolies. Competitive prices, on the other hand, fell by 36 per cent and the prices of farm products were cut in half. These discrepancies were only partially corrected during the subsequent recovery, and the controlled prices were considerably higher relative to the competitive prices in 1938 than in 1929.[23]

[22] These indexes, kindly prepared by the Dominion Bureau of Statistics, are weighted geometric means. The weights are those used by the Bureau in computing its index of wholesale prices; they represent in most cases the importance of the commodity in 1926, though adjustments have been made in a few cases. The sample of commodities included in the table, though numerically small, represents a large part of the annual value-product of Canadian manufacturing. The representative character of the results is impaired, however, by a rather wide dispersion among the individual commodity indexes. The underlying wholesale price data are also open to well-known objections.

[23] The behavior of these indexes, of course, may be due in part to extraneous factors. The "competition" group is composed largely of industries engaged in processing agricultural products, and one would expect the sharp decline of farm prices from 1929–32 to be reflected in the price of the processed goods.

At one stage of the work separate indexes were prepared for competitive industries in which producers are few and those in which many producers are present. It is interesting to note that the two indexes fell equally far during the depression. While the "many producers" index fell steadily,

TABLE 6

WHOLESALE PRICE INDEX NUMBERS OF SELECTED COMMODITIES, CLASSIFIED ACCORDING TO TYPES OF MARKET *

(1926 — 100)

Year	(1) Monopoly	(2) Price Agreement	(3) Competition	(4) Farm Products
1927	96.4	98.3	98.5	102.1
1928	96.0	97.2	99.6	100.7
1929	96.2	94.3	98.1	100.8
1930	93.5	90.2	91.5	82.3
1931	87.7	84.3	74.4	56.3
1932	87.0	82.4	65.9	48.4
1933	87.0	81.3	62.6	51.0
1934	87.4	81.7	68.2	59.0
1935	86.6	80.1	68.6	63.5
1936	87.2	80.5	70.4	69.4
1937	90.6	85.2	79.7	84.9
1938	88.8	83.2	77.5	...

* The composition of the sub-groups is as follows:

Monopoly: rayon, pig iron and steel billets, cement, asbestos, inorganic chemicals, explosives, nickel, aluminum (sheet), lead and copper.

Price agreement: sugar, cotton yarn and thread, rolling mill products, fertilizers, agricultural implements, leather, tobacco, salt, and wool cloth.

Competition: canned fruit, flour and milled products, bakery products, meats and poultry, newsprint and wrapping paper, paper pulp, boots and shoes, wool yarns, furniture, fishery products, silk hose, silk fabrics and coal.

These results must be interpreted with caution. It is possible that controlled prices fell more than appears from Table 6 because of secret discounts below the published prices on which the Bureau's indexes are based. Further, the statistical rigidity revealed by the table is not conclusive proof of rigidity in the theoretical sense of failure to adjust to changed demand and supply conditions.[24] It seems likely, however, and it will be

however, the "few producers" index held up well until 1931 and then fell rapidly, possibly indicating successful price maintenance in the early stages of the depression followed by complete collapse.

[24] For an elaboration of the distinction between the statistical and theoretical concepts of price rigidity, see E. S. Mason, "The Inflexibility of Prices," *Review of Economic Statistics*, May, 1938.

assumed here that controlled prices fell less than they would have under conditions of competition.

What were the effects of this situation on the depth and duration of the depression? Discussion will be confined to the effect of the level of producers' goods prices, in part because

Chart I

WHOLESALE PRICES BY TYPE OF MARKET

37 Commodities 1926=100

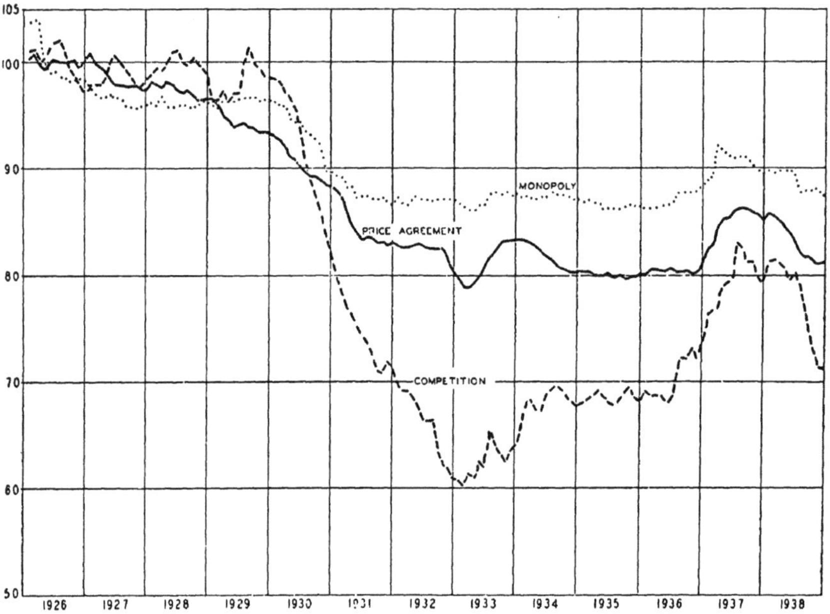

these prices seem to be of crucial importance at certain stages of the cycle, and in part because most of the controlled articles included in Table 6 are basic raw materials: pig iron, rolling-mill products, chemicals, non-ferrous metals, cement, asbestos.[25] Producers of these materials argue that the demand for their

[25] Group 2 includes also a number of consumers' goods: sugar, tobacco products, petroleum products, salt, cotton yarn and cloth, rayon yarn. For a good discussion of some possible effects of rigidity of consumers' goods prices on the length and intensity of depression, see D. H. Wallace, "Monopoly Prices and Depression," in *Explorations in Economics*, Cambridge, 1936, pp. 346–356.

products is highly inelastic and that to reduce prices in bad times would make very little difference in the quantity sold. The decline of output, they contend, is due entirely to a fall in demand and prices have very little to do with it. What is the merit of this argument? Would greater flexibility in the prices of basic materials materially reduce cyclical fluctuations of investment?

It seems generally agreed that the demand for one of a group of materials is markedly inelastic.[26] Cement, for example, is usually demanded jointly with several other materials and with construction labor. A reduction of 10 per cent in cement prices, unaccompanied by similar reductions elsewhere, would probably have a very slight effect on the volume of building construction. The chief effect of such a reduction would be to transfer a certain amount of income from cement manufacturers to cement purchasers. During a recession, the purchasers would probably use this additional income to reduce indebtedness and accumulate liquid reserves, and investment would increase little if any. From a purely individual point of view, therefore, the producers of capital goods and the trades unions in the capital goods industries are probably serving their own interest best by the present policy of stabilizing prices and wage-rates.

If, however, the prices of *all* materials (and the wage-rates of workers in the capital goods industries) could be reduced during a recession as rapidly as other prices, might not the decline of investment be checked? The answer evidently turns on the shape of the general demand curve for capital goods. It

[26] Not, however, *completely* inelastic, as producers often contend. Whitman, studying the course of steel prices in the United States, found that the *immediate* effect of a price reduction is a reduction in sales, and that a price increase causes an increase in sales. If the data are corrected for this tendency, however, a lower level of steel prices is associated with a larger volume of sales and *vice versa*. R. J. Whitman, "Elasticity of Demand for Steel," *Econometrica*, April, 1936.

is suggested as a working hypothesis that the demand for capital goods is inelastic at all times and that it becomes more inelastic during the depression and prosperity phases of the cycle. It seems reasonable to expect inelasticity in the demand for capital goods, for (1) it is a derived demand. It will normally be inelastic, therefore, where the demand for the finished good is inelastic or where capital costs form a small proportion of total costs. (2) There are at all times industries whose demand for capital goods is inelastic for special reasons. In the railroad industry, for example, new physical investment has declined almost continuously since the War, and lower material prices would probably have made little difference. (3) Opportunities for unusually profitable investment seem to be linked with the progress of discovery and invention. If a "crop" of inventions suddenly produces opportunities to earn from 20 to 200 per cent by installing new equipment, the demand for capital will increase, and this increase will be little affected by a moderate rise in the rate of interest or the cost of equipment. Conversely, a slackening in the rate of technical progress will make for a decline of investment regardless of equipment costs.

The view that the demand for capital goods becomes more inelastic in prosperity and depression rests on the well-known bias of producers' anticipations during these periods. During the course of recession and depression the temper of the business community shifts from qualified optimism to pessimism and even despair. It seems that the decline in demand for finished products will go on indefinitely. Riot and revolution are felt to be imminent dangers. Producers are therefore unwilling to offer hostages to the future by expanding their plants, and may not even replace existing equipment as it depreciates. Toward the peak of the cycle the opposite situation prevails. Producers, carried away by the buoyancy of the period, project the rising trend of demand into the future and build, not on the basis of present needs, but on the basis of expected future requirements. The demand for capital goods was probably almost as inelastic during 1928 and 1929 as during 1931 and 1932, though for opposite reasons. Higher prices for capital goods would probably have had little effect in the face of the prevailing optimism and the easy marketability of securities.

If this view is correct, it follows that the level of capital goods prices has little effect on sales during certain phases of the cycle. Once recession is well under way, reduction of basic material prices can probably do little to check it; conversely, moderate increases in these prices during prosperity will probably not prevent boom conditions from developing. In the early stages of recovery, however, when favorable anticipations incline producers toward expansion, low prices for capital goods will certainly stimulate the recovery process. Again, a prompt reduction of capital goods prices might help to check the development of a recession. In the early stages of a recession, business men usually regard the decline as merely temporary, and the demand for capital may retain considerable elasticity. It is therefore possible to argue that, if the cost of equipment were reduced at a time when producers are still reasonably optimistic, they might be induced to make fresh investments, and that this increased spending would in itself help to make their anticipations come true.[27]

A further qualification may be added, having to do with investment in residential housing. It seems reasonable to suppose that the demand curve for medium-sized, single-family homes is inelastic at the top, quite elastic in the central part because of the competition of apartments and other substitutes, and inelastic once more at the lower end. This demand prob-

[27] This line of argument, unfortunately, may easily be turned in the opposite direction. If, in order to reduce prices, capital goods producers cut wages and reduce their disbursements in other directions, the result may be a decline in purchases of consumers' goods. The anticipations of business men will be unfavorably affected and investment may be reduced rather than stimulated.

ably does not fall nearly so far during depression as does the demand for producers' goods. If the cost of building construction is held rigid, however, the decline may well be sufficient to bring the elastic portion of the demand curve below the price of new houses. This would explain the great decline in residential construction which occurs during depression. It would also follow, if this hypothesis is correct, that through a prompt reduction of building costs the volume of construction might be maintained at a relatively high level.

While greater flexibility of producers' goods prices would probably not alter the general outlines of the cycle, it would undoubtedly have an alleviating influence. The desirable policy might be termed one of "selective flexibility" — cutting the right prices at the right time. In practice, however, most monopolists and cartels follow an ultra-conservative price policy during depression periods. This sort of policy hampers the operation of the system, and it is doubtful whether it serves even to maximize the monopolist's profits. It is extremely difficult, however, to persuade business men to accept policies which go against conventional business practice, even though those policies might be in their own interest.

SUMMARY

Three disadvantages of monopolistic control have been examined. Output is restricted and prices are maintained at a level which yields unduly large profits. Closely related to this is the practice of price discrimination, which is simply a method of collecting larger tolls from the more vulnerable groups of consumers. Under certain conditions price discrimination may result in a larger output of the product, but most of the practices described above cannot be justified in this way. Finally, the maintenance of monopoly prices at about the same level over good and bad years probably makes depressions deeper and longer than they otherwise would be. The fact that most of the monopolized products enter into the construction of capital goods is particularly significant. Relatively high prices for capital goods must retard the growth of new products and new industries, and must be held at least partly responsible for the stagnation of investment during the past decade.

The other advantages and disadvantages of monopoly are more difficult to assess. Unified control of an industry obviously eliminates competitive selling expenditures. Whether unit production costs are reduced is more doubtful. Where a single plant of moderate size is sufficient to supply the market for the product, monopoly is desirable and probably inevitable. It is not so clear that a chain of cement, meat packing or chemical factories extending across Canada can be managed more economically from a central office. Administrative expenses mount at an alarming rate in these large concerns and may easily outweigh any savings in direct production costs. Detailed studies in this field are highly desirable, but would require data which only the companies possess and which they would not voluntarily reveal. It must also be considered that even though a single management may *potentially* be more efficient than several managements, it may actually be less efficient. Slack morale, wasteful methods, and technical stagnation are apt to set in when the pressure of competition is removed. The problem of bureaucracy is probably as acute in large business enterprises as in large government departments.

No remedy for monopoly is attempted at this point. Some reasons have been given for doubting the effectiveness of the "trust-busting" approach. Even were it possible to dissolve the large Canadian monopolies into several smaller concerns, the economic gains would probably be slight. It is suggested in Chapter X that the only real alternative to private monopoly is public monopoly, and an attempt is made to weigh the possible gains from public ownership and operation.

IV

THE PROBLEM OF INEFFICIENCY: AGREEMENT AND COMPETITION

AGREEMENT

MUCH of what was said above concerning monopoly applies also to price agreement. Cartels as well as monopolies try to fix prices at a profitable level, to resist the pressure for lower prices during depression, and to increase their profits by discriminating among buyers. In many industries, indeed, the economic results of price agreement are probably about the same as those of monopoly. Where entrance to the industry is virtually closed and selling expenses are relatively small — as in sugar, cotton yarn and cloth, copper, iron and steel, hardware and machine tools — the fact that there are several producers instead of a single firm probably makes little difference to the level of prices, profits and output. Under other conditions, however, agreement may yield results quite different from those of monopoly, and it is these cases which we wish now to examine.

It is noteworthy that in many cases the parties to a price agreement are able to earn only moderate profits. Producers usually regard this as conclusive evidence that their prices are "fair," and that consumers are being adequately served. But this conclusion does not necessarily follow. Profits may be low, not because prices are reasonable, but because costs are too high. Unit costs may be high because plants are being operated below capacity, because selling expenditures are large, or for a number of other reasons. Where this is the case, prices may be unduly high even though only moderate profits are being earned. It is necessary, then, to discuss the level of costs under price agreement, and this inevitably involves some discussion of selling expenses and unused capacity.

Unused capacity may be said to exist when a plant is being used at less than the rate which would give lowest unit costs (henceforth called the capacity of the plant).[1] Measurement of unused capacity, however, is extremely difficult. Business men often estimate capacity as the absolute maximum which the plant can produce. Lowest unit costs, however, may be obtained at a rate of operation considerably below the technical maximum. The point of lowest cost, too, will depend on the rate of wages, the cost of materials, and the valuation placed on plant and equipment. Even if the capacity of a plant at a particular time can be determined, and if it can be shown that the plant produced less than the capacity output in a given month or year, it does not follow that unused capacity exists. Seasonal fluctuations may make continuous full operation impossible. A plant large enough to meet boom demands, too, will necessarily operate below capacity in depression years, and unused capacity must therefore be measured in a "normal" year or perhaps averaged over a complete business cycle.

In spite of these difficulties of measurement, there are cases in which the existence of unused capacity is reasonably clear. One such case is that of the baking industry. The leading bakeries in most Canadian cities are owned or controlled by the "big five" flour-milling companies. In 1931 the capacity of these mill-controlled plants was estimated by company offi-

[1] It is necessary to distinguish carefully between *unused* capacity, as defined above, and *excess* capacity. Excess capacity properly refers to an industry rather than to an individual firm. It may be said to exist when, if all equipment in the industry were used to capacity, profits would be reduced below normal. This is the typical situation of an over-expanded competitive industry. Under competition, it is quite possible for considerable excess capacity to exist with very little unused capacity, while under monopoly or price agreement there may be much unused capacity but no excess capacity.

cials at 1,144,488,609 pounds per annum, or 20 per cent more than the production of *all* bakeries in Canada for the year. These estimates, however, were computed on a basis of 24-hour operation for 304 days in the year. Because of the necessity of providing for long week-ends and holidays, such regularity of production is impossible in practice. A revised estimate of "practical capacity" was accordingly prepared, and data for the larger cities are presented in Table 7.[2] The bakeries in question were apparently operating in 1931 at roughly 50 per cent of capacity. Making due allowance for the fact that 1931 was a depression year, it seems clear that there was (and still is) a large amount of unused capacity in this industry.

TABLE 7

PRODUCTION OF BREAD IN SELECTED CITIES, 1931

	Production of Bread			Mill-Controlled Plants		
	Mill plants	Other plants	Mill plants % of total	Capacity	Pro-duction	Production as % of capacity
Montreal	67,023	56,587	54	111,742	67,023	60
Toronto	71,366	58,058	55	158,255	71,366	45
Hamilton	10,409	22,139	32	28,377	10,409	36
Ottawa	15,894	8,603	65	22,928	15,894	70
Winnipeg	29,162	12,344	70	60,614	29,162	48
Vancouver ...	21,822	16,153	57	36,704	21,822	59

The same situation exists in the dairy industry. The Saskatchewan Royal Milk Inquiry Commission of 1933 reported that the number of milk distributors in Regina had increased from 2 in 1924 to 8 in 1933, and that "plants have been provided for at least double the needs of the City." [3] In Moose Jaw, "there are two important dairies . . . which operate at

[2] Evidence before the Price Spreads Commission, Vol. VI, p. 3668.

[3] Province of Saskatchewan, Royal Milk Inquiry Commission, 1933, Report, p. 5.

about 50 per cent of their capacity."[4] Similar conditions were found in every part of the province. "The facilities in operation have for some time greatly exceeded the requirements of all cities . . . except Saskatoon, yet additional plants and equipment continue to be provided."[5] Although sales of milk have increased since 1933, there must still be much unused capacity, not only in Saskatchewan but throughout the country.

Baking and dairying have been selected because information concerning them happens to be available, but it is highly probable that unused capacity exists in steel, gasoline, cotton cloth and many other industries in which prices are fixed. Price agreement, indeed, tends naturally to produce unused capacity. If prices have been set at an unusually profitable level, and if entrance to the industry is not prevented, new producers may be expected to arise. This will reduce the markets of those already in the industry and will curtail both their output and their profits. The process can go on until profits sink to the level prevailing in comparable industries.[6] The prices fixed by the large baking companies, for example, have made it profitable for others to enter the industry, and the problem of unused capacity has been aggravated by a great influx in small bakeries.[7] Even if new producers are excluded, unused capacity may develop through the expansion of existing producers. In a controlled industry it may sometimes be profitable to construct capacity which is not needed or desired for actual production. If production quotas are set on the basis of plant capacity,

[4] *Ibid.*, p. 13. [5] *Ibid.*, p. 36.

[6] In technical terms, the entrance of new producers will force the demand curves of existing producers to the left. Equilibrium will be reached when the demand curves of all producers (or of a "representative" producer) become tangent to their average total cost curves.

[7] The number of establishments in the industry increased from 1,658 in 1921 to 3,173 in 1934. Dominion Bureau of Statistics, Census of Manufactures: Annual Reports on the bread and other bakery products industry, 1919–1934.

for example, a larger plant may enable a firm either to enlarge its share of total sales or to obtain benefit payments for not producing.

Under competition, unused capacity would tend to be eliminated through the bankruptcy of the least efficient producers. Under price agreement, however, there seems no reason why it may not continue indefinitely. Each producer will have relatively high unit costs because of the necessity of recovering his overhead expenses from a low volume of output. Since prices are controlled, however, they can be adjusted to cover these high costs. Normal profits can still be earned, and there is no pressure for elimination of productive capacity.

Fixed prices and unused capacity lead naturally to high selling costs. When a plant is operating considerably below capacity there is a strong pressure to spread overhead costs by increasing sales. Producers are forbidden, however, to increase their sales by cutting prices and are therefore forced to embark on sales campaigns. Each firm attempts to differentiate its product from rival products by giving it a high-sounding name and placing it in a fancy package. The name of the product and its real or mythical advantages are kept constantly before the public through advertising. It is made available at as many retail outlets as possible. Frequent delivery, liberal credit terms, free premiums and a wide variety of other services are offered as inducements to buyers.

The object of these activities is to increase the demand for the product and to hold this demand steady in the face of counter-attacks by other companies. The actual outcome, however, is likely to be different. If one company alone increased its selling efforts, it might secure a considerable increase in sales. But when *all* firms increase their selling expenditures, their efforts tend to neutralize each other in much the same way as the efforts of rival nations to outstrip each other in military strength. Unless the advertising works a change in consumers' tastes, so that they desire more of this good and less of other goods than before, the market for the industry as a whole will not be increased. All companies will thus have higher unit costs than before, and it will be necessary to raise the price of the product to cover these costs.[8] It is a unique disadvantage of price agreement that it enables consumers to be taxed to pay for an armament race among producers.

While a single firm may temporarily increase its sales and its profits by a particularly ingenious sales campaign, competitive selling activities probably reduce the profits of the industry as a whole. It is a curious fact that, while price cutting is commonly condemned by business men as "cutthroat" and "unethical," sales campaigns, which have a similar effect on profits, are generally regarded as "sound business." One reason may be that price cuts are quickly imitated by other producers, and it is impossible to foresee how far price cutting may go. There is less danger of runaway competition in selling expenditures. Moreover, the effect of price cutting on profits is felt immediately. The consequences of selling competition take some time to work themselves out, and appear as a general increase of costs which cannot be blamed on any particular firm. The main reason, however, may be simply that salesmanship has insinuated itself so effectively into the *mores* of business that to question its merit is regarded as a major heresy.

An incidental result of selling competition has been the creation of two price levels for many consumer goods — one price

[8] This point has been well stated by the Combines Investigation Commissioner: "What the present inquiry has disclosed is that high prices have been due not so much to combination as to this costly form of competition in quality, service and salesmanship. The additional costs have quickly become absorbed into normal costs, ultimately appearing to be as necessary as any other items of expense. Such increased costs are all but certain to lead to higher prices, and the baker's explanation of these higher prices is that they do little more than reimburse him for his actual outlays." Department of Labour, Report of investigation into an alleged combine in the baking industry, 1931, p. 46.

for nationally advertised brands sold through a quality appeal, and a lower price for unadvertised goods sold on a price basis. There may be little or no difference in quality between the two groups. The situation is simply that selling expenses have increased both the cost of and the demand for the advertised brands, and their equilibrium price is therefore higher. It would be interesting to examine the distribution of consumers between these two types of product at any one time, and the changes in the distribution over time. It seems likely that the demand for low-priced goods comes very largely from the low-income groups who cannot afford to pay for prestige, and that the demand for such goods rises considerably in depression years.

The importance of selling expenses is now recognized, but their extent is still not generally known. The baking, gasoline, and dairy industries may serve to illustrate the methods used and their costliness. The baking industry, as was pointed out above, has suffered for many years from extensive unused capacity, while at the same time price competition has been held in check by agreements among the larger bakers.[9] The pressure for increased sales has therefore been turned in the direction of selling expenditures. Each manufacturer has endeavored to attract buyers by wrapping his bread in paper of a unique design, by giving it an attractive name, by preparing it sliced and in fancy shapes, by advertising that it is "slo-baked" or that it contains vitamins not found elsewhere. Deliveries have been made more frequent, credit services have been extended, and sales pressure has been increased. The delivery man is now usually termed a salesman. In addition to delivering the product, it is his duty to solicit new orders, which in many cases can only be obtained at the expense of rival bakeries. He is paid a small salary and is expected to

[9] For a fuller discussion of this industry, see my article in the *Quarterly Journal of Economics*, August, 1938.

earn the remainder of his income from a commission on sales.

These selling efforts are reflected in the cost figures of baking companies. A summary of unit costs of large and small bakeries in 1929 appears in Table 8.[10] It will be observed that

TABLE 8

SUMMARY OF COSTS OF MAKING AND SELLING BREAD, CANADA, 1929

(cents per lb. of bread)

	Mill-controlled bakeries	Large independents	Smaller independents
Number of bakeries reporting	76	12	31
Flour	2.38	2.39	2.58
Other Ingredients	0.78	0.87	0.69
Baking costs:			
Wages	0.59	0.52	1.02
Wrappers and wrapping	0.14	0.13	0.24
Other baking costs	0.33	0.39	0.21
Total baking costs	1.06	1.04	1.47
Delivery and sale:			
Wages and commissions	1.11	1.16	0.73
Other delivery costs	0.59	0.59	0.23
Advertising	0.12	0.14	0.02
Other selling costs	0.04	0.02	0.06
Total delivery and sale costs	1.86	1.91	1.04
Overhead	0.84	0.71	0.61
Total costs	6.92	6.92	6.39

for the larger concerns the cost of selling and delivering a loaf of bread was nearly as great as the cost of the flour used. In the city of Toronto, where competition of the sort described above has been particularly keen, the cost of delivery and sale in 1929 amounted to 2.45 cents per pound of bread, or rather more than the cost of flour.[11] Selling costs are not only large, but appear to be increasing. "A comparison of the present re-

[10] Department of Labour, Report of investigation into an alleged combine in the baking industry, 1931, p. 36. The sample of "smaller independents," it will be noticed, is very small, and perhaps biased.

[11] *Ibid.*, p. 40.

turns of five Montreal bakers with their statements in the 1925 bread inquiry (only five are comparable) indicates that distribution costs were increased in the case of four plants (from 1.00 to 1.98¢ per pound of bread, from 1.30¢ to 1.97¢, from 1.99¢ to 2.36¢, and from 1.04¢ to 1.80¢)." [12] Such increases in a period of less than five years are remarkable.

Additional evidence of the increase of selling costs is presented in Table 9.[13] It will be observed that the spread between the cost of the flour contained in a pound of bread and the retail price of a pound of bread more than doubled between 1913 and 1930. From a level of 2.40 cents in the former year it advanced steadily to 5.13 cents in 1930. While the price of flour was only 30 per cent greater in the latter year, the retail price of bread had advanced by nearly 80 per cent. Part of the increased spread may represent the use of more expensive ingredients — sugar, shortening, milk — while part of it represents the cost of wrapping, a sanitary practice which was not common in 1913. But when these have been allowed for, there remains a considerable price increase due to competitive advertising, competitive delivery service and other sales promotion devices for which there is probably little genuine consumer demand. The close analogy between this situation and that which exists in the marketing of milk will be readily apparent.

The small baker ordinarily sells his bread for two, three, even five cents less than the price of the standard brands. He can do this partly because of lower overhead, partly because he works himself and his family long hours for a low return, partly because he has an inadequate system of accounting and leaves some cost items out of consideration. His greatest advantage, however, lies in the fact that his selling costs are only half as great as those of the large producers. The small baker sells much of his bread over the counter in his shop. He spends nothing for delivery and little or nothing for advertising. Lower

[12] *Ibid.*, p. 33.

[13] *Ibid.*, p. 13.

costs and lower prices have enabled small bakers to maintain their position in the industry and even to increase their sales at the expense of the large producers during the depression.

TABLE 9

"SPREAD" BETWEEN FLOUR AND BREAD PRICES, 1913–30 *

(*cents*)

Year	Cost of flour used in making 1 lb. bread	Retail price of bread per pound	Amount of "Spread"
1913	1.80	4.2	2.40
1914	1.99	4.3	2.31
1915	2.45	4.7	2.25
1916	2.67	5.0	2.33
1917	4.07	7.0	2.93
1918	4.13	7.8	3.67
1919	4.04	7.9	3.86
1920	4.94	9.3	4.36
1921	3.41	8.1	4.69
1922	2.65	6.9	4.25
1923	2.36	6.7	4.34
1924	2.56	6.9	4.34
1925	3.30	7.8	4.50
1926	3.08	7.6	4.52
1927	2.87	7.7	4.83
1928	2.66	7.7	5.04
1929	2.71	7.8	5.09
1930	2.37	7.5	5.13

* Price series used: Flour — Manitoba 2nd Patent, car lots, delivered Montreal (Dominion Bureau of Statistics); Bread — white bread, retail prices monthly in 69 localities (Department of Labour). Flour cost computed on the basis of 270 lbs. of bread from a 196 lb. barrel of flour.

The price of gasoline is set in most areas by tacit agreement among the larger producers, led by Imperial Oil. The struggle for sales is thus forced into non-price channels. Each producer tries to secure control of as many retail outlets as possible, and most "independent" dealers are now bound by contract to take all of their gasoline from one company.[14] In addition, the major producers have built large numbers of company stations, most of which are leased to operators though a few are operated by company employees. The purpose of these stations is both to increase sales and to serve as advertising

TABLE 10

GASOLINE SOLD THROUGH SERVICE STATIONS, BRITISH COLUMBIA, 1934 *

	Number of stations	Gasoline sold (thousand gallons)	Percentage of gasoline sold
Company owned (wholly or partly) ..	535	9,301	42.5
100 per cent accounts	1,344	10,770	49.2
Split accounts	144	1,817	8.3
Total	2,023	21,888	100.0

* British Columbia, Report of Royal Commission on Coal and Petroleum Products, Vol. 1, pp. 39–41.

media. Building is highly competitive, and when one company builds in a locality other companies feel compelled to locate there also. There seems also to be a systematic buying-up of good sites in order to prevent rivals from occupying them.[15]

These policies have resulted in a serious overbuilding of service stations. In Victoria, for example, there is a gasoline pump for every 43 cars, and in Vancouver one for every 48 cars, as compared with one for every 114 cars in Seattle.[16]

[14] The British Columbia Commission found that retailers who were willing to sign such a contract were given an additional discount of 1 per cent on their gasoline and equivalent discounts on oil and other supplies. As a result nearly all dealers in the province are "100 per cent accounts." Report, Vol. 1, pp. 48–49.

[15] An independent refiner and marketer testified as follows before the British Columbia Commission: "When we come to buy a site for a service station we invariably find, if there is a service station in one corner, that the same company owns the other corner, in order to prevent — at least I surmise that is the reason, I do not see any other — another competitive station being erected on the other side of the street." Report, Vol. 1, p. 73.

[16] *Ibid.*, p. 37.

The British Columbia Commission concluded that in most towns one half or more of the stations could be eliminated with no loss in convenience to the public. The volume of sales available to each station is further reduced through direct sales by the companies to consumers. In some areas company tank-wagons go about the country peddling gasoline to farmers in much the same way that milkmen compete for business in the cities. The average amount sold by Victoria service stations in 1934 was 21,000 gallons. With a margin of 4 cents per gallon, this provides the operator with only $840 to cover his operating and living expenses.

Company stations, however, operate only nominally on a 4 cent margin. The company comes to the operator's assistance by leasing him the station for a nominal sum, installing expensive equipment, providing free supplies and repairs, and even giving cash subsidies. Heavy losses are incurred by all of the companies on their retailing operations. Imperial Oil lost 3.88 cents per gallon on sales through its own stations in British Columbia during 1934, and the other major companies had even larger losses. Operating expenses of company stations ranged between 8 and 10 cents per gallon sold.[17] The companies are able to afford these losses because of their large refining and wholesaling profits, made possible by price control. Consumers have been taxed, in short, in order to erect unnecessary service stations and to provide subsidized competition for the independent retailer. While prices to consumers are high, the net profits of the companies are only moderate, and the earnings of independent retailers are very low.

A similar duplication of distributive facilities has occurred in the dairy industry. Dairy companies, faced with unused capacity, have tried to increase their sales by sending wagons to all parts of the city. Many blocks are covered by five or even ten

[17] *Ibid.*, pp. 46–47.

wagons,[18] each of which sells relatively little. Since it costs almost as much to deliver 200 quarts from a wagon as to deliver 400 quarts, low sales mean high delivery costs. These high costs reflect the fact that the driver is being paid for touring the neighborhood rather than for delivering milk.

Montreal dairies in 1931 paid producers 4.85 cents per quart of fluid milk and obtained a margin of 5.46 cents for themselves, of which 1.60 cents went for processing, 2.93 cents for delivery, and 0.90 cents for selling and administration.[19] The figures for Quebec dairies were almost identical. Processing cost Winnipeg dairies 1.80 cents per quart in the first half of 1938, while delivery cost 3.00 cents per quart.[20] The Saskatchewan Milk Commission found that in the Regina market delivery wagons were "at least 75 per cent in excess of actual needs,"[21] and the evidence was similar with regard to other cities and towns. It is amazing that the cost of delivering milk should be almost twice as great as the cost of receiving, pasteurizing, bottling and storing it. Yet evidence from all parts of the country leaves no doubt that this is the case.

Without attempting to assess the full effect of selling expenditures, a few suggestions may be offered. It seems necessary to distinguish between activities which serve merely to differentiate the product and activities necessary for the transfer of the product to the consumer. Informative advertising, typified by the classified advertisement, obviously serves a useful function. Advertising designed merely to promote a par-

[18] A study made in Milwaukee, Wisconsin, showed that, while there were only 1,097 miles of streets in the city, milk wagon routes aggregated 11,830 miles. Each block was covered on the average 7 times, while one block was served by 17 wagons. Agricultural Adjustment Administration, A Study of the Milwaukee Milk Market, 1933.

[19] Bond, *op. cit.*, p. 44.

[20] Milk Control Board of Manitoba, Statement with reference to Order No. 8, June 1, 1938.

[21] Report of the Commission, 1933, p. 6.

ticular brand, on the other hand, is usually either irrelevant or actually misleading, and could probably be eliminated with no economic loss.[22] Those engaged in this sort of activity are really being maintained on an indirect form of relief, since they are being paid by the community for producing nothing. If they were thrown out of employment there would be no loss to the community even in the short run and in the long run there would be a considerable gain, since most of them would probably be reabsorbed into productive occupations. The service station and the delivery wagon occupy an intermediate position. They perform a necessary service, but the cost of this service is needlessly high and could be greatly reduced by a consolidation of distributing facilities.

The consequences of price agreement may be summarized tentatively at this point. Eagerness to secure the profits made possible by price fixing leads to the construction of too much productive capacity, which leads in turn to intensive selling efforts. The chief effect of selling expenditures, however, is to raise costs rather than to increase sales. Unit costs are thus higher than they need be for two reasons: high unit overhead resulting from under-utilization of plant, and high unit selling costs. If an industry in this condition is attacked for price fixing it usually replies that its profits are not large and that consumers are therefore not being exploited. The fallacious nature of this argument should now be clear. It is entirely

[22] Against this it may be contended (1) that advertising may increase the *total* sales of a product, thus reducing unit costs and making possible lower prices. This is not likely to be important, however, except in the case of informative advertising necessary to introduce a new product to consumers. (2) That consumers derive increased satisfaction from using advertised articles. This proposition also seems very doubtful, except perhaps for a limited range of high-priced "prestige goods." (3) That advertising yields certain direct satisfactions, e.g., the pleasure of listening to privately-sponsored radio programs. Against this, however, must be balanced the unpleasantness of billboard advertising and "high pressure salesmanship."

possible for both costs and prices to be too high even though earnings are low. It is quite possible, indeed, that price agreement may result in a price higher than that which a monopolist would charge.

It is not contended that all cases of price agreement conform to this pattern, or that the pattern itself has been clearly established. It is presented merely as the hypothesis which seems most nearly to fit the available facts. Thorough studies of additional industries in which prices have been fixed are highly desirable.

COMPETITION

In economic writings the term "competition" usually carries an overtone of beneficence. In business circles, however, "cutthroat" and "competition" are regarded as virtually one word. Price reductions are also termed "ruinous," "chaotic," "insane," "unethical."[23] It is necessary to explore the reasons for these complaints, and to consider the remedies which business men propose.

"Cutthroat competition" and similar terms are used by business men in at least two ways. They sometimes refer to misrepresentation of goods, commercial bribery, defamation of competitors, and other dubious trade practices. There would be general agreement that these practices are undesirable, and most of them are already prohibited by law. In other cases "cutthroat competition" refers to practices which undermine the existing price structure, either through direct price reductions to particular buyers, or through indirect reductions —

[23] The bitterness of business men on this point is strongly impressed on one by even a small amount of reading in trade journals. The following is a typical outburst: "The price-cutter is worse than a criminal. He is a fool. He not only pulls down the standing of his goods; he pulls down himself, and his whole trade. He scuttles the ship in which he, himself is afloat, . . . Price-cutting is not business any more than smallpox is health." (Editorial in the *Canada Lumberman* for November 15, 1925, entitled, "Price Cutting is Peanut Salesmanship.")

advertising allowances, free deals, rebates, and the like.[24] It is important to draw a clear distinction between these two uses of the term. In what follows we shall be concerned only with price cutting.

The language used by business men in denouncing price cutting often implies that any price reduction constitutes cutthroat competition. Such a definition, however, is too broad to be useful. It seems better to define cutthroat competition as existing when prices have fallen so low that a large part of the capital invested in an industry is unable to earn a reasonable return. Practical application of this definition, of course, is extremely difficult. In addition to the difficulties involved in erecting a standard of reasonableness, determination of the actual rate of return in an industry is by no means easy. It is necessary, too, to consider the earnings of the industry over a considerable period, since in some years nearly all industries will show low earnings because of general depression. In what follows we shall be concerned only with industries which have experienced subnormal earnings over at least a complete business cycle, and which therefore have some claim to be regarded as chronic problems.[25]

[24] Most large manufacturers have an elaborate price structure comprising thousands of individual prices. The price charged to a particular buyer will depend on the quantity and quality of the goods bought, on the trade classification in which the buyer falls, and perhaps on personal or strategic considerations. The actual price may be cut without any change in the nominal price by altering quantity discounts, credit terms, freight allowances, or some other term of the bargain. A cut to one buyer, moreover, need not be extended immediately to others. News of the cut is likely to leak out, however, and other buyers will demand similar reductions. In this way the existing price structure is gradually undermined. In most manufacturing markets, then, price cutting is a tortuous, complex and secretive process, the full effect of which may not appear for a considerable period.

[25] In periods of general depression most industries complain that competition is cutthroat because their profits are falling. It is necessary, however, to distinguish clearly between this situation and that of a single industry which shows low earnings over a long period. There is a presump-

Cutthroat competition, defined in this way, requires the existence of excess capacity.[26] The conditions under which excess capacity may develop are so well known that they can be summarized very briefly. The demand for a product may turn downward unexpectedly because of a change in public taste or the appearance of a substitute product, and may decline more rapidly than productive capacity can be reduced. In the capital goods industries, a non-recurring demand may induce the building of plants for which there is no permanent need. Where demand is increasing, producers may overbuild because of a misjudgment of the rate of increase. Even though the rate of growth of total demand has been correctly estimated, an individual producer may overestimate the share of the new business which will fall to him, either because of ignorance of the expansion programs of his rivals or because of undue confidence in his selling ability. Or he may reason that if he does not expand ahead of demand his rivals will do so anyway, and his caution will leave him with a smaller share of the market than before. He may thus feel obliged to over-expand in order to maintain his relative position in the industry.[27]

Insufficient attention has been given to the possibility that the capacity of an industry may be increased considerably with little or no new investment. Machinery may be made to run faster or more continuously by relatively small alterations. A better routing of materials through the plant, the use of conveyors, faster chemical reactions which reduce the time required

---

tion that the remedies for low earnings due to a general decline of business activity will differ from those appropriate to low earnings caused by maladjustment of a particular industry.

[26] This is a truism. Excess capacity was defined above as a situation in which, with all equipment being used at capacity, the profit ratio of the industry would be below normal. But when excess capacity is defined in this way it becomes synonymous with cutthroat competition.

[27] This point is well argued in D. H. Wallace, Market Control in the Aluminum Industry, Cambridge, Mass., 1937, pp. 333–342.

for important processes, may give increases in productivity quite out of proportion to the investment required. An industry may thus find itself with excess capacity, not because of the building of new plants, but because of revolutionary changes within existing plants. Somewhat analogous is the discovery of a new and superior location for production. This may lead to extensive construction of plants in the new, low-cost area even though the result is excess capacity and low earnings for the industry as a whole.

The existence of excess capacity does not lead necessarily to subnormal earnings, provided producers can prevent the excess from being used.[28] Cutthroat competition arises only when excess capacity is accompanied by inability of producers to control production and prices. Some of the conditions which may make control difficult were indicated in Chapter I. Where the number of producers is large it is difficult to reach a consensus of opinion and to enforce this on all members of the industry. Moreover, control in such industries necessarily takes the form of a trade association, whose extensive records and formalized enforcement machinery render it relatively open to investigation and prosecution under the Combines Act. In other cases price control may be prevented by the presence in the market of a few large buyers. The heterogeneity of the industry may be a source of difficulties. High-cost and low-cost producers, makers of national brands and of "price lines" may disagree concerning the general advisability of control and the details of particular proposals. Personal factors, finally, cannot be neglected. The desire of a particular producer to remain independent, or to expand his business, or to worst a rival whom he dislikes, may prevent agreement even when all other conditions appear favorable.

[28] That is, provided the excess capacity can be turned into unused capacity. It is not unused capacity which renders a competitive industry unprofitable, but excess capacity which is used.

Inability to control prices and output in the face of excess capacity produces similar results in all cases, but the similarity of the result is veiled by apparent differences in the process. Where the number of producers is large, excess capacity produces its consequences gradually and apparently inevitably. Prices decline by small stages. Trade journals plead with producers to restrict their output. Individual producers, however, are unwilling to undertake restriction without an assurance that others will do likewise. The continued high rate of output reduces prices and profits still further. Since no one producer can be blamed for the situation, it is attributed to impersonal forces or to the collective unwisdom of the group — to "chaotic competition," "overproduction," "a mania for volume."

Where producers are few (and this is the more common case in practice), more spectacular developments may be expected. Each producer is closely watched by his competitors, and there is a subtle pressure on all not to reduce prices. Prices may be maintained for a considerable period because of the strength of this group opinion. When the break comes, however, it is likely to be sharp. One or more firms make reductions. The others denounce this action but are soon obliged to follow, and prices go down hand-over-hand. Secret discounts are given, price warfare breaks out, prices tumble, then recover as a "truce" is arranged. Prices move less regularly than where there are many producers, the future is less predictable, nervousness is greater, and bitter feeling develops more frequently. The firms which have shown greatest willingness to reduce prices are stigmatized as "price cutters," and the whole blame for the industry's misfortunes is placed on their shoulders.

Unless the industry is rescued from this situation by an increase of demand, some firms will fail, and some plants will probably be closed down or transferred to other uses. Many examples of this process could be given from Canadian manufacturing. The milling industry, which had been greatly expanded to meet war demands, had in 1919 an annual capacity of almost 43 million barrels. In the post-war period, however, annual production never rose above 21 million barrels. Over the period 1919–32, the industry operated on the average at only 47 per cent of its stated capacity. The result was severe price competition, low earnings for many companies, and the shutting down of many mills. Capacity in 1934 was only 32 million barrels, and the process of liquidation is doubtless still continuing.[29]

The high profits of the newsprint industry in the early twenties led to a burst of plant construction quite out of proportion to the growth of demand. The daily capacity of the industry increased from 5,830 tons in 1924 to 12,618 tons in 1930, or 117 per cent.[30] Over the same period the consumption of newsprint in the United States increased by only 26 per cent. As a result, the operating ratio of Canadian newsprint mills fell from almost 100 per cent of capacity in 1923 to 83 per cent in 1929 and 50 per cent in 1932.[31] Even this rate of production forced newsprint prices down from $73 per ton in 1923 to $40 per ton in 1933. By this time seven large companies controlling 58 per cent of total capacity were in receivership or had been reorganized.[32] There has as yet been little withdrawal of Canadian newsprint capacity from production. This might mean that newsprint prices are still above the level which would be reached were competition entirely free. Probably more important is the fact that most of the old, high-cost mills in the

[29] Price Spreads Report, p. 89.

[30] House of Commons: Committee on Banking and Commerce, 1934. Minutes of Proceedings and Evidence, p. 890.

[31] Financial Post, October 1, 1932.

[32] J. Guthrie: The Newsprint Paper Industry (Doctoral dissertation, Harvard University, 1939, unpublished), p. 103. These failures, of course, were not due entirely to the decline of prices. Probably a more important cause was the inflation of capital accounts during the mergers of the late twenties (see Chapter VII).

industry are located in the United States. Newsprint capacity in the United States fell by almost 50 per cent between 1928 and 1936, part of the equipment being transferred to the production of fine papers and part being abandoned entirely.

The experience of these and other industries indicates that a situation of cutthroat competition tends in time to correct itself through the elimination of excess capacity. As plant capacity is scaled down to market requirements, prices and profits rise once more toward a normal level. The length of time required for this readjustment will depend on the extent of the initial excess capacity, the trend of demand, the specialization and durability of equipment, the ease or difficulty of closing down part of a plant without disrupting the productive process, the extent to which corporation directors are motivated by economic considerations, and other factors. It is clear that the process may easily require fifteen or twenty years.

The fact that bankrupt companies can be reorganized and resume production with lower fixed charges is often said to prolong the period of adjustment. This argument, however, seems to rest on a misunderstanding. The possibility of writing down capital does enable a plant to continue in operation so long as it has any value whatever — that is, so long as its output yields anything above the direct cost of production. When the plant no longer yields any surplus above direct costs, however, it can no longer be rehabilitated through reorganization, and will be closed down. This is exactly what would happen under the conditions of individual proprietorship assumed by classical writers on competition. Reorganization is simply a device intended to give the corporation something of the financial flexibility of the proprietorship, and to provide for legal recognition of a reduced rate of earnings.

It must be admitted, however, that under certain conditions competition does not provide an automatic corrective for excess capacity. Where workers are unorganized and have a limited choice of jobs — as, for example, in an isolated company town — an employer can make large wage cuts with impunity. In many industries, therefore, at least part of the producers will be able to escape the consequences of falling prices by reducing wages. Firms which would otherwise have been eliminated are thus enabled to remain in production, excess capacity is perpetuated rather than reduced, and the incidence of cutthroat competition is shifted to wage earners instead of being borne by profits.[33]

Another possibility usually overlooked by earlier writers is the existence of general unemployment. Where unemployment is widespread and persistent, many of the unemployed will try to establish themselves in industries which require little capital, such as baking, the garment industries, printing, retailing, and the repair and service trades. These men require no return on their meagre investment, and will often work their entire families long hours for little more than could be obtained on relief. Thus although their methods of production may be relatively inefficient, they are able to sell at prices low enough to take business away from larger and more efficient establishments. This sort of situation does not correct itself automatically. If some of the larger firms are forced out of existence because of their rigid cost structures, and if some of the small men do fail through mismanagement or lack of resources, their places will quickly be filled by others who prefer work at low wages to unemployment.

Cutthroat competition, then, appears frequently, persists for relatively long periods, and in some cases assumes the proportions of a chronic illness. What remedies have been suggested for this situation? The proposal which finds greatest favor among business men is to fix prices at a level sufficient to cover

[33] An incidental result is that the firms which are eliminated are not necessarily the least efficient, but may be simply those which have greatest difficulty in cutting wages.

"cost" or "cost plus a reasonable profit." While there can be no doubt that this policy would increase business profits, it would seem to be against the interest of the consuming public.[34] The direct effect of fixing (and presumably raising) prices is to reduce consumption and turn excess capacity into unused capacity, supporting the burden of overhead charges by a tax on consumers.[35]

The attempt to demonstrate that price fixing is really in the public interest has gone through much the same evolution as the business argument for a protective tariff, and like the latter has now come to rest mainly on a professed desire to protect wage rates. Price cutting, it is argued, leads to wage cutting which reduces the worker's standard of life. This can occur, however, only where the workers are for some reason in a weak bargaining position. The proper approach to the problem, therefore, would seem to be through measures designed to increase the knowledge, mobility, and organization of labor. If it is desired to set a minimum level of earnings below which no worker can fall, this can be accomplished through adequately enforced minimum wage legislation. The fact that most employers would object to this sort of solution probably indicates that their real concern is with profit margins rather than with wage rates.

The superficial fairness and simplicity of price fixing schemes

[34] There are a few exceptions to this statement. In the mining industries, for example, very low prices may lead to an undesirably rapid use of exhaustible resources, and also to wasteful methods of mining. Producers tend to respond to low prices by "picking the eyes from the vein," a practice which increases ore yields and reduces unit costs for the time being but renders the rest of the vein irrecoverable.

[35] It should be noted that the effect is the same if the scheme includes the buying up and scrapping of surplus equipment. Any equipment bought will presumably be priced on the basis of anticipated earning power under the control plan. While the equipment itself is scrapped, its conjectural value is added to the capitalization of the survivors, and consumers must still pay a return on this capital.

rest on an ambiguity of statement which appears as soon as one inquires what is meant by "cost." Cost is a highly equivocal concept, and accounts can be set up to show almost any cost which is desired. To allow producers to set a price which will cover cost, then, is to give them virtually a blank check. Moreover, producers almost always think in terms of average cost. It is desirable, however, that goods should be produced so long as the additional cost of producing them is covered. Where excess capacity exists, a price designed to cover average cost will be too high to permit the most desirable utilization of plants.

It must be remembered, too, that different producers will have different costs. In 1934 the costs of the larger Ontario flour mills ranged from $3.49 per barrel to $4.03 per barrel, while the costs of large Alberta mills varied from $3.25 to $4.06 per barrel.[36] Again, in 1935 the costs of corrugated and solid fibre box producers varied from 84.7 to 104.2 per cent of the selling price.[37] Other studies indicate that a spread of 20 per cent between high-cost and low-cost producers is not at all unusual. It would thus make a great deal of difference whose costs were selected as the basis for price fixing.

An impartial commission might conceivably determine an average cost for the industry, and set prices at this level. High-cost producers, however, will be faced with failure under such an arrangement and, since this is about what would have happened anyway, government intervention will have produced no result. It is much more likely that the producers themselves will determine "cost," either directly as under the NRA codes, or indirectly through the data which they supply and the influence which they exert. So far as one can judge from existing trade association practice, there will be a strong tendency to

[36] Report on the Flour Milling and Baking Industries, prepared for the Royal Commission on Price Spreads, 1935, p. 42.

[37] Department of Labour: Report of investigation into an alleged combine in the manufacture of paperboard shipping containers, 1939, p. 25.

"hold an unbrella over the industry" by setting prices high enough to cover the costs of the least efficient producers. This is necessary in order to secure coöperation of the marginal firms, and is satisfactory to low-cost producers as well since it enables them to earn larger profits.[38]

Price fixing based on the costs of the least efficient firms has several undesirable results. The pressure on producers to effect economies is reduced, for the fear of failure is a far sharper spur than the desire for larger profits when profits are already large. Low-cost firms are prevented from increasing their sales through price cutting, and are forced to reap their reward in high profits. The triumph of efficiency over inefficiency is retarded or prevented altogether. The problem of excess capacity, which under competition tends to be solved through liquidation, is perpetuated and even aggravated by price fixing. Not only are the existing producers protected and enabled to remain in the industry, but new producers may be attracted as described in the preceding section. The other disadvantages of fixed prices — high selling expenses, price rigidity, etc. — may also make their appearance.

These harmful consequences of price fixing may be illustrated from the experience of the paper box industry. It was pointed out above that the costs of individual producers in this industry differ by as much as 20 per cent. Under competitive conditions one would expect the price to settle somewhere in the middle of this range, resulting in failure of some of the high-cost firms and a steady expansion of the more efficient producers. A strong combination, however, has been able to maintain prices at a level several per cent above the cost of the least efficient pro-

[38] It is conceivable that a price high enough to protect the marginal firms might be too high to yield the maximum profit to other producers. The low-cost firms, however, would probably still be willing to coöperate, regarding the profits which they were obliged to forego as an insurance premium against the risk of price competition.

ducer. During the year 1935–37 all producers showed net profits, and the group as a whole made average profits of 15.1 per cent.

The production quotas allotted to each producer remained almost unchanged over the period 1931–37, the more efficient firms showing no tendency to expand relative to the others. The high-cost firms, it is true, tended to produce less than their quotas and to draw large bonuses from the central pool, while contributions to the pool on account of excess production came almost entirely from the low-cost firms.[39] This indicates that the low-cost firms could expand their production considerably, and would probably do so except for the quota restriction. They are willing to observe the quota arrangement, however, in order to insure themselves against unrestrained price cutting. An additional consequence of the plan has been the entrance of several new producers since 1931, reducing the share of the market held by the combine and aggravating the problem of excess capacity.

Finally, it has already been pointed out that many manufacturing industries contain two types of firm: producers of national brands, who provide their customers with the satisfaction of consuming an advertised product at a relatively high price, and producers of "price lines," not necessarily inferior to the national brands, but available at a lower price because of relatively low selling expenses. It is against small producers of this type that the charge of "selling below cost" is most frequently directed. It is quite possible, however, that the small firm, while selling below the cost of the large producer, is selling above its own cost. The real grievance of the large producer may be that the small firm's costs are too low.[40] A code author-

[39] Department of Labour: Report of investigation into an alleged combine in the manufacture of paperboard shipping containers, p. 25.

[40] The complaint of the "regular" retailers against chain and cut-rate stores, discussed in the next chapter, is exactly the same. These new types

ity dominated by the larger firms would tend to set a minimum price geared to the higher costs of advertised products. The small producer would then be compelled to enter the advertising race himself or drop out of the industry. This result could not be regarded as an economic gain, for the previous success of the small firm must have indicated a demand for the unadvertised good at a low price, and this demand will now go unsatisfied.

It is no doubt unfortunate that excess capacity should develop and that firms should fail. Business men, however, must face the possibility of failure along with the prospect of gain. If they are allowed to take shelter from economic storms behind a fixed price, to tax consumers in order to repair errors of business judgment, much of the theoretical argument for private enterprise disappears.

It is highly unreal, of course, to discuss cutthroat competition in abstraction from cyclical fluctuations of business activity. It is in depression years that the effects of excess capacity are most keenly felt and that the demand for price fixing becomes most insistent. If cyclical fluctuations could be reduced or eliminated, most of the complaints against competition would also disappear. The persistent argument that price fixing itself constitutes a remedy for depression, however, would seem to rest on very doubtful grounds.[41]

---

of retail outlet provide fewer services with the good and exact a smaller retail margin. Independent merchants feel that they should take a larger margin and provide more services. Among both retailers and manufacturers this desire is rationalized as solicitude for consumers and a desire to protect them against "inferior" products or "cheap" stores.

[41] It is argued, for example, that fixing (and raising) prices will increase profits and thus encourage businesses to expand their production, employment and payrolls. This increase in purchasing power will enable more goods to be bought, and the spiral of recovery will be under way. But is it not more reasonable to suppose that the first effect of increased prices will be to force consumers to restrict their purchases, and that production and employment will be reduced? And is not the real requisite for recovery

SUMMARY

While competitive industries do not attain the standard of efficiency set up in Chapter III, they probably come considerably closer to this standard than do industries in which prices are set by agreement. Excess capacity and selling expenses appear where prices are free as well as where they are controlled. Under competition, however, a condition of excess capacity tends to correct itself, while under agreement it may persist indefinitely. Selling expenses, too, are not likely to be so large under competition as under agreement. Where buyers can be won by price reductions salesmanship is less likely to attain large proportions. Producers, moreover, are unlikely to have large profits available for dissipation in sales campaigns. Under competition, finally, the pressure for efficient management tends to be continuous and severe. The producer in a competitive industry knows that he must keep his costs below the market price under penalty of extinction. Where prices can be adjusted to cover costs and where producers are to a large extent assured of survival, the incentive to efficiency is much reduced. Even with a fixed price, of course, individual producers can increase their profits by reducing their costs. But it is doubtful whether this is a very strong incentive in a corporate system where the hired managers who do the economizing do not receive the resulting profits.

Whether price agreement is on the whole more efficient than monopoly is a more difficult question. Selling expenses, excess capacity and plants of less than optimum size may in some cases

---

the maintenance and expansion of consumers' incomes? Certainly the experience of the United States under the National Recovery Administration lends little support to the view that price fixing can promote recovery. The most thorough non-governmental survey of N.I.R.A. concluded that its effect on recovery was neutral or perhaps even negative. (Leverett S. Lyon and others: The National Recovery Administration, Washington, 1935.)

make prices higher under agreement than they would be under monopoly. On the other hand, rival producers may be more active in improving the product, developing new products and new methods of production than a single seller would be. Agreement, too, is not such an efficient control device as monopoly. There is always the possibility that someone may cut the fixed price — openly or secretly — or that competitive expansion of plants may lead to the breakdown of the agreement. Rival producers, too, offer the consumer at least a nominal choice of delivery, credit, repair and other services, while there is no appeal from the monopolist's decisions.

The fact that most of the statements in the present chapter have been expressed as hypotheses or probabilities indicates how unsatisfactory is our knowledge in this field. There is a great need for detailed studies of the efficiency of particular industries. Only when a considerable number of such studies has accumulated can the suggestions of the last two chapters be reframed as valid generalizations.

V

THE PROBLEM OF INEFFICIENCY: RETAIL TRADE

THE LAST FEW DECADES have seen a marked increase in the importance of marketing activities and striking shifts in the channels of trade. The value added by marketing was three-fourths as great as value added by manufacturing in 1930, while the number of persons engaged in marketing was almost as large as the number engaged in manufacturing. The percentage of Canadian workers engaged in marketing increased from ten to thirteen per cent between 1911 and 1931, while the percentage engaged in manufacturing fell from eighteen to fifteen per cent.[1] The reasons for this increase are not entirely clear. It does not seem to be due to a lengthening of the distributive chain, which has tended rather to become shorter. The increased selling efforts of manufacturers described in the preceding chapter are no doubt partly responsible. The ease of entrance into retailing and the tendency of men displaced from other trades to seek refuge in this field is also an important factor. The rapid growth of chain and department stores has aggravated this chronic condition of excess capacity.

We are accustomed to think of the manufacturer-wholesaler-retailer — consumer chain as the "normal" channel of trade. In 1930, however, only 28 per cent of the domestic sales of Canadian manufacturers were made to independent wholesalers. Manufacturers made 50 per cent of their sales directly to retail-

[1] These estimates, of course, are only approximate. For a discussion of the methods by which they were derived see my article "Some Notes on the Distributive Trades in Canada," *Canadian Journal of Economics and Political Science*, November, 1938.

ers, 12 per cent to industrial consumers and 10 per cent to home consumers.[2] While corresponding figures for earlier periods are not available, it is highly probable that the proportion of sales passing through wholesalers has declined. Only in groceries, food products, dry goods and hardware do wholesalers still make more than half of the total sales. The independent retailer has also declined in importance during the past twenty years. In 1930 chain stores made 18.3 per cent and department stores 12.9 per cent of all retail sales, and their share of the market has probably grown since that year.[3] Meats, groceries, gasoline and variety products were the staples of chain store trade in 1930 (Table 11), while more than half of all department store sales were made in furniture, home furnishings, dry goods, shoes and clothing.[4]

TABLE 11

SALES OF CHAIN STORES IN SELECTED BRANCHES OF RETAIL TRADE, 1930 *

Type of business	Per cent of net sales made by chain stores	Type of business	Per cent of net sales made by chain stores
Variety	93.6	Drugstores	18.6
Meat and groceries	33.2	Restaurants	18.5
Groceries	28.5	Women's clothing	15.8
Filling stations	24.8	Men's clothing	14.3
Shoe stores	21.1	Country general stores	2.4

* Dominion Bureau of Statistics, Census of Merchandising and Service Establishments: Retail Merchandise Trade, 1934, pp. 40–41. The figures given include only chains of four or more units. They do not include voluntary chains or manufacturer-controlled chains.

[2] These percentages relate only to sales of finished goods, and do not include inter-manufacturer sales of semi-finished products.

[3] For detailed information concerning the growth of chain stores in Canada see Dominion Bureau of Statistics: A Decade of Retail Trade, 1923–33, pp. 6–7, 28–31. See also the Price Spreads Report, Chapter VII.

[4] In 1930 department stores had 60 per cent of the trade in home furnishings, 52 per cent of dry goods, 42 per cent of women's clothing, 46 per cent of furniture, 32 per cent of shoes, and 27 per cent of men's clothing. (Price Spreads Report, p. 206.)

The rise of the mass distributor has brought loud complaints from wholesalers and retailers, who foresee a steady decline in their volume of sales and possible extinction of their business. Publicity campaigns have been launched charging the chains with oppressive buying tactics, predatory price cutting, unduly low wages, misleading advertising, short weight and other unfair practices. Manufacturers have been urged to prevent price cutting by maintaining fixed resale prices. These methods proving inadequate to meet the menace, appeals have been made to government for protection. Since the merchants are well-organized and sufficiently numerous to form a strong pressure group, they have been able to secure anti-chain legislation, particularly in the provinces. It is the purpose of the present chapter to appraise the economic issues at stake in this struggle. By what methods have the chains attained to their present size, and what have been the effects of these methods? To what extent is it desirable that free use of these methods be curbed? Is the anti-chain store legislation now being enacted in Canada calculated to promote or hinder economic efficiency?

SOME CHARACTERISTICS OF RETAIL MARKETS

Before considering these questions it will be well to review briefly the principal characteristics of retail markets. The retailer, in the first place, usually sells in a smaller market than the wholesaler or manufacturer. In rural districts it is fairly easy to delineate market areas by drawing circles around the towns which serve as shopping centers. In cities the neighborhood shopping center performs a similar function. Prices within each area have a measure of autonomy. Prices which are too far out of line with those in adjacent areas, however, will lead to transference of consumers at the margins, and all retail markets are thus linked in an endless chain. The size of the retail market depends to some extent on the product. A city which contains dozens of food markets may form a single market area for clothing. Improved means of transportation have enlarged nearly all retail markets in recent years.[5]

Even within a single market area, several different prices can usually be found for the same article.[6] Merchants set their margins with an eye to their retailing costs. But these cost calculations may differ widely because of inadequate cost data, or differences in methods of cost calculation, or differences in the services provided. Perfectly rational consumers would correct these discrepancies by shopping about for the lowest price. Many consumers, however, will not take the trouble to hunt bargains. Others buy consciously in the dearer market because they prefer to deal with a particular merchant or because of the prestige gained by buying at a certain store. Where goods are unstandardized, exact comparisons are difficult. Prices which appear to be the same may differ widely because of differences in the quality of the goods. Most consumers and many dealers are poor judges of quality, and buying thus becomes to a large extent a game of chance.

Because of the small capital required and the widespread belief that anyone can manage a store, retail trade is very attractive to the would-be business man. Each year sees a fresh influx of men who have lost their jobs in other fields or who prefer to be independent proprietors rather than employees. A

[5] The fact that 55 per cent of retail sales in 1930 were made in cities of 30,000 or more persons, while only 29 per cent of the population lived in these cities, is evidence of the willingness of country dwellers to drive considerable distances to shop. Department stores, five and ten cent stores, second-hand stores, restaurants, furniture stores and clothing stores did two-thirds or more of their business in these cities in 1930. Food products, automobiles, building materials and hardware were the mainstays of small-town trade.

[6] A study of drug prices in New York City showed that the cheapest stores were selling for only 65 per cent of the prices charged by the dearest stores. Within this range, stores were distributed so as to yield a rather regular bell-shaped curve. (E. R. A. Seligman and R. Love: Price Cutting and Price Maintenance, New York, 1932, p. 376.)

large proportion of these men have had no previous experience of retailing, and it is not surprising that the business mortality rate is high. Of the stores operating in 1930, 48 per cent had been under the same ownership for less than five years, and 25 per cent for less than two years. A study of Buffalo stores from 1918–28 found that 35 per cent of grocery stores, 16 per cent of hardware stores and 12 per cent of drug stores withdrew from business each year.[7] Similar studies in Canadian cities would probably yield very similar results.

It was pointed out in Chapter IV that easy entrance to an industry combined with fixed prices leads to unused capacity for which there is no automatic corrective. This situation, common in manufacturing, is almost universal in retail trade. Unemployment and the desire for independence lead to the opening of new stores even in areas which are already adequately served. This reduces the sales and profits of existing merchants, and might conceivably result in a period of price warfare. General price reductions, however, are strongly against the traditions of retail trade. Particularly in small towns and closely-knit neighborhoods, retail prices are maintained by informal pressures too strong to be ignored. The opening of a new store, then, is likely to lead in time to a raising of prices and retail margins to the point where normal profits can once more be earned on the diminished volume of business. Additional stores result in a still finer fragmentation of the available trade, and still higher margins. This process can go on until the sales and net earnings of some retailers become so small that they are barely able to remain in business.

Measures of the extent of unused capacity in retail trade are not available. Casual observation, however, leads one to believe that most stores could handle a large increase in sales

[7] E. D. McGarry, *Mortality in Retail Trade*, Buffalo, 1930. McGarry also found that 50 per cent of those entering retail trade during these years had had no previous experience.

with no increase in store space or staff. The fact that 56.6 per cent of retail stores in 1930 had annual sales of less than $10,000 (approximately $33 per day) confirms this observation.[8] These figures suggest also that most stores are too small for maximum operating efficiency. It must be remembered, of course, that the convenience of a near-by store is worth something, and that many consumers prefer a personal relationship with an independent proprietor to the impersonal treatment received in a super-market. Taking these considerations into account, it still seems likely that consolidation of stores and lowering of operating costs could go considerably farther than it now has with a net gain in satisfaction to consumers.

THE RISE OF THE MASS DISTRIBUTOR

Into this archaic industry have come the chain and department stores, buying in large quantities and selling in a large number of local markets. These organizations are able to buy more cheaply than independent merchants for a number of reasons. It is apparent that the cost to the manufacturer of filling a single large order will be less than that of filling several small orders. Selling and clerical expenses are small. Machinery can be operated steadily with relatively few changes of patterns and sizes. If the order is given sufficiently far in advance of the delivery date, it can frequently be filled in periods of slack operation. The retailer takes delivery at the factory door and performs the wholesaling functions for considerably less than the normal wholesale margin.

There is evidence, too, that mass distributors are frequently able to buy goods for less than their full cost. Table 12 shows the prices charged by bakeries to chain stores, independent stores, and consumers in certain Canadian cities in June, 1933. Tires are sold to regular dealers at a standard discount of 20

[8] Dominion Bureau of Statistics: Retail Merchandise Trade in Canada, 1934, pp. 38–41.

TABLE 12

BREAD PRICES, JUNE, 1933 *

(*cents per pound*)

	Grade 1			Grade 2		
	Chains	Inde-pendents	Con-sumers	Chains	Inde-pendents	Con-sumers
Montreal	4.17	6.00	6.00	3.17–3.33	4.00	4.67
Toronto	3.66–5.17	6.00	6.67	2.83–4.00	4.67	5.33
Hamilton	...	...	...	3.33	4.00	4.67
Ottawa	...	...	...	3.17–3.50	4.67	5.33
Winnipeg	4.00–4.75	5.00	6.00	3.00	4.00	...
Vancouver	4.50	5.00	7.00	...	...	...

* Evidence before the Price Spreads Commission, p. 3707.

per cent off the list price, while mass distributors purchase private-brand tires of comparable quality at from 38 to 44 per cent below list price.[9] Similar evidence was presented to the Price Spreads Commission with regard to clothing and furniture.[10] It is impossible to be sure that these sales were made below cost since cost figures were not obtained and since it is not certain that the quality of the goods sold to chains was exactly the same as that of the goods sold through independent retailers. It seems likely, however, that these prices, while covering the direct cost to the manufacturer, contributed little or nothing to overhead. The one case in which cost data were obtained corroborates this view.[11]

Price concessions of this sort seem most likely to occur when the manufacturer is using his plant at less than the optimum rate. Considering that he has idle capacity, and fearful that other manufacturers will seize the opportunity should he reject

[9] Evidence before the Price Spreads Commission, pp. 2153–3154.

[10] *Ibid.*, pp. 125–126, 174–176.

[11] Thirty-eight purchases of furniture by the Eaton and Simpson companies were analyzed by Commission accountants. It was found that the average total cost per piece to the manufacturers was $76.19, while the average selling price was only $65.77.

it, he will usually be willing to take a chain order at something less than full cost. Again, a manufacturer may be dependent on a mass distributor for a large part of his business. Cancellation of the chain order would leave his plant idle until new outlets could be developed. He may be willing to sell below full cost for a considerable period rather than suffer this inconvenience. The price in any particular case is set by a process of higgling. The manufacturer will not sell below direct cost, and his minimum price may be somewhat above this. The maximum which the mass distributor will pay depends on the price at which he estimates the good might be obtained elsewhere. Within these limits, the determination of price will depend on the bargaining strength of the two parties. The advantage probably rests with the buyer in most cases, since it will usually be easier for him to place his orders elsewhere than for the manufacturer to find alternative sales outlets. Studies which have been made in the baking and milling industries indicate that manufacturers commonly have a separate price for each chain with which they deal, the most powerful chains receiving the lowest prices.[12]

The most obvious effect of sales below cost to mass distributors is upon independent merchants. By passing on to consumers part of its buying advantage, the chain is able to undersell the independent and cut into his business, and at the same time to earn large profits which may be used to build additional stores. There is an indirect effect on the manufacturer, however, since independent retailers and wholesalers come to him demanding lower prices to meet chain store competition. Unless the manufacturer is prepared to sacrifice his

[12] The range of bread prices appears from Table 12. The milling investigation revealed that one company was making sales to chains at prices ranging from $5.00 to $5.40 per barrel, while another company's prices ranged from $5.30 to $5.60 per barrel. (Evidence before the Price Spreads Commission, p. 3613.)

independent outlets, he must reduce prices to them also. He is thus placed in the position of competing with himself, and the result is a general reduction of prices.[13] In the baking industry the price structure agreed on among manufacturers has been repeatedly undermined and broken down in this way, and this must be true also of many other industries. If manufacturers have already correctly calculated their points of maximum return, they will be injured by this lowering of the price structure. But this will not always be the case. Manufacturers tend to assume inelasticity of demand and to be very cautious about reducing prices. They may find that demand is more elastic than they had supposed and that the new prices are more profitable than the old. The profits of some companies have probably been reduced through the buying policies of mass distributors, but the general lack of enthusiasm among manufacturers for resale price maintenance legislation[14] leads one to doubt whether the injuries have been serious or widespread.

Mass buying also has repercussions on wage rates. In industries in which payroll is the main cost item, the price at which the manufacturer can afford to sell depends largely on the wages which he pays. Severe pressure for lower prices tends to be passed on to the worker through wage reductions. The result under pure competition would be a withdrawal of workers from the industry. Where transference is difficult, however, because of general unemployment, distance, ignorance, or the

[13] This illustrates the familiar principle that price discrimination is possible only where the markets involved can be kept separate. In this case the goods sold to mass distributors come into direct competition with the goods sold to independent merchants, and discrimination is therefore impossible over a long period.

[14] Manufacturers in the United States showed little interest in the Robinson-Patman Act, which was intended to prevent the granting of discriminatory prices to large buyers. The bill was supported almost entirely by retailers and wholesalers, and these groups have taken the lead in promoting similar legislation in Canada.

possession of a specialized skill, the worker is exploitable, and a considerable reduction in wages can take place.

The spread between chain and independent selling prices varies with the place, product and time under consideration. In groceries, for example, the spread in recent years has varied between 5 and 10 per cent, while drug chains appear to undersell independents by about 20 per cent.[15] Only part of this spread, however, and perhaps only a minor part, can be attributed to the buying advantage of the chain store.[16] A large part is traceable to the markedly lower retailing costs of the chains. The expenses of chain drug stores in Canada in 1930 were 26.3 per cent of net sales, as compared with 29.8 per cent for independent stores. Chain grocery expenses were 13.6 per cent of sales, compared with 19.1 per cent for independents. The reasons for the lower operating expenses of the chains have never been fully explored. Chain stores, of course, have much larger average sales than independent stores.[17] This probably means, not only that chain stores are larger and secure certain economies of scale, but also that they operate

[15] Investigators for the Price Spreads Commission found that the cost of a selected food budget of 32 articles in chain stores was 90.8 per cent as great as the cost in independent stores in January, 1930. In July, 1934 the chain store price was 94.4 per cent of the independent price. (Report, p. 217.) The United States Federal Trade Commission made a similar study of food and drug prices in Washington, Memphis, Detroit and Cincinnati. It found that the chains undersold the independents by from 6 to 10 per cent in groceries and from 17 to 22 per cent in drugs. (F. T. C.: Final Report on Chain Stores, pp. 30–32.)

[16] The Federal Trade Commission found that the buying advantage of grocery chains was sufficient to account for only 30 per cent of the spread in selling prices, while only 15 per cent of the spread in drug prices could be explained through lower buying prices. (F. T. C.: *op. cit.*, pp. 53–57.)

[17] Chain drug stores in 1930 had average sales of $49,390, compared with $20,149 for independents. Chain groceries had average sales of $49,863, while independent groceries averaged only $13,251. These figures, together with those on expense ratios, were obtained from special tabulations prepared by the Dominion Bureau of Statistics from schedules collected in the 1930 Census of Merchandising.

more nearly at capacity. Since the cost of operating a store is almost entirely overhead, a larger volume of sales per employee and per square foot of floor space means correspondingly lower unit costs. Centralized planning of store layout, selection of stock, advertising and display of goods by capable specialists contributes to operating efficiency. Chain store managers are obliged to pass through a period of apprenticeship, and their average ability may possibly be above that of independent merchants.[18]

The charge of price cutting so frequently launched against the chains does not refer to this moderate under-selling, but rather to deep price cuts on particular items. It is evident that a chain system is in a good position to engage in predatory price cutting.[19] Prices could be cut sharply in one local market and the losses spread over the whole system. When independent merchants had been weakened or eliminated in this area, prices could be cut in another market, and so on. Chains do not actually pursue this policy, partly because of the pressure of public opinion and the fear of political consequences, partly because of the presence in most markets of other chains which would enter the struggle with equal resources. They do tend to assume, however, that it is their right to undersell independents by a conventional margin. Any attempt by independents to narrow this margin is met by price cuts in the chain store. If the independent cuts again a price war may break out, in which the chain has a great advantage. It can pursue the conflict indefinitely and can almost always secure a settlement favorable to itself.

Chain stores also make systematic use of "price leaders." Instead of underselling independents by an even five or ten

[18] It has also been alleged that the chains "save" by giving short weight to customers. The Price Spreads investigation, however, did not show that this practice is more prevalent in chain stores than in independent stores.

[19] That is, price cutting designed to force competitors into bankruptcy.

per cent on all items, they prefer to sell most items only slightly below independent prices and to cut prices sharply on a selected list of products. These "leaders" are emphasized in advertising and store display, in the hope of attracting customers who will buy other products as well. A good leader must be a standardized product, not too high or too low in price, the demand for which is large and regular, and the usual price of which is widely known. The advertised brands of manufacturers are most commonly used, though chain brands and even unbranded goods such as sugar also serve as leaders. Selling below cost appears to be exceptional, the usual practice being to sell leaders at or slightly above their cost to the chain.[20] Leaders escape almost entirely the burden of retailing costs, which is thus loaded more heavily on to other articles.

The leader policy has different effects on different groups. Independent retailers are adversely affected, since it is difficult for them to use leaders successfully.[21] Yet without leaders they stand to lose, both directly through smaller sales of the cut-price articles, and indirectly through the diversion of customers to the chain stores. It is not clear, however, that they lose more under these conditions than they would if the chains undersold them by an even margin on all items. The root of the independent retailer's problem lies in the fact that the chains are able to afford lower prices to consumers, not in the technique by which these concessions are given.

It might be thought that the manufacturer of a cut-price article will gain through increased sales of the article at the lower price. Independent merchants, however, may lose interest

[20] See on this point the conclusions of the Price Spreads Commission (Report, p. 228) and of the Federal Trade Commission (Final Report on Chain Stores, pp. 38–42).

[21] This is due, among other things, to the fact that a chain store system can present the same leaders simultaneously throughout a city, and give them wide publicity in the daily newspapers. The independent cannot hope to compete in advertising, and must depend largely on window displays.

in a brand which has become unprofitable to them as a result of price cutting and may push alternative brands. The manufacturer may therefore lose sales and, since his sales will be confined increasingly to chain stores, may be forced by them to accept lower prices for his product. While sales of the product as a whole are increased, the producer of the particular brand used for price cutting purposes may find his profits reduced. The fact that manufacturers have shown little interest in resale price maintenance, however, and have usually accepted it only under pressure from retailers and wholesalers, probably indicates that they have not suffered seriously from retail price cutting.

Consumers pay less for some articles and more for others than they would if the chains followed a policy of uniform mark-ups. Consumers who watch and wait for cut prices and who sternly resist the temptation to buy other chain store offerings at regular prices may gain considerably by the leader policy. Consumers as a whole probably neither gain nor lose.[22]

THE PRICE MAINTENANCE MOVEMENT

Retail merchants have been most directly and seriously affected by the rise of the mass distributor. Their organizations have consequently been most active in voicing protests and preparing counter-attacks. Wholesalers, whose existence depends on that of the independent retailer, make common cause with them. The principal object of these two groups has been to secure fixed retail prices on branded products. Maintenance of uniform retail prices would protect the margins of both

[22] This is not strictly true, since under the leader policy the prices of goods no longer correspond to the cost of producing and distributing them. Consumers are induced to buy more of the cut price goods and less of other goods than they would have chosen at prices corresponding to costs. The leader system thus involves some loss in economic efficiency, but this loss is probably quite small.

wholesaler and retailer, check the use of price leaders, and slow up if not prevent the expansion of chain store sales.

A large number of nationally-advertised products, particularly in the drug and toilet articles trade, are now "price protected." A common technique is to require all wholesalers and retailers dealing in the article to sign a contract in which they promise, among other things, to adhere to the manufacturer's prices. Dealers breaking this contract are refused supplies and are sometimes required to pay damages to the manufacturer.[23] Another method is to appoint all wholesalers and retailers agents of the manufacturer and ship goods to them on consignment with specific instructions as to selling prices. Selling below these prices is punished by withdrawal of merchandise.[24] The chief difference between the two methods is that the latter is clearly within the law, while the legal status of the former is doubtful.[25] Neither method is completely effective. The fact that the courts will usually not enforce a resale price maintenance contract places the burden of enforcement on the parties themselves. The manufacturer, however, who has probably

[23] The methods used in the tobacco industry were described in Chapter I.

[24] This method has been used successfully by manufacturers of electric light bulbs since 1919. Prices to consumers are very rarely cut. (*Hardware and Metal*, August 8, 1936.)

[25] Several cases have come before the courts in which a retailer, having signed and then broken a resale price maintenance contract, was sued for damages by the manufacturer, and entered as a defense that the contract was in restraint of trade and therefore not binding. The court has usually, though not always, accepted this view and refused to grant the manufacturer damages or an injunction. (The Ozone Co. v. Lyons, 7 Que. P. R. 65–66, 1902; Wampole v. Lyons, 25 Que. S. C. 390, 1904; Wampole v. Karn, 11 O. L. R., 619–29, 1906; Stearns v. Avery, 33 O. L. R. 251–52, 1915; Berliner Gramaphone Co. v. Scythes, 9 Sask. L. R. 365–71, 1916; Berliner Gramaphone Co. v. Phinney, N. S. R. 295–309, 1921; Berliner Gramaphone Co. v. Musical Merchandise Co. et al., 31 Révue Légale, 453–65, 1925.)

The first prosecution of parties to a resale price maintenance agreement under the Combines Act occurred in 1939, when a number of tobacco manufacturers and dealers were brought to trial in Alberta.

adopted the scheme only under pressure from distributors, has neither the interest nor the facilities for effective policing, nor are the distributors themselves always unanimous. Where other brands of the product are subject to price cutting, departure from the fixed price is particularly likely. Effective price maintenance probably cannot be secured without organization of all producers and dealers in an industry, and the establishment of an enforcement authority similar to that of the book and drug trades in Great Britain.

The most notable attempt at industry-wide organization in Canada was made by the drug trade. Sir William Glyn-Jones, who had successfully organized the Proprietary Articles Trade Association of Great Britain, was invited in 1926 to organize a similar association in Canada. The response from the trade was enthusiastic, and a Proprietary Articles Trade Association was quickly formed. It included 157 manufacturers, 28 wholesalers and 2,732 retailers, and covered some 600 products. A retail price was set for each product, of which the manufacturer was to receive one-half, the wholesaler one-sixth, and the retailer one-third. Any manufacturer or dealer who cut prices was to be boycotted by all P.A.T.A. members.[26] The scheme was evidently aimed at the mass distributors, who prior to this time had been selling proprietary articles for from 10 to 25 per cent less than the independent druggists. Its main beneficiaries were wholesalers and independent retailers, who were sheltered from price competition and whose margins were increased by about one-quarter.[27] The generous margins offered by the plan

[26] Department of Labour: Interim report of the investigation into the P. A. T. A., 1926. Final report of the investigation into the P. A. T. A., 1927.

[27] Just previous to the organization of the P. A. T. A., retail margins had averaged about 27 per cent and wholesale margins 14 per cent. (Department of Labour, Interim Report, pp. 23–4.) The 1930 Census of Merchandising shows that in that year retailers' expenses formed 26.9 per cent and wholesalers' expenses 13.1 per cent of the final selling price. It is apparent that the margins allowed by the P. A. T. A. were unduly generous.

would probably have led in time to an increase in the number of drug stores, a finer subdivision of the available business, and a demand for still larger margins.

The P.A.T.A. was hailed by retailers throughout Canada as the beginning of a new era. Under the auspices of the Retail Merchants' Association a much broader movement, the Fair Trade League of Canada, was launched. Officers of the R.M.A. toured the country carrying the message into all the larger cities. Members were enrolled, conventions held, and much enthusiasm developed. In the meantime, however, the P.A.T.A. had been investigated under the Combines Act, found to be "against the public interest," and had dissolved without waiting for prosecution. With it vanished the Fair Trade League and similar ventures.

The desire of the retailers for price maintenance has continued undiminished, however, and in some cases this desire has triumphed over fear of the Combines Act. Toronto electrical appliance dealers, for example, formed an association in 1935 intended to prevent both direct price cutting and indirect cuts disguised as trade-in allowances. Forty-five members were enrolled, representing about 90 per cent of the total business. Members agree to observe the manufacturers' list prices, which yield them a margin of about 30 per cent. The agreement is policed by hired shoppers who go from store to store trying to obtain price reductions. Any store granting such a reduction is reported to manufacturers and blacklisted. Members are required to boycott any manufacturer who will not "coöperate," but this has not been necessary, since manufacturers seem to approve the plan. One result of the scheme was the entrance of between 15 and 20 new dealers into the trade within 18 months. The most recent report (April, 1937) indicates that prices had been well maintained until that time, and that the

There would probably have been a tendency, too, for these margins to increase with the passage of time.

dealers were well satisfied with the plan.[28] Associations of this sort, of course, are often of a transitory nature, and break down under the strain of a business depression or the prospect of a government investigation.

After 1929 most manufacturing plants operated below capacity, and mass distributors were able to secure particularly favorable prices. They were thus able to reduce their selling prices more rapidly than independent stores, and to intensify the use of leaders. Independent stores found themselves handling a shrinking percentage of a shrinking volume of business. Balked in their efforts at voluntary organization, they turned to government for aid. The Price Spreads inquiry, though its scope was eventually widened to cover almost the entire economy, was at the outset a witch hunt directed against middlemen, and in particular against the mass distributor. One result of the inquiry was the insertion of a new section (498A) into the Criminal Code in 1935. This section, among other things, forbids the granting of different prices to different purchasers "in respect of a sale of goods of like quality and quantity." [29] This provision, which is almost identical with that of the Robinson-Patman Act in the United States, is intended to eliminate the advantage which mass distributors sometimes secure by buying from manufacturers at less than cost.

[28] Details of the association's methods appear in *Electrical Appliances and Supplies* for April, 1937. The journal points out with pride that "the plan is working so well that the association is receiving enquiries from Hamilton, Oshawa and other centers. Mr. Binnington recently acceded to a request to address dealers in Hamilton to explain how the plan works." This is typical of the way in which such plans spread from city to city unless checked by investigation.

[29] "Every person . . . is guilty of an indictable offence . . . who is a party or privy to, or assists in, any transaction of sale which discriminates, to his knowledge, against competitors of the purchaser in that any discount, rebate or allowance is granted to the purchaser over and above any discount, rebate or allowance available at the time of such transaction to the aforesaid competitors in respect of a sale of goods of like quality and quantity."

The section in its present form raises many problems of interpretation. Moreover, the task of determining the facts in a particular case is too large for a private complainant. Cost figures are a morass in which almost endless time and money may be sunk. It is significant that no actions have been brought under section 498A during the first four years of its life. The force of the section could be increased by creating a staff of accountants and economists to investigate alleged cases of price-discrimination.[30] The desirability of such a step, however, is very doubtful. The only important benefit would be the protection of independent retailers against an illegitimate advantage sometimes secured by their rivals. Manufacturers' profits would also be protected, but this probably counts against the legislation rather than in its favor. Many manufacturing industries in Canada have long been in a condition of partial or complete monopoly, and can well afford some reduction in their profits. Wage rates would be protected to some extent by enforcement of section 498A, but minimum wage laws and trade union organization afford a more direct means to this end. The tendency of the legislation to increase the rigidity of prices must also be counted as a disadvantage. Price reductions seem to occur in practice through the granting of a lower price first to one customer, then to a few others, and finally to all. Official announcement of a price reduction usually merely confirms a *fait accompli*. The prevention of price discrimination would probably tend to check all price reductions. When to these considerations is added the heavy cost of effective enforcement, the disadvantages of the legislation appear to outweigh its advantages.

[30] The Combines Investigation Commission may investigate instances of price-discrimination at present, of course, if it is alleged that their effects have been detrimental to the public interest. The Dominion Trade and Industry Commission may also receive complaints under section 498A. It has no special staff to investigate these complaints, however, and has taken little action in this field.

The evidence now available suggests that the mass distributor is considerably more efficient than the independent merchant. He makes genuine savings by mass buying, his stores are large enough to secure important economies of scale, they are operated more nearly at capacity than independent stores, and their integration in a large system makes possible more effective management. Under these conditions, some displacement of independent stores is inevitable. This displacement does not seem to have taken place primarily through elimination of existing businesses. Large numbers of independent stores fail each year in any event, mainly because of insufficient capital and inexpert management. The primary effect of the chain store has probably been to prevent new independents from arising by occupying the best locations and by hiring capable young men who at an earlier time would have set up their own stores.

The campaign by independent merchants against the chain store is analogous to the smashing of machines by hand workers during the Industrial Revolution. Most of the arguments employed in this campaign rest on the assumption that what hurts the independent merchant hurts the community, and on serious distortion of chain store selling practices. It is also argued at times that the growth of chain and department stores will lead to monopoly in retail trade, but this cannot be taken very seriously at present. There are natural limits to the displacement of the independent, and the chains thesmelves will offer vigorous competition to each other within the visible future. At the moment, indeed, the mass distributors must be counted as an anti-monopolistic influence, since they offset to some extent the power of manufacturers' associations and help to break down fixed price structures.

The best thing that can be said about the anti-chain legislation of recent years is that most of it will have little effect. Certainly it is not sufficient to prevent, though it may retard, the expansion of chain store sales. One is inclined to object to this legislation, not because of its strength, but because of the tendency which it represents. The Retail Merchants' Association may be expected to press for more and more stringent legislation, designed to freeze price structures and to maintain the channels of distribution in their present form. Only if preservation of large numbers of small independent merchants on political or social grounds is considered more important than economic efficiency can such measures be justified.

SUMMARY OF CHAPTERS III–V

It is apparent that the Canadian economy falls far short of the standard of efficiency set up in Chapter III. This standard, of course, could probably not be reached under any conditions. Even if perfect competition prevailed throughout the economy, changes in demand and in the technique of production would lead to a considerable waste of labor and capital. The presence of monopoly and price agreement, however, leads to additional wastes which are by no means inevitable. Six main types of inefficiency have been discussed above, and may be summarized briefly here.

In some industries prices are much in excess of costs, and profits are unduly large. In general, profits in Canadian industry are considerably larger than appears on the surface because of the inflation of capital values during corporate reorganizations.[31] A nominal profit of 6 per cent may be 15 or 20 per cent on the actual cash investment. Profits of this magnitude indicate that it would be desirable to have more of the good produced and sold at a lower price. Where price control exists, however, this desirable development is unlikely to occur.

In many industries plants are operated on the average at considerably less than capacity. Part of this unused capacity, of course, is due to cyclical and seasonal fluctuations of production. A large part, however, can be traced fairly directly to

[31] See Chapter VII.

price control, which makes it possible to earn good profits even at a low rate of operation. This situation encourages the building of unnecessary plants and prevents the price cutting which under competition would tend to eliminate them. The result is underemployment of both equipment and workers. Each plant tends to gather around itself a labor reserve, based not on its normal rate of operation but on the capacity rate, and a considerable part of this labor force must at any one time be unemployed.

Partly as a result of unused capacity, large numbers of persons are engaged in advertising and selling activities for which consumers must pay but which probably add little to consumers' satisfaction. Moreover, necessary distributive facilities, such as delivery wagons, filling stations and other retail outlets, have been grossly overexpanded in the struggle for business. Each filling station or milk wagon accordingly operates much below capacity and the unit cost of distribution is needlessly high.

Productive units seem in some cases to be too large, in others too small. Retail stores are almost certainly too small for maximum efficiency, and this is probably true also of many manufacturing industries. The development of consumer preference for particular brands through trade-marking and advertising may easily keep in existence too many producers, each of less than the most efficient size. In other industries, however, the desire for price control or promoters' profits has led to the merging of many companies into huge concerns which invite mismanagement. Inflated salaries, high administrative expenses, the difficulty of coördination and supervision may make the unit costs of these concerns considerably higher than those of smaller and more compact firms.

Under monopoly and price agreement there can be no assurance that the operations of an individual establishment are performed with least cost. They may be, but they do not have to be. Increased operating costs resulting from slack supervision, errors of judgment, and bureaucratic procedure can be made up by raising the controlled price. Only in the small competitive sector of the economy is there that pressure for efficiency which was supposed to be one of the major virtues of private enterprise. For this reason as well as for the reasons given above, unit cost is ordinarily higher than it need be, and the fact that the price merely covers costs does not prove that the price is reasonable.

The fact that controlled prices fall relatively little during depression probably makes depressions deeper and longer than they otherwise would be. The rigidity of capital goods prices, in particular, has unfortunate effects not only on the course of the business cycle but also on the long-run trend of investment. New products and new processes are continually being developed and struggling for acceptance. A high level of capital goods prices must hamper the construction of new plant and equipment, while a lower level of prices would facilitate industrial investment, building construction, and public works programs.

In the face of these inefficiencies, what policies have Canadian governments followed? Do the policies adopted indicate a clear conception of the underlying problem? Or have they been largely irrelevant to the real issues? To what extent have they been dictated by political pressures rather than by careful analysis of facts? These are a few of the questions which should be kept in mind throughout the next three chapters.

VI

PUBLIC POLICY TOWARD COMPETITION: PRESERVATION

Competition may be eliminated either by agreement or by amalgamation. There are important legal and economic differences between these methods, and they have been sharply distinguished in Canadian policy. Canadian legislators have tended to assume that amalgamation is beneficial and, though the danger of monopoly has been given verbal recognition, there have been no attempts at "trust busting." Price agreement, however, has been regarded with suspicion and has been attacked by both legal and administrative methods.

LEGISLATIVE HISTORY

Charges of "rings" in coal, salt, binder-twine and other necessities were frequently heard in Parliament after Confederation, and cases involving such agreements occasionally came before the courts. In dealing with these cases, Canadian courts followed the British common law dealing with restraint of trade. British common law has been and continues to be very lenient toward trade combinations. To be valid, a restraint must be demonstrated to be reasonable in reference to the interests of the parties concerned and reasonable in reference to the interests of the public.[1] In practice, however, the public has come off

[1] "All interference with individual liberty of action in trading, and all restraints of trade of themselves if there is nothing more, are contrary to public policy, and therefore void. That is the general rule. But there are exceptions: restraints of trade and interference with individual liberty of action may be justified by the special circumstances of a particular case. It is a sufficient justification, and indeed it is the only justification, if the restriction is reasonable — reasonable, that is, in reference to the interests

second best, and almost any sort of agreement which would further the interests of the parties has been held valid and binding. Regulation of supply and maintenance of an agreed price has been held lawful in several important British cases.[2] In the leading Canadian case of this period, a price agreement among salt manufacturers was held to be "reasonable" and an injunction was granted against a company which had broken the agreement.[3] This attitude not only allowed combinations to exist with impunity but strengthened them by enabling them to use legal sanctions against any firm which tried to break away from the group.

During the eighties the growth of such large concerns as the Imperial Oil Company, and the multiplication of agreements among manufacturers and dealers, brought increasing protests in Parliament and in the press. The sources of the complaints are not clear, but it is likely that they came primarily from small business men who felt their position menaced by the growth and tactics of the large concerns. The Conservative

---

of the parties concerned and reasonable in reference to the interests of the public." (Nordenfelt v. Maxim Nordenfelt Co., 1894, A. C. 535.)

[2] "Unquestionably the combination in question was one the purpose of which was to regulate supply and keep up prices but an ill-regulated supply and unremunerative prices may in point of fact be disadvantageous to the public. Such a state of things may, if it is not controlled, drive manufacturers out of business or lower wages and so cause unemployment and labour disturbances. It must always be a question of circumstances whether a combination of manufacturers in a particular trade is an evil from a public point of view." (Viscount Haldane in North-Western Salt Case, 1914 A. C. 461.)

And in a case involving two coachmakers who had agreed to charge the same price, Lord Ellenborough said in part: "How can you contend that it is in restraint of trade? They are left to charge what they like, though not more than each other. This is merely a convenient mode of arranging two concerns which might otherwise ruin each other." (Hearne v. Griffin, 2 Chitty's Reports, 407.)

[3] Ontario Salt Co. v. Merchants Salt Co., Ontario Chancery, 1871, 18 Gr. 540–56.

government took no action, but a Conservative private member, Mr. Clark Wallace of Toronto, in 1888 moved the appointment of a select committee to investigate the charges of combination. The committee, after sitting for two months, reported combinations among manufacturers of sugar, coffins, binder-twine, stoves, oatmeal, biscuits and confectionery, and also among certain wholesalers and retailers.[4] The tone of the report was mild. The agreements were criticized on the ground that they interfered with the business of non-members of the combination rather than on the ground that prices to consumers were raised. The Toronto coal dealers' combine, for example, was criticized mainly because non-member dealers could not get coal. The Wholesale Grocers' Guild was condemned because "establishments, which in some cases are the growth of half a century of toil and honourable dealing, and rich in valuable experience and public confidence, are threatened with extinction."

Immediately after the filing of the Committee report, Mr. Wallace introduced into the House a strongly-worded bill "for the prevention and suppression of combinations formed in restraint of trade." It forbade combination for the purpose of: (a) Limiting, lessening or preventing the production, manufacture or sale of any commodity, (b) Unreasonably enhancing prices, (c) Securing any special concession for members of the combine which was denied to non-members, (d) Preventing or restricting competition in the production, manufacture or sale of any commodity. Any company incorporated under Dominion charter was to forfeit its charter upon conviction under the Act, in addition to the usual remedies of fine and imprisonment.

The subsequent history of this measure illustrates very well the obstacles which such legislation is bound to encounter. The Prime Minister gave it cautious verbal approval, but allotted it so little time that it was held over until the following year. Early in the session of 1889, Mr. Wallace once more introduced

[4] Report of Select Committee, May 16, 1888, pp. 6–17.

the measure. Once more the government showed no enthusiasm for its passage, and did not give it a place in the government schedule of legislation. Opponents of the measure moved that it be referred to the Committee on Banking and Commerce. Large lobbies of manufacturers and traders descended on Ottawa to oppose the bill, and were heard by the Committee.[5] Apparently as a result of this business pressure, the original measure was withdrawn while still in Committee, and a startlingly different bill was substituted. The clause which forbade the securing of special concessions was dropped, as was also the provision concerning forfeiture of the corporate charter. The insertion of the word "unlawfully" greatly weakened the effect of the measure, for it carried a clear implication that only acts previously unlawful at common law were to be unlawful under the new Act. Another new clause cast considerable doubt on the legal status of trade unions. Mr. Wallace reluctantly accepted the new act, which passed the House and went to the Senate. It came back from the Senate in still more emasculated form, for that body inserted the words "unduly" or "unreasonably" in each of the sub-sections. As finally placed in the statute books, then, the measure read as follows:

"Everyone is guilty of an indictable offense . . . who conspires, combines agrees or arranges with any other person . . . unlawfully —

(a) to unduly limit the facilities for transporting, producing, manufacturing . . . any article or commodity . . .

(b) to unduly prevent or lessen competition . . ." etc.

A more half-hearted statute can scarcely be imagined. Members of a combine could not be convicted unless the Crown

[5] Mr. Wallace referred in debate to " . . . those men who have formed those illegal combinations and who came down in great force to defeat the Bill . . . they came down before the Banking and Commerce Committee at its last meeting, with a great array of lawyers from Montreal and Toronto, and with amendments carefully considered, to legislate this Bill out of existence." (Hansard, April 22, 1889.)

proved that they were "unduly" doing something which was already unlawful at common law. It is not surprising that the Attorneys General of the provinces took no steps to bring prosecutions under the new act, and that Mr. Wallace was obliged to admit in 1892 that the combinations were still in existence.[6] In the only case which arose under the Act during the nineties, the American Tobacco Company was acquitted on the ground that its dealer contracts, which forbade the dealer to sell the tobacco of any other manufacturer, were not illegal under the common law.[7]

Another act of this period, commendable in principle, failed of its effect for administrative reasons. In 1897 the Liberal government added a section (Sec. 18) to the Customs Act, providing that, whenever the Governor in Council had reason to believe that a harmful combination existed, he might order an investigation by a Superior Court judge. If the judge reported the existence of such a combination, the Governor in Council was empowered to place the articles in question on the free list, or so to reduce duties on them as to give consumers the benefit of foreign competition. There seems no *prima facie* reason why this provision should not have been highly effective. It has been applied, however, only in the case of newsprint. It is significant that this case involved a well-organized group of consumers able to spend the sums necessary for adequate defense of their interests.[8] Small and unorganized consumers rarely possess the

[6] Hansard, 1891, Vol. II, p. 2553.

[7] The Queen v. American Tobacco Company of Canada, 3 Revue de Jurisprudence, 453–64 (1897).

[8] Paper manufacturers formed an association in 1900 to stabilize the price of newsprint and other less important products. The Canadian Press Association complained to the government in 1901, and an investigation was ordered. The investigation lasted for three months; the Press Association employed counsel and spent about $2,000 to make the most of its case. The judge reported that the paper-makers association was a combine whose operations had been undue and oppressive. In consequence the duties on certain sorts of paper were reduced by 40 per cent.

knowledge or influence necessary to lodge a forceful complaint, nor are they able to bear the expense of engaging counsel and contesting a case.

In 1900 the Act of 1889 was put into workable form by deleting the word "unlawfully," and appeared thereafter as Sections 496–498 of the Criminal Code. After this date the enactment was interpreted by the courts as going beyond the common law and creating a new criminal offence.[9] Prosecution, however, was still dependent on the Attorneys General of the provinces, and remarkably few prosecutions occurred. Only five reported cases were tried between 1900 and 1910,[10] and only one between 1910 and 1923.

The first merger movement swept over the country during the years 1909–1912. The rise of prices during these years was attributed to the mergers by many people. Newspapers, particularly in the smaller centers, published frequent editorials

[9] The definitive statement of this view appears in Weidman v. Shragge, 46 Can. S. C. R. 1–44, 1912. Idington, J. said in part: "It cannot be said to be a purely declaratory act. It covers ground not covered by the then existing law. In no sense can the field it covers be held to be co-extensive with the field of law relative to restraint of trade. . . . The legislative history demonstrates as clearly as possible that it was not as against something already unlawful, but the unduly doing that then lawful so far as the criminal law extended that the amended statute was aimed at."

See also Clute, J., in Dominion Supply Co. v. T. L. Robertson Mfg. Co., 39 O. L. R. 495–518, 1917. "The result of the consideration of the cases is, I think, that the provisions of the Code in question are to be construed differently from cases at common law in England."

[10] The Ontario Coal Dealers' Association, an organization designed to maintain retail prices and to prevent direct sales to consumers (Rex v. Elliott, 9 O. L. R. 648–63, 1905); the Alberta Retail Lumber Dealers' Association, which limited entrance to the trade and maintained prices (Rex v. Clarke, I Alta. L. R. 358–83, 1908); and two groups whose operations were described in Chapter II — the Toronto plumbers and jobbers of plumbing supplies (Rex v. Master Plumbers and Steamfitters, 14 O. L. R. 295–321, 1907) and the Dominion Wholesale Grocers' Guild (Rex v. Beckett et al., 20 O. L. R. 410–32, 1910). Convictions were secured in the first three cases, while the Wholesale Grocers' Guild was acquitted.

calling for regulation of the "combines." Agricultural sentiment was strongly in favor of regulation. The Minister of Labour, Mr. Mackenzie King, was sympathetic to these proposals, and in 1910 introduced into Parliament a bill to provide for the investigation of alleged combines.[11] The bill encountered severe opposition, but was passed without substantial alteration as the Combines Investigation Act of 1910.

"Combine" was defined by the Act to mean "any contract, agreement, arrangement or combination which has, or is designed to have, the effect of increasing or fixing the price or rental of any article of trade or commerce or the cost of the storage or transportation thereof, or of restricting competition in or of controlling the production, manufacture, transportation, sale or supply thereof, to the detriment of consumers or producers of such article of trade or commerce . . . and also includes what is known as a trust, monopoly or merger." Although monopolies are included in this definition, the Act was evidently aimed primarily at agreements among a number of firms. The phrase "to the detriment of consumers or producers" is also significant. Mr. King pointed out repeatedly during the debates on the Act that it differed from the Sherman Act in

[11] Mr. King's ideas on this subject are important, since he was Prime Minister of Canada from 1921–1930 and from 1935 to date and was also the sponsor of the effective Combines Investigation Act of 1923 as well as the ineffective Act of 1910. Mr. King, who obtained a doctorate in economics from Harvard University in 1909, is a liberal in the British tradition. He prefers to leave business men to run their own affairs, though it may occasionally be necessary for government to intervene as a mediator or to protect the interests of defenseless groups. The growth of large-scale enterprises should be encouraged, he believes, and amalgamation of business units is in most cases beneficial. Monopolies and trade agreements must be carefully watched, however, to see that they do not abuse their economic power. Mr. King believes strongly in the preventive value of publicity, and considers that the possibility of investigation will do more to deter potential wrong-doers than any amount of criminal legislation. His speeches in Parliament on the two Combines acts are able expositions of these beliefs.

being directed, not against all restraints of competition, but only against those whose harmful effects could be proven.

Any six persons who believed a combine to exist might apply to a judge. The judge was to order a hearing, at which the applicants and the parties complained against were to be represented. If in his opinion the hearing gave reasonable ground for believing an injurious combine to exist, he was to order an investigation. The Minister of Labour was then to proceed with the appointment of an investigatory board. One member of the Board was to be suggested by the complainants and one by the parties complained against. The third, who was to be chairman, was to be chosen by the first two, or, if they could not agree, by the Minister himself. There is an evident parallel between this arrangement and that of the Industrial Disputes Investigation Act.[12] The Board was given wide investigatory powers; its report was to be presented to the Minister and to be made public, after which the Board was to disband.

No penalty was provided in the Act for past actions of a combine. If the combine continued its activities after the publication of an adverse report by a Board of investigation, however, a penalty of not more than $1,000 per day of such continuance might be levied against it. Adverse report of a Board was almost made *prima facie* ground for reduction of tariff duties on articles produced by the combine, and also for revocation of patent rights. There can be no doubt from the debates, however, that the penalty provisions of the Act were not regarded as highly significant by its author. It was in his

[12] This Act, passed in 1907, was also drafted under Mr. King's supervision. It provided that in the event of an industrial dispute in the mining, railroad, or public utilities industries, either party might apply to the Minister of Labour for appointment of a board of investigation and conciliation. One member of the board was to be chosen by the workers, one by the employers, and the third, who was to be chairman, by the first two, or, if they could not agree, by the Minister of Labour. No strike or lockout was permitted until the Board had submitted its report.

mind primarily a vehicle of investigation and publicity. If the facts of a combination were made known, the pressure of public opinion would in most cases force the firms involved to mend their ways. Penalties would only need to be invoked as a last resort against incorrigible offenders, and the number of prosecutions would thus be greatly reduced.

In spite of the impressive appearance of the Act, it was invoked only once during its nine-year lifetime. This case, which involved the United Shoe Machinery Company, was long, expensive, and resulted in only a paper victory for the applicants.[13] The defects of the Act seem to have been the same as those of the Customs amendment of 1897. Complainants were obliged to make out a *prima facie* case before a judge. To do this required more knowledge, courage and money than the average consumer possesses. The complainants were openly named throughout the proceedings, and were therefore open to future retaliation. The procedure was cumbersome, and could be obstructed for long periods by skillful lawyers. Finally, no machinery was provided to ensure compliance with the orders of a Board. Both of these measures, while potentially useful as weapons in feuds between large business groups, were ill-calculated to serve the interests of the small consumer.

The War brought a rapid rise in prices, a shortage of many

[13] Any manufacturer leasing machines from the U. S. M. Co. was obliged to sign a contract, which contained a "tying clause" binding the manufacturer not to use the machines on shoes on which the machinery of any other maker had been used. This meant in effect that the manufacturer must use U. S. M. Co. machines only. Late in 1910 a shoe manufacturer applied for an investigation of these contracts under the new Combines Act. The Company used almost every known legal device to prevent the appointment of an investigating Board, and later to hinder its work. In consequence a report was not handed in for nearly two years. The majority report declared the Company's contracts to come within the definition of a "combine" and ordered them changed. The Company replied, not by changing the contracts, but by granting to lessees the privilege of terminating the lease on thirty days' notice in writing!

commodities, and charges of "profiteering." Late in 1916 an Order-in-Council was passed to allay popular discontent. This Order,[14] which reads like a modern version of the Elizabethan statute against "forestallers, regraters and engrossers," provided that no person should accumulate necessaries of life beyond the amount reasonably required for home or business. Anyone holding an excess stock of necessaries was to offer them for sale "at prices not higher than are reasonable and just." The Minister of Labour was empowered to investigate fully any situation in which profiteering was suspected. If the Minister considered that the Order had been violated, he was to turn over all the evidence collected to the Attorney General of the Province concerned for prosecution. There is no record of any prosecutions under the Order, however, and it is doubtful whether any were instituted.

A Cost-of-Living Commissioner was also appointed at this time, and devoted himself primarily to the preparation and publication of statistics. Monthly returns were required from sugar refiners, textile manufacturers, coal merchants and others engaged in producing or distributing necessaries of life. The returns were designed to reveal the component elements of cost, and the net profit per unit of the commodity. From the material collected, the average cost of producing and distributing the various necessities was computed and published by provinces and localities. The expectation apparently was that residents of (say) Barrie, Ontario, on reading that the average cost of producing and distributing bread in Barrie was twelve cents per loaf, would promptly boycott any baker who attempted to charge more. No attempt, however, was made to compute ratios of profit to capitalization, or to inquire into the fairness of the capitalization figures themselves. The effect of these activities on the course of prices and profits was probably insignificant. The most important result seems to have been that business

[14] Privy Council 2777, 1916.

men acquired the habit of answering government questionnaires. The records accumulated by the Commissioner were taken over by the Dominion Bureau of Statistics in 1918.

Prices continued to rise after the end of the war, and the public continued to demand that prices should be brought down. The coalition government, alarmed by this agitation and by the widespread labor unrest, appointed a committee of the House of Commons to inquire into the reasons for the high cost of living. The Committee reported that the rise in prices was due primarily to the War demand for materials and to the increased quantity of currency, that distributors' margins were for the most part reasonable, and that "profiteering" was probably no more common than in time of peace. They recommended, however, "that legislation be enacted . . . creating a tribunal with power to investigate mergers, trusts, monopolies . . . also with regulative power in connection with discriminations in price between different purchasers of commodities, exclusive purchase and sale arrangements, inter-corporate shareholding and interlocking directorates, and unfair methods in Commerce" — in short, a Canadian equivalent of the United States Federal Trade Commission.[15] This recommendation, which is in no way connected with the factual part of the Report, seems to have sprung full-grown from the head of some member or adviser of the government. This suspicion is strengthened by the fact that the Report was presented on June 26, while the bills implementing the recommendations were introduced into Parliament on June 28.

These bills, the Board of Commerce Act and the Combines and Fair Prices Act, were passed with little debate in the dying hours of the session. They attempted to synthesize ideas drawn from a wide variety of sources, including the Combines Act of 1910, the three American anti-trust statutes, the sections of the Railway Act which relate to the Board of Railway Commis-

[15] Second Report of the Commission on Cost of Living, June, 1919.

sioners, and the Australian Industries Preservation Act. Administration of the two acts was entrusted to a Board of Commerce, composed of three members appointed for ten-year terms. The board was to have the powers of a court in securing evidence, and its determinations on matters of fact were to be conclusive. The board was given very wide powers in two directions. It might initiate investigations of suspected combines of its own accord or on the written complaint of a single person. If hearings and investigations confirmed the existence of a combine, the board might issue a cease and desist order, violation of which was an indictable offence. No prosecution either under the 1919 acts or under Sec. 498 Cr. Code might be initiated, however, without the written authority of the board. The entire anti-combine machinery was thus centralized in the hands of three individuals. Secondly, the board was empowered to inquire into and restrain the taking of unfair profits on the necessaries of life. It could determine what was a fair profit, compel holders of goods to sell at a prescribed price, and even order the distribution of the stocks of individual firms. Violation of an order of the board in any of these matters was made an indictable offence.

The initial board was composed of Judge H. A. Robson, Mr. W. F. O'Connor, a lawyer who had served as Cost-of-Living Commissioner from 1916 to 1918, and Mr. James Murdock, a trade union official. One of the first acts of the board was to issue an elaborate set of rules governing formal complaints, evidently modeled on the regulations of the Federal Trade Commission. Few formal complaints were made to the board, however, and almost all of the cases investigated were undertaken on informal complaints or on the board's own initiative. The combines side of the board's jurisdiction received little attention. A sweeping order was issued in January, 1920, requiring all parties to existing or proposed combines to submit full details of these combines to the board, together with evidence that their activities were not against the public interest. In response to this order the board received copies of some forty price-fixing agreements from two trade association secretaries, but no action was taken on them.

The major activity of the board was the regulation of prices and profits. Its career in this field was brief but dramatic. It went about from city to city, admonishing and exhorting, holding a steady succession of hearings and issuing dozens of orders covering a wide range of products. The cost studies initiated by Mr. O'Connor in 1916 were continued by the Economic Division of the board. On the basis of these studies and of the evidence produced at hearings, the board proceeded to set "fair" retail prices — sometimes directly, in other cases indirectly by fixing the retailers' margin.[16] In the six months of its active life the board issued more than fifty "Orders" and more than seventy-five "Decisions."

The attempt to control prices by beginning with the retailer instead of with the manufacturer was distinctly unfortunate. It meant, in the first place, a burden of work with which the board could not possibly cope, and a problem of policing whose dimensions can be imagined. There is little evidence as to whether the board's orders were generally complied with, but it would be surprising if this were the case. Attempts to regulate such numerous groups as retailers and milk producers,

[16] Board decisions which were particularly unpopular were No. 33B of Dec. 23, 1919, restraining milk producers and distributors in the Toronto market from advancing prices, and No. 38 of Jan. 8, 1920, fixing the price of sugar at 16 cents per pound. This latter order read in part as follows: "This Board orders a positive limitation of the retail price at 16 cents per pound. The wholesalers and refiners will have to mutually arrange so that the retail price can be kept for three months at not higher than sixteen cents." Order No. 30 of Nov. 24, 1919, provided that retailers' gross profit on sliced bacon should not exceed 22 per cent of the selling price, and on other pork products not more than 25 per cent of the selling price; this order brought loud protests from butchers. For a full list of Board orders see the First Annual Report, March 31, 1920.

moreover, at once made the Board a center of political controversy. Deputations from the Retail Merchants' Association waited on the board and on the Cabinet time after time, angry editorials appeared in the *Canadian Grocer* and other journals. The board had other difficulties. There was internal dissension and political intervention. The chairman, a political appointee, does not seem to have been in sympathy with the purposes of the legislation,[17] and the vigor of the Board's activities was due to Mr. O'Connor and Mr. Murdock. The government, surprised and alarmed at the activities of its creature, and besieged by delegations of business men, seems to have done its best to hamper and soften the board's actions.[18] There was difficulty in securing staff appointments, though whether the Board or the Civil Service Commission was at fault is not clear. There was doubt, finally, as to the constitutionality of the two acts. The chairman of the board resigned in February, 1920; Mr. O'Connor and Mr. Murdock resigned in June of that year, and the board ceased to function. It was given formal burial in 1921 by an adverse judgment of the Privy Council.[19]

It seems safe to say that the anti-combination laws passed

[17] See his letter of resignation from the board. (Hansard, 1920, p. 86.)

[18] Mr. Murdock, in his letter of resignation, made the following charges: i. That most of the Cabinet had never been in sympathy with the provisions of the Acts. ii. That they only recommended their passage because of the temporary alarm incidental to the Winnipeg strike. iii. That the chairman was appointed because he was considered a "safe man," and that he saw that the board did not tread on the toes of important business interests. iv. That the board's activities were continually thwarted by Cabinet intervention. (Hansard, 1921, pp. 3603–3607.)

[19] In the matter of the Board of Commerce Act and the Combines and Fair Prices Act. (1921), 1A. C. 191–201. It is worth pointing out that the judgment was concerned primarily with the second half of the Combines and Fair Prices Act which gave the board the power to determine "fair" profits; this portion was held unconstitutional as interfering with "property and civil rights in the provinces." It is not proper to infer from this judgment, however, that any federal trade commission would be held invalid; if its powers were more restricted and more clearly defined, it might possibly pass the scrutiny of the Privy Council.

between 1889 and 1920 had little effect on the actions of business men. Sections 496–498 Cr. Code were legally adequate after 1900, but no administrative machinery was provided for detecting offenders and bringing them into court. The Combines Investigation Act of 1910 attempted to meet this need by providing for judicial hearing of complaints, but this method was so costly and inconvenient that "small men" could not be expected to take advantage of it. The Acts of 1919 moved in the right direction by setting up a permanent administrative body. The function of the Board of Commerce was not clearly defined, however, and the attempt to endow it with enormous and varied powers proved completely impracticable.

Effective legislation dealing with combination may be dated from the Combines Investigation Act of 1923, introduced into the House of Commons by the Prime Minister, Mr. King. This Act, like that of 1910, was designed primarily to detect and publicize undesirable combinations, leaving prosecution to the provincial Attorneys General. Two advances, however, were made over the 1910 statute. The lodging of a complaint was made easier and cheaper. A sworn statement, signed by six citizens, alleging the existence of a combine and presenting supporting evidence was now sufficient to set an investigation in motion. Moreover, a permanent official, the Registrar, was appointed to conduct investigations on receipt of a complaint, or when instructed by the Minister of Labour, or on his own initiative. The bill encountered vigorous opposition. Powerful newspapers misrepresented it completely. Deputations of protesting business men visited Ottawa. Circulars were distributed to members of Parliament. Most Conservative members of the House opposed it strongly, as did several Liberal members from manufacturing areas. The strongest supporters of the bill were Progressives and Liberals from western Canada. In spite of this opposition, Mr. King and Mr. Dandurand, Liberal Leader in the Senate, steered the bill through without substantial alternation.

The Combines Investigation Act of 1923, with certain amendments, is still in effect, and its provisions are discussed below. Reasons will be given for believing that it has not seriously frightened the larger Canadian cartels and monopolies. But it is equally clear that there has been more activity and more effective activity under the Act than under any previous statute. Several hundred complaints have been received and investigated since 1923. Twenty major investigations have been carried out, sixteen reports published, eight separate groups of prosecutions instituted and over $300,000 collected in fines.[20] The Registrar's office, moreover, has become a focal point of industrial information, and his thorough reports form an excellent introduction to realistic economics.

Before examining the administration of the Combines Investigation Act, it is necessary to mention recent legislative developments. As depression deepened after 1929, more and more voices were raised in lament and denunciation. Farmers, workers and their representatives cried out against "monopoly." Business men, on the other hand, denounced the "price-cutter," the "mean man" who "demoralized" the market, and limitation of competition was proposed with increasing frequency. The Conservative government, swept into power in 1930 by depression discontent, tended to listen to business men, and to support the efforts at combination by a policy of non-intervention.[21]

[20] These figures are as of March 31, 1939.

[21] This viewpoint is well represented by the Minister of Trade and Commerce, Mr. H. H. Stevens. As early as 1923, Mr. Stevens had opposed the Combines Act in the following terms: "My chief criticism of the bill is that in effect it declares to be a crime that which is, without question, ordinary, sound business sense." He pointed out with approval the growing tendency of business men to eliminate "vicious, useless competition — competition which simply seeks to slay a competitor"; such agreement of business men improves the efficiency of distribution and stabilizes both prices and production. (Hansard, 1923, 2524.)

The administration of the Combines Act from 1930 to 1935 was definitely unsympathetic to the Act's purposes. A narrow view was taken of the powers conferred by the Act,[22] and several important reports of investigations made during this period were not published. Appropriations for the work of the Act were reduced. At the same time, members of the government spoke favorably of protective combinations of business men, and the launching of the "code" idea by President Roosevelt in 1933 was received enthusiastically by a number of Cabinet members.

A special committee of Parliament, later constituted a Royal Commission, was set up in 1934 to investigate the marketing of agricultural products, labor conditions, and the effects of chain and department store buying. The Commission sat at intervals for nearly a year, took several thousand pages of oral evidence and received a large number of memoranda and special statistical reports. Its conclusions, embodied in the Price Spreads Report of April, 1935, form the most comprehensive existing treatment of the Canadian economy, and the volumes of evidence are a mine of information. The report recommended, among other things, the creation of a Federal Trade and Industry Commission. This body was to have the following main functions:

i. Rigorous administration of an amended Combines Investigation Act, for the purpose of retaining and restoring competition wherever possible.

A speech of 1934 shows that Mr. Stevens' ideas had not basically changed since 1923. He points out with approval that the United States has apparently abandoned its anti-trust policy and substituted a policy of regulated combination [the NRA codes]; Canada, he thinks, should follow this lead — any attempt to enforce the Combines Act would be "an entirely retrograde movement." He condemns "the selling of goods at less than legitimate cost" and suggests that "we try to find out whether the indulgence in unfair and unethical practices is prevalent in this country." (Hansard, 1934, p. 200.)

[22] See answers given by Mr. Bennett to questions in the House of Commons. (Hansard, 1931, pp. 501 and 2374.)

ii. Regulation of monopoly in those industries where competition cannot be restored or enforced.

iii. Approval and supervision of agreements regulating prices and production, in industries where competition has proven wasteful or demoralizing.

iv. Prohibition of unfair competitive practices, using methods similar to those of the United States Federal Trade Commission.

v. Administration of existing and proposed laws for the protection of the consumer.

vi. Regulation of new security issues.

vii. Conduct of general economic investigation, and such special inquiries as may be necessary for fulfillment of the above functions. Full publicity was to be given to all findings of the Commission.

The bill introduced into Parliament by the government in June, 1935, gave the Commission only five of these powers, regulation of monopoly and of unfair competitive practices being omitted.[23] The most surprising feature of the bill, however, was the provision that the three members of the Tariff Board were also to constitute the new Trade and Industry Commission. This provision greatly weakened the effect of the measure. The regular duties of the Tariff Board are sufficient to keep it fully occupied. Moreover, its confidential relationship with business men unfits it for the rôle of policeman. The

[23] At the same session, however, a new section (498A) was inserted into the Criminal Code. The first part of this section, which forbids sellers to discriminate among buyers "in respect of a sale of goods of like quality and quantity," was discussed in Chapter V. In addition, the section forbids the charging of different prices in different areas of Canada or the sale of goods "at prices unreasonably low," provided that these policies are followed "for the purpose of destroying competition or eliminating a competitor." In spite of the commendable purpose and clear construction of the section, its effect has been negligible to date because of the failure to provide adequately for its enforcement.

bill was passed with only one important change: the clause empowering the Commission to regulate new issues of securities was deleted in the Senate.

The Combines Investigation Act was also amended in several directions during the 1935 session. Administration of the Act was transferred from the Minister of Labour to the new Trade and Industry Commission. It was provided that documents required to be produced before the Commission during an investigation might not be used as evidence in subsequent criminal proceedings. A combine might thus destroy the possibility of a successful prosecution by filing all of its incriminating documents with the Commission. Finally, it was provided that persons might not be prosecuted under both the Combines Act and Section 498 Cr. Code. It is evident that these changes considerably reduced the effectiveness of the Act.

Conservative policy, as crystallized in the statutes of 1935, accepted in the main the business view that competition should be limited whenever its consequences become unpleasant to the competitors. The Trade and Industry Commission Act permitted control of prices and production in any industry, subject only to possible veto by the Commission.[24] At the same time the Combines Act, which had in some measure served as a check on the growth of price agreements, was crippled by amendments. The two measures were positive and negative aspects of a single policy, sometimes described as "self government of industry."

A few months later the government was defeated at a general election and the Liberal party returned to power. The new government, led by Mr. King, immediately referred the Trade and Industry Commission Act to the Supreme Court for an opinion as to its validity. The Supreme Court, while sustain-

[24] Specifically, the Act provided that after any price and production agreement had been approved by the Commission, the parties to the agreement should be immune from prosecution.

ing parts of the Act, rejected the section legalizing price and production agreements. The government evidently welcomed this decision, and did not tempt fortune by carrying the matter to the Privy Council. Administration of the Combines Act was removed from the Commission in 1937. The Commission (i.e., the Tariff Board) thus retains only the power to investigate commodity standards and grant the trademark "Canada Standard" to articles meeting established specifications, to investigate alleged violations of various laws relating to commodity standards and trade practices, to hold fair trade conferences, and to conduct general economic investigations. Little action has been taken as yet under any of these heads, the limited staff of the Board being preoccupied with tariff investigations.

The Liberal government also attempted to salvage the Combines Act and restore it to approximately its previous form. During the 1937 session the Minister of Labour, Mr. Norman Rogers, introduced an amending bill providing for: (1) Transfer of the Act from the Trade and Industry Commission to a single Commissioner reporting to the Minister of Labour. (2) Admissibility of documents produced during an investigation in subsequent criminal proceedings. (3) Prosecution of offenders under both S. 498 Cr. Code and the Combines Act. (4) A new and clearer definition of "merger, trust or monopoly." (5) Seizure of documents, and their retention after the end of an investigation for purposes of prosecution. (6) Performance of certain functions of the Trade and Industry Commission (fair trade conferences, investigation of unfair trade practices) by the Commissioner. (7) Increase of the maximum penalties for breach of the Act. (8) Other changes designed to strengthen the Act.

The first three of these provisions were necessary to restore the Act to its 1923 form, while the remainder were new fortifying clauses. The bill passed the House with little change, but the

Conservative majority in the Senate tore it to pieces.[25] Only the first two provisions listed above were passed. In addition, the Senate inserted an amendment providing that before the Commissioner can compel production of evidence he must obtain an order from the President of the Exchequer Court of Canada or the Chairman of the Dominion Trade and Industry Commission or a judge of a provincial Supreme Court. The present Combines Investigation Act, then, is in some respects str..nger, in other respects weaker, than the Act of 1923. The chief administrator now has the title of Commissioner, more extensive offices and a larger permanent staff. He can also secure publication of his reports whenever this seems desirable. On the other hand, he can no longer begin investigations on his own initiative but must wait for either a formal application by six citizens or instructions from the Minister of Labour. A more serious handicap might develop through the necessity of applying to a judge before powers of compulsion can be exercised. This delay might be sufficient to enable the destruction of essential evidence.

ADMINISTRATION OF THE COMBINES INVESTIGATION ACT

The structure of the amended Combines Act is relatively simple. "Combine" is defined as an actual or tacit agreement having or designed to have the effect of lessening competition or enhancing prices, or a merger, trust, or monopoly,[26] "which

[25] Familiar arguments were used against the bill. The Conservative leader in the Senate, Mr. Arthur Meighen, said at one point: "I have very grave misgivings about granting to any government department these extraordinary functions which can be exercised to the harassment of business, to the penalizing of any special business or section of business, subjecting it to tremendous expense, and attaching to it a degree of obloquy which is even more serious than the expense; I say I have very grave misgivings about granting these extraordinary functions to any government department without the supervision of something in the nature of a judicial tribunal." (Committee Proceedings on the Bill, p. 42.)

[26] "'Merger, trust or monopoly' means one or more persons (a) who

combination, merger, trust, or monopoly has operated or is likely to operate to the detriment or against the interest of the public, whether consumers, producers or others." Any six persons who believe a combine to exist may apply to the Commissioner for an investigation, and inquiries may also be undertaken at the request of the Minister of Labour. An investigation may be conducted either by the permanent Commissioner or by a special commissioner appointed for the purpose, and temporary technical assistants may be employed. The Commissioner may require the attendance of witnesses and the production of documents. Proceedings are to be private unless the Commissioner orders that they be conducted in public. At the end of an investigation a report is to be presented to the Minister of Labour, and this report must be made public unless the Commissioner recommends against publication. If a combine has been found, the Commissioner may remit the report and the supporting evidence to the Attorney General of the province within which the offense occurred. If within three months the provincial Attorney General has taken no action, an action may be commenced by the Attorney General of Canada. Individuals convicted of an offense under the Act are liable to a fine not exceeding $10,000 or to two years' imprisonment, while corporations are liable to a fine not exceeding $25,000.

How has the Act been administered during the past fifteen years, and what results have been achieved under it? [27] The

---

has or have purchased, leased or otherwise acquired any control over or interest in the whole or part of the business of another; or (b) who either substantially or completely control, throughout any particular area or district in Canada or throughout Canada the class or species of business in which he is or they are engaged." (Section 2 (4).)

[27] The amended Act is very similar to the Act of 1923 in both structure and intention. The Registrar under the 1923 Act, moreover, was made Commissioner under the amended Act in 1937. The experience of 1923–1937, therefore, probably affords a fair indication of the administrative methods which will be followed in the future.

administrative procedure may best be described in terms of the stages through which a typical investigation passes. The machinery of investigation is in most cases set in motion by a complaint to the Commissioner.[28] It was assumed in 1923 that consumers would be the most frequent complainants. A majority of the complaints received, however, have come from manufacturers, jobbers and retailers. A manufacturer complains that his rival is cutting prices in order to ruin him, a retailer writes that manufacturers will not sell to him because he cuts prices, a jobber reports that he must pay more for merchandise because he is not a member of a jobbers' association, and so on. Farmers have frequently complained that the buyers of their products are combining to depress prices. A number of inquiries have been initiated at the request of city councils and other public bodies. Only a small proportion of the complaints have come from consumers. The well-informed consumer, rationally protecting his own interest, seems to be rarer than is commonly assumed. A large majority of the complaints, however, have related to consumers' goods. A few staple products — bread, milk, coal, tobacco, gasoline — recur frequently in the list of cases.

The original complaint is in most cases vague and unsubstantiated. The first step, then, is to write to the complainant for additional information. This is usually the last heard from him, for he probably has no facts and is either unable or unwilling to secure any. If additional evidence is received, however, the Commissioner must decide whether he shall proceed with a preliminary investigation. The following appear to be the main criteria used in making this decision: 1. Disputes between business men which do not to any extent involve the public interest will usually not be investigated. There has been no attempt,

[28] This official, as has been pointed out above, was known as the "Registrar" previous to 1937. It will be less confusing, however, to use a uniform terminology and refer to him throughout as the Commissioner.

for example, to regulate "unfair" trade practices as such. Only in cases which appear to affect directly or indirectly the interests of consumers or primary producers has action been taken. 2. Attention has been given largely to cases involving agreement, and the single-firm "merger, trust or monopoly" has been left relatively untouched. 3. The commodity must be of considerable importance in commerce, and the agreement in question must cover a considerable area. It is evident that it would be administratively impossible to investigate the activities of small tradesmen in every village of the Dominion. 4. Valid enactments of a provincial legislature or a city council are held to be *prima facie* in the public interest, and agreements concluded under them will not be investigated.[29]

If these requirements of public interest, an important article and a considerable territory are met, a preliminary investigation is made. A good deal of information about the product in question can be compiled by writing to the parties complained against, and from publications of the Dominion Bureau of Statistics and other government departments. The price and output history of the article, imports and exports, the degree of tariff protection received, comparison of prices in Canada with those in the United States and elsewhere, profit statements of the companies involved, are all studied. The Commissioner or an assistant may visit and question officials of the companies at their offices. On the basis of this research, a written report is prepared for the Minister of Labour. In most cases, the original complaint is found to have had little basis. It was either grounded on inaccurate information, or else the actions com-

[29] In November, 1934, for example, the Montreal city council passed a by-law limiting the number of taxicab licenses which might be issued in the city. An application was made almost immediately for an investigation under the C. I. A., but this application was refused. Applications have also been received for investigations of milk distribution, and where this matter is regulated by provincial commissions the Commissioner has declined to intervene.

plained of, while harmful to the complainant, have had no effects of public importance. In a few cases, dissolution of the combine has resulted directly from the preliminary investigation. In twenty cases, however, full investigation has been deemed necessary. These twenty full investigations have constituted the most publicized and probably the most valuable part of the activities under the Act.[30]

Well over half of these inquiries have been directed by the permanent Commissioner. Informal methods of investigation have been used wherever possible. The Commissioner or his representative have visited the offices of the companies complained against, asked questions, requested documents and special reports. This procedure has the advantages of being less costly than a formal investigation and of avoiding all

[30] These investigations, with the date of the Report, are listed below:

Marketing of fruit and vegetables in western Canada	Report,	Feb. 18, 1925
Retailing of coal in Winnipeg	"	Feb. 28, 1925
Marketing of New Brunswick potatoes	"	June 9, 1925
Bread-baking in Montreal	"	March 25, 1926
Marketing of fruit and vegetables in Ontario	"	July 31, 1926
Proprietary Articles Trade Association (Distribution of drugstore products)	"	Oct. 26, 1927
Amalgamated Builders' Council (plumbing contractors, Ontario)	"	Dec. 18, 1929
Electrical Estimators' Association (electrical contractors, Toronto)	"	Oct. 4, 1930
Motion-picture distribution, Canada	"	April 30, 1931
Bread-baking, Canada	"	Feb. 5, 1931
Manufacture of radio-tubes, Canada	"	1932 (Unpublished)
Manufacture of fruit baskets, Ontario	"	1932 (Unpublished)
Distribution of anthracite coal, eastern Canada	"	April 21, 1933 (Not published until March 10, 1936)
Buying of tobacco, Ontario	"	March 4, 1933
Manufacture of rubber footwear, Canada	"	1934 (Unpublished)
Sale of gasoline, Ontario	"	1934 (Unpublished)
Coal distribution, eastern Canada	"	Feb. 3, 1937
Tobacco distribution, Canada	"	August 31, 1938
Manufacture of paperboard shipping containers, Canada	"	March 14, 1939
Wholesale fruit distribution, western Canada		Pending

appearance of a trial. It is sometimes easier to obtain the truth from a man by talking with him across a desk than by arraigning him before an investigating body which has many of the appurtenances of a court. Where formal hearings seem desirable, these are usually conducted by the permanent Commissioner, though in earlier years it was the practice to appoint a special Commissioner. The Commissioner is assisted in these hearings by a small staff, consisting at most of an economic adviser, a lawyer, an accountant and stenographic reporters. Hearings are usually private. The Commissioner and his counsel question at length a large number of witnesses. While the Commissioner is not bound by the strict rules of evidence, every effort is made to give the parties being investigated full opportunity to be heard either in person or by counsel. Counsel are permitted to raise questions at any time, but cross-examination of witnesses is not usual. The hearings are not a trial but a piece of economic research, and it is important to bring out as much information as possible in a minimum of time. At the end of the hearings, counsel for the parties under investigation sometimes make a more or less formal argument before the Commissioner, who weighs this argument along with the evidence in making his report.

The Act of 1923 gave the Commissioner the powers of a court in summoning witnesses and compelling the production of documents, and these powers have proven adequate for the purpose. Companies have usually been willing to produce documents when requested, and the largest companies have been the most ready to make their records available. In the only case in which it has been necessary to institute contempt proceedings, the Commissioner was upheld by the court.[31] In the same

[31] Mr. Louis Singer, organizer of the Amalgamated Builders' Council, a combination of plumbing contractors, denied that the Commissioner appointed to conduct the investigation had any jurisdiction over him and refused to answer any questions or produce any documents. The Commis-

case, the group being investigated endeavored to obtain an injunction to prevent the preliminary investigation from proceeding. Mr. Justice Raney decided that such an injunction would amount to an injunction against Parliament, which cannot be granted. Further, "the defendant McGregor has gone no further than to issue invitations to certain persons to meet him and tell him what they are doing. There cannot be an injunction against an invitation."[32] The legal position of the Commissioner has been rendered less secure by the Senate amendment of 1937. It remains to be seen whether this will prove a serious obstacle to the Act's operation.

Half of the major inquiries have been concerned primarily with manufacturing. The remaining ten investigations have centered mainly on the activities of wholesalers and retailers, though manufacturers were also involved in several cases. Most of the early investigations were concerned with marketing, but during the past ten years manufacturing industry has received increased attention. It should also be observed that most of the inquiries have related to agreement among a number of firms. In only four cases (British Columbia fruit distribution, motion-picture distribution, tobacco buying, and tobacco manufacture and sale) were the policies of a single large firm the main object of investigation.

Combines were found in nine of the fifteen cases which have been made public. The reports are judicial in tone, well-written, and make informative reading for the layman as well as for the economist. With one possible exception, the evidence presented seems fully adequate to support the conclusions based upon it.[33]

---

sioner, Mr. Waldron, had him committed to jail for contempt, and was upheld by a judge in so doing. (*Re Singer*, 37 O. W. N. 3–6, Aug. 1, 1929.)

[32] A. B. C. v. McGregor and Heenan, 36, O. W. N. 34406, June 28, 1929.

[33] The possible exception is the report on tobacco buying, which concluded that no combine had been discovered. It would appear from evidence given before the Price Spreads Commission that the buying policies of the Imperial Tobacco Company did in fact work to the detriment of the grow-

In only one case has the judgment of the courts differed from that of the Commissioner.[34]

What criteria have been used by the Commissioner in determining whether or not a particular arrangement constitutes a "combine"? The terms of the Act are very general. "Combine" is defined to include "fixing a common or resale price," "preventing or lessening competition," "limiting facilities for transporting, producing, manufacturing, supplying," etc., but only when the arrangement has operated or is likely to operate "to the detriment or against the interest of the public, whether consumers, producers, or others." Such phrases as "the interest of the public" require interpretation. How has the phrase in fact been interpreted? The Commissioner has looked first of all for evidence as to the lessening or elimination of competition, and has regarded the lessening of competition as *prima facie* evidence of injury to the public. The injury need not necessarily consist in the reaping of undue profits. In nearly all of the combines investigated under the Act, large profits have in fact been reaped, and evidence to this effect has been included in the report. Even without this, however, the Commissioner has held that agreement on prices and production may serve to discourage efficiency and perpetuate over-capacity. Prices may therefore be too high, even though no producer is making large profits. Methods used to eliminate rivals or to shut out potential competition are also cited, where necessary, as additional evidence.

Business groups have frequently consulted the Commissioner

---

ers. The Combines investigation succeeded in unearthing enough evidence to arouse justifiable suspicions, but not enough to warrant the finding of a combine. The report was inadequate and unsatisfactory rather than wrong.

[34] In the motion pictures case, Famous Players Canadian Corporation, Ltd., and several other defendants were acquitted by Mr. Justice Garrow of two charges under Sec. 498 Criminal Code and one charge under the Combines Investigation Act. (The King v. Famous Players et al., 1932, O. R. 304–49.)

for advice as to the probable legal status of proposed price-maintenance or production-control schemes. If the scheme as submitted seems definitely in conflict with the Combines Act, the group concerned is notified to that effect. If the plan seems on its face innocent, no guarantee is given that there will not be a subsequent inquiry under the Act. If the scheme appears to have dangerous possibilities, the parties are advised that if they proceed they must take their chance of an investigation and an adverse court judgment. There are several reasons for this policy. Since almost any scheme of combination might be so presented as to appear lawful, full investigation would be necessary before any stamp of government approval could be given. If approval were given, the scheme could then be described to the public as government inspected, yet it might be so altered in operation as to have harmful effects. The operation of the plan would need to be examined from time to time, and this would require a large staff and heavy expenditures of public funds. In any event, the final decision as to the legality of an agreement rests with the courts, and the Commissioner cannot predict what their opinion would be.

The action taken on a case depends largely on the report of the Commissioner to the Minister of Labour.[35] If the Commis-

[35] The Minister may help or hinder the work of the Commissioner in a number of ways: (1) He may severely limit the scope of any inquiry of which he disapproves. He cannot prevent the Commissioner from proceeding with an investigation if an application has been filed. But he can refuse to appoint a special commissioner to continue the investigation, since this requires an Order-in-Council which he must recommend. In addition, since he recommends appropriations for the work of the Department, he can prevent the Commissioner having sufficient funds to proceed with further inquiry on his own account. (2) He could formerly, though this is no longer true, decide whether a report of the Registrar should be published. Of the important investigations carried on during 1930–35 only four were made public. One of these (tobacco buying) was only published after repeated pressure in the House of Commons, and another (anthracite coal) was not published until three years after it had been completed. (3) He

sioner finds that no combine exists, the report is published and the matter ends there. If a combine has been found, the report is published and sent to the Attorney-General of the province in question. Ten reports have thus far been sent on for prosecution. No action was taken by the province in the New Brunswick potato case, possibly because of political considerations. In another case involving several large manufacturers, Ontario declined to prosecute on the ground that prices had been reduced sufficiently as a result of the investigation. In the remaining cases prosecutions were instituted, though sometimes only after a certain amount of negotiation between the federal and provincial authorities.[36] Charges are laid either under the Combines Investigation Act or under the very similar prohibitions [37] contained in Sec. 498 of the Criminal Code.

The final decision as to whether an offense has been committed rests with the courts, and it is therefore necessary to ask how they have interpreted the terms of the statutes. It has been clear since *The King v. Elliott* (1903) that S. 498 Cr. Code

---

could formerly decide whether or not the Registrar's report is to be sent on to a provincial Attorney-General for prosecution. If this is not done, the effect of the investigation may be largely lost.

With the exception of the years 1930–35, the work of the Act does not appear to have been hampered by direct political intervention. There has, however, in the writer's opinion, been a persistent tendency to underestimate the importance of the Act and to provide insufficient funds and staff for its operations.

[36] The Western Fruit case was turned over to the Dominion by British Columbia; there was some ground for this, as the case involved the four western provinces. Ontario handed the A. B. C. case to the Dominion, on the ground that the province was at the time contesting the constitutionality of the Combines Act. The anthracite coal case was passed back and forth between Quebec and Ottawa several times before the province finally began the prosecution.

[37] Similar, but not identical. S. 498 makes it an offense to combine to *unduly* prevent or lessen competition. The Combines Act makes it an offense to prevent or lessen competition *against the interest* of the public. The courts have tended, however, as is pointed out below, to regard these two provisions as having the same effect.

goes beyond the common law and creates a new offense. But what is the precise nature of this offense? What does it mean to "unduly prevent or lessen competition," to "unduly prevent, limit or lessen the manufacture or production of any article or commodity"?

The courts have consistently held (and there can be no doubt that in so holding they have correctly interpreted the view of Parliament) that competition is beneficial, and that any substantial restraint upon it is likely to be against the public interest. This view was first emphatically stated in *Weidman v. Shragge:* "I have no hesitation in holding that as a rule an agreement having for one of its direct and governing objects the establishment of a virtual monopoly in the trade is an important article of commerce throughout a considerable extent of territory by suppressing competition in that trade, comes under the ban of the enactment" (Duff, J.); "One thing which must appear in any given case is that the agreement or arrangement is one designed to prevent or lessen competition" (Idington, J.); ". . . the prime question certainly must be, does it, however advantageous or even necessary for the protection of the business interests of the parties, impose improper, inordinate, excessive, or oppressive restrictions upon that competition the benefit of which is the right of every one?" (Anglin, J.).[38] The same view, variously expressed, runs through other leading cases.[39]

But when is restraint of competition "undue," or "against the interest of the public"? Mr. Justice Duff in *Weidman v. Shragge* set up three criteria, which have been frequently cited in subsequent cases: 1. The combination in question must

[38] Weidman v. Shragge, 46 Can. S. C. R. 1–44, 1912.

[39] "Injury to the public by the hindering or suppressing of free competition notwithstanding any advantage which may accrue to the members of the combine, is what brings an agreement under the ban of Section 498." (Mignault, J., in Stinson-Reeb Builders' Supply Co. v. The King, 1929, S. C. R. 276–82.)

deal with an "important article of commerce." 2. It must cover a considerable extent of territory. (In the *Electrical Estimators* case and the *Master Plumbers* case, however, combinations of contractors within a single city — Toronto — were held illegal.) 3. The combination must aim at a virtual monopoly of the trade. In an earlier case, too, it was held that a combination may not be illegal provided a sufficient number of firms remain outside to provide adequate competition.[40]

The courts have consistently refused to apply any specific yardstick, such as the amount of profit made by members of the combine. Counsel for the defense have argued in several cases that the combinations in question were innocent because prices had not been enhanced, or because profits had not been excessive, or because combination was necessary to avoid losses. All of these contentions have been rejected by the courts; a combination, it has been held, may be detrimental to the public even though prices and profits may appear "reasonable." [41]

[40] In the Ontario Coal case, after pointing out that a partial combination may be legal, MacMahon, J. went on to say that in this case *all* dealers in coal were included. "That without more is sufficient to show that the combination was of a character which must 'unduly' prevent competition in the sale of coal." Hately v. Elliott, 9 O. L. R. 185–91, 1905.

[41] See in this connection the opinion of Chief Justice Sifton of Alberta in the Alberta lumber dealers' case: "The question does not necessarily arise as to whether the price of lumber has been lowered or raised in the province of Alberta. This does not constitute the essence of the crime that is made by the statute in connection with this case. As I understand it, the essence of that crime is that men should agree to do something that would unduly prevent competition. In my estimation, you can unduly prevent competition without raising the price of lumber." (The King v. Clarke, 1908, 1 Alta L. R. 358–83.)

In Weidman v. Shragge, Idington, J. points out that the use of any standard of profit "must, as evidence, be of trifling value"; profits which might be justified for a vigilant and able firm would be undue for an antiquated, overcapitalized, inefficient concern. In deciding each case many things must be taken into account, including: "The enhancing or lowering of prices; the variation thereof without obvious causes other than the evil

Several decisions have emphasized the fact that Sec. 498 Cr. Code relates only to the suppression of competition by *agreement*. Monopoly, price leadership, and the use of economic power by large firms do not come within its scope.[42] Nor does it prevent a producer or dealer from buying out a competitor, though to form an agreement with him might be illegal.[43] The

---

purpose the Act forbids; the margin of profit; the scale of business; the operative field; the frame of the contract, the devices used therein and its execution; the refusal to deal with others without assigning any reasonable cause. . . ."

In the Electrical Estimators' case, the contention of defense counsel that the Association was necessary to protect the industry from price-cutting, that prices charged were not exorbitant and that in some cases losses were suffered, was answered as follows by Raney, J.: "But the system adopted by the Electrical Estimators' Association is not to be judged by its accidents, but by its tendency — not by the circumstance that sometimes the members of the association made no profit, or sometimes made too much, but by what the thing was in essence that the defendants were seeking to accomplish. That thing was the prevention or lessening of competition . . . and in my view, apart altogether from its effect on prices, that scheme was . . . likely to operate to the detriment or against the interest of the public." (The King v. Alexander, Ltd., et al., 1932, 2 D. L. R. 109–28.)

[42] The Famous Players Canadian Corporation, for example, owns more than half the theatre capacity in all except seven Canadian cities of more than 10,000 population. This position was attained by steady buying of theatres during the twenties, some of which were then kept closed, and by buying up theatre sites to prevent competitors from securing them. Since the Company is much the largest buyer of films in Canada, no film distributor can afford to run counter to its wishes. Famous Players is able to obtain first choice of all films, leaving only the inferior products for independent exhibitors. It has also been able in some cases to cut off the film supplies of independents in order to induce them to sell their theatres or to raise their admission price to the level set by Famous Players. (Department of Labour: Report of investigation into an alleged combine in the motion picture industry, 1931.) When the Company was brought to trial for these practices, however, it was acquitted on the ground that it had acted independently and without collusion with any other firm. (Rex v. Famous Players et al., 1932, O. R. 304–49.)

[43] In the anthracite coal case the action of the F. P. Weaver Company in buying control of a competitor was held lawful, since this action had been taken independently. (The King v. Canadian Import Co. et al., 61 C. C. C.

Combines Act, on the other hand, includes "mergers, trusts and monopolies" in its definition of a combine. Until a few charges have been laid under this section, however, it is impossible to tell how far the courts will go in holding illegal the acts of single firms.

A few judges have relied on reasoning strongly tinged with the common law point of view to justify leniency even toward combinations. In some instances they appear to have been impressed by the drawing of a sorry picture of an industry brought to its knees through price cutting, and of the erstwhile competitors magnanimously coöperating to save each other from disaster. Chief Justice Falconbridge of Ontario gave as one reason for acquitting the Wholesale Grocers' Guild the fact that they had acted in good faith to protect their own interests and those of all wholesalers. In *Weidman v. Shragge*, the majority of the Manitoba Supreme Court and one member of the Supreme Court of Canada held that "unduly" should be interpreted in the same way as "unreasonably" under the common law, which would have greatly reduced the scope of the statute. In a lengthy dissenting judgment in the *Stinson-Reeb* case, Mr. Justice Howard contended that members of the gypsum cartel had merely taken steps which they deemed reasonable in their own interest; if manufacturers prefer stable to fluctuating prices, why should there be any complaint? A more extreme example is the case of *Tanguay v. Laing* in which Mr. Justice Surveyer, dismissing charges against the Canadian Fire Underwriters' Association, in effect placed the whole judgment on a common law basis.[44] A similar sort of argument was

114–68.) Again, Chief Justice Harvey of Alberta upheld the purchase by a coal company of its chief competitor on the ground that S. 498 does not apply to "an arrangement to buy out the property of a competitor who is left free to acquire other properties and so to continue in competition with his vendees." (Stewart v. Thorpe, 36 O. L. R. 752–60, 1917.)

[44] "If the real purpose of the combination is not to injure another, but to forward or defend the trade of those who enter it, no wrong is com-

used by Mr. Justice Logie in dismissing charges against an association of cement block makers.[45] These judgments, however, run counter to the general trend of judicial opinion, which has been strongly opposed to combination.

A few additional points of interpretation should be noted. Agreement must be actually proven to exist, and suspicious circumstances do not in themselves constitute adequate proof.[46] It is not necessary, however, to prove that parties to an agreement intended to break the law.[47] Nor is it necessary that the combination should actually have operated; the mere formation of the agreement is in itself an offence. It is also important that a wide interpretation has been given to "article of commerce." In the *Famous Players* case a motion-picture film was held to be an article of commerce, while in the *Electrical Estimators'* case and the *Amalgamated Builders' Council* case building and

---

mitted, and an action will not lie, although damage to another ensues." (Tanguay v. Laing et al., 35 Revue de Jurisprudence, 444–59, 1928.)

[45] Ratcliffe v. Crawford, Supreme Court of Ontario, Oct. 10, 1928. (Not reported.) Mr. Justice Logie said in part: "An agreement among traders to prevent competition, and even to keep up the price, is not necessarily invalid, if it is carried out under the provisions of an agreement reasonably necessary for the purpose, and not detrimental to the public interest. . . . (After pointing out that most of the cement block makers had been losing money, he continues) . . . this condition of affairs was not in the interest of the public."

[46] Mrs. Mary Floyd, an Edmonton ice-cream dealer, persisted in selling double-header ice-cream cones, to the annoyance of other retailers; they brought pressure to bear on the manufacturers of ice-cream, who thereupon cut off Mrs. Floyd's supply of ice-cream. She brought suit, charging a conspiracy to injure her business. The action was dismissed on the ground that each of the manufacturers seemed to have acted separately, and that no agreement had been proven. (Floyd v. Edmonton City Dairy Ltd., et al., 1935, 1. D. L. R., 754–9.)

[47] "Under both these laws, the evil results attained seem to replace the intention." (Laliberte, J. in The King v. Canadian Import Co. et al., 61 C. C. C., 114–69.) Under the Australian Industries Preservation Act it is necessary to prove "intent to injure Australian industry"; this is of course very difficult to prove, and the effect of the law is thereby weakened.

installation contracts were held to come under the statute, since they include materials supplied as well as labor services performed.

Of the six groups of prosecutions completed to date, five have resulted in convictions. The Ontario basket makers pleaded guilty at once, apparently to avoid the publicity of a trial, and received light fines. The other five cases (western fruit, plumbers, electrical contractors, motion pictures, and anthracite coal) came to trial, the trials being largely a repetition of the evidence secured during the investigation. In all except the motion picture case the prosecution was successful, and fines of moderate severity were imposed.[48] The adverse publicity received by the defendants in the course of the trials doubtless resulted in much greater losses than the fines themselves.

As a result of fifteen years' operation under the Act, then, nine combines have been reported to the public, and eight groups of prosecutions have been conducted. There is evidence that at least four of these combinations have been dissolved. Recent investigations indicate that the Nash interests no longer dominate the fruit and vegetable trade in Western Canada. The Proprietary Articles Trade Association broke up after the unfavorable report of the commissioner without waiting for prosecution. The Amalgamated Builders' Council and the Electrical Estimators' Association also broke up under investigation, and were definitely laid to rest by the prosecutions which followed.[49] In three cases the outcome is uncertain. The New Brunswick potato dealers were not prosecuted, and there is no

[48] The Nash fruit houses were fined $200,000, the coal importers $40,000, members of the plumbing combination $45,200, and the electrical contractors $26,000. Considering the number and size of the firms involved, these fines are not large.

[49] The A. B. C. case also resulted in the break-up of a number of other "guilds" which Mr. Singer had organized on similar lines, including the Canadian Millinery Guild, Canadian Furriers' Guild, Canadian Cap Manufacturers' Guild, and Amalgamated Garment Manufacturers' Council.

evidence as to whether the combine has continued to operate. The Famous Players Corporation, acquitted in the courts, has probably not modified its practices materially. The Ontario fruit basket makers managed to escape publicity by pleading guilty at a preliminary hearing, and it is not known whether the association has been reëstablished. In the anthracite coal case, while the combine itself was not broken, the object of the Act was achieved through the stimulation of competition from new sources. The importation of Welsh anthracite coal into Ontario and Quebec is still closely controlled. Anthracite is now entering Canada, however, from Belgium, Germany and other sources, and coal prices have been considerably reduced.[50] In two cases, finally, prosecutions are pending, and the outcome can therefore not be predicted.

Since the purpose of a law is to deter possible offenders, it would be improper to judge the Combines Act solely by the number of prosecutions under it. It is impossible to obtain conclusive evidence concerning the effectiveness of the Act in preventing price agreements. Retailers, wholesalers, and building contractors seem to regard it as a serious obstacle to such activities. The widespread existence of price agreement among manufacturers indicates either that manufacturers do not take the Act so seriously or that they do not consider their price fixing activities to come within its scope. They do tend, however, to regard it as an annoyance which should be repealed or rendered innocuous. In a memorandum presented to the Minister of Trade and Commerce in 1934, the Canadian Manufacturers' Association suggested the repeal of the Act, or, if this were impossible, the following amendments: (1) Transfer of the administration of the Act from the Department of Labour to the Department of Trade and Commerce. (2) That "combinations of employers, producers, distributors or others for the

[50] Report of the Royal Commission on Anthracite Coal, February 3, 1937, pp. 115–18.

reasonable prevention of unfair practices" be exempted from the operation of the Act. (3) That the Commissioner (at that time, the Registrar) should be allowed to proceed with investigations only after the passing of an Order in Council. (4) That the Minister may at his discretion substitute a cease and desist order for prosecution. The effect which these amendments would have in crippling the Act is evident.[51]

Most investigations under the Act receive little publicity. If a report is published, copies are distributed to the publishers of newspapers and other periodicals, libraries, universities, and others, including those with a particular interest in the investigation. A copy of the Motion Picture report, for example, was sent to every motion picture exhibitor in Canada, and a copy of the P. A. T. A. report was sent to every druggist. These reports are not extensively reported in the daily press. Prosecutions receive more newspaper space, and are the main way in which the ordinary citizen learns of the combine's activities. The publicity resulting from the Act does not seem to have justified the claims made by its proponents in 1923.

SUMMARY

Canada has oscillated between two distinct policies of trade regulation. The Liberal party has endeavored to prevent harm-

[51] For the full text of the memorandum, and the comments of the Commissioner on it, see the Price Spreads Report, pp. 473–483.

The manufacturers' point of view is well represented in the evidence of Mr. C. H. Carlisle, then President of the Goodyear Rubber Company of Canada, before the Price Spreads Commission: "My third recommendation is to require all members of an industry to operate in a common organization, but subject to government supervision . . . the things I complain of in the Combines Act are that it prohibits organization that is economic and constructive . . . by turning over to the government full power of regulation you can give to the public the same measure of protection or greater protection than they have under the Combines Act." (Evidence, p. 2177.) It is interesting that Mr. Tom Moore, then leader of Canada's trade unionists, also advocated code organization of industry, checked by government supervision to protect the consumer. (Evidence, Vol. 1, p. 150.)

ful combinations by means of publicity and penalties. Free competition, they believe, will serve as adequate regulation for industry, and will in most cases make further government intervention unnecessary. The Conservative party, on the other hand, has tended toward the view that business men should be allowed greater freedom to combine for the defense and furtherance of their common interests. The function of the government should be to protect business against the "unfair" competition of "unethical" firms, "price cutters" and the like. The idea of codes of fair competition under government supervision has been welcomed by some Conservative leaders in recent years. The division between these two points of view, of course, does not run strictly on party lines, nor is the division as clearly defined as this brief statement would suggest. The alternation of Liberal and Conservative governments, however, has brought frequent and distinct shifts of emphasis which have prevented the emergence of any clear-cut policy.

While eight important statutes have been passed since 1889, nearly all of the effective action in this field has been taken under the Combines Investigation Act of 1923. The wording of this Act is less severe than that of United States anti-trust legislation. The Sherman Act forbids any restraint of trade. The Combines Act forbids only combinations which have operated or are likely to operate against the public interest. Canadian courts, however, have tended to take the position that any substantial restraint on competition extending over a considerable area is *prima facie* against the public interest. At the same time United States courts have moderated the severity of the Sherman Act by holding that only "unreasonable" restraints of trade are unlawful. Moreover, United States courts have used much the same criteria in deciding what is "unreasonable" that Canadian courts have used in determining what is "against the public interest." [52] The process of judicial interpretation has

[52] Compare, for example, the language of Mr. Justice Sifton in the Al-

thus brought the two statutes into much closer agreement than one would judge from their wording. In some respects, indeed, the Combines Act is even stronger than the Sherman Act. It can be applied to agreements within a single province, while the jurisdiction of the United States extends only to interstate commerce. Moreover, it prohibits market control by a "merger, trust or monopoly," while the Sherman Act makes no mention of monopoly.[53]

Much valuable work has already been done under the Combines Act. Several combines have been broken by full investigation and prosecution, others have dissolved as a result of preliminary investigation, and there is some evidence that the mere existence of the Act has checked the formation of price agreements. There is no doubt that the costs of administration have been repaid many times over in savings to consumers.

---

berta Lumber Dealers case with that of the United States Supreme Court in the Trenton Potteries case:

"The question does not necessarily arise as to whether the price of lumber has been lowered or raised in the province of Alberta. That does not constitute the essence of the crime . . . the essence of that crime is that men should agree to do something that would unduly prevent competition. In my estimation, you can unduly prevent competition without raising the price of lumber." (Rex v. Clarke, 1908, 1 Alta. L. R., 358–83.)

"The aim and result of every price-fixing agreement, if effective, is the elimination of one form of competition. The power to fix prices, whether reasonably exercised or not, involves power to control the market and to fix arbitrary and unreasonable prices. . . . Agreements which create such potential power may well be held to be in themselves unreasonable or unlawful restraints, without the necessity of minute inquiry whether a particular price is reasonable or unreasonable as fixed. . . ." (U. S. v. Trenton Potteries Co., 1927, 273 U. S. 392.)

[53] It is true that the Standard Oil Company, the American Tobacco Company, and other monopolies have been held unlawful under the Sherman Act. The judgments in these cases, however, were concerned mainly with the tactics used in driving out or excluding competitors from the industry. It is the *monopolizing* of an industry, rather than the mere existence of a monopoly, that has been condemned by the Supreme Court, and it is not at all certain that a monopoly which had made no attempt to exclude competitors would be held unlawful.

Moreover, a large body of valuable economic information has been accumulated. At the same time it must be admitted that the possibilities of the Act have by no means been fully realized. Too little money has been spent, too few combines have been investigated, an intrinsically good policy has not been carried far enough. Until the Act has been applied to a wider range of manufacturing industries and to a considerable number of single-firm monopolies, it will not have the full effect which it might have on business behavior.

The limited effectiveness of the Combines Act is not due to inherent weaknesses. The machinery of the Act is well conceived, it has been fully sustained in the courts, it has been sympathetically and ably administered. The difficulty is that both Liberal and Conservative governments, for political reasons, have not favored too vigorous enforcement of the Act, and have not given the administrators either the definite encouragement or the larger staff necessary for effective action. If these requisites were provided, the Combines Investigation machinery could perform important work in that sector of the economy within which competition is still possible. The area within which competition now prevails — described in Chapters I and II — might be policed fairly effectively. It is also possible that competition might be restored in some industries now regulated by agreements. The possibilities in this direction are explored in the concluding chapter, which contains also some suggestions for amendment of the Combines Act.

VII

PUBLIC POLICY TOWARD COMPETITION: LIMITATION

A STUDY OF THE COMBINES ACT ALONE would lead one to believe that preservation of competition has been the main object of Canadian policy. It is necessary, however, to set this Act in perspective against other Canadian statutes bearing on competition, many of which go directly against the policy expressed in the Combines Act. These other measures may be divided into two groups. Statutes such as the Companies Act, the Tariff Act, and the Patent Act, while concerned primarily with other objects, have incidentally permitted and even encouraged the limitation of competition. By skillful use of the powers conferred by these acts and by the common law, manufacturers in most industries have been able to restrict competition within narrow limits. Direct price fixing legislation has not been necessary, and there has accordingly been little demand for it from manufacturing industry.

The situation of farmers, retailers and other small enterprisers is quite different. For obvious reasons they are unable to make effective use of the statutes mentioned above. Their businesses are usually conducted as individual proprietorships, using immemorial skills which cannot be patented, and producing goods and services which cannot take advantage of tariff protection. Voluntary price control is difficult to secure and almost impossible to enforce. These industries therefore tend to react to any sharp decline in effective demand by appealing to government for agricultural marketing acts, resale price maintenance acts, and similar price fixing legislation. Since the power of the Dominion to regulate production and trade has been held within narrow bounds by Privy Council decisions, most of this legislation is of provincial origin. These statutes, then, differ in several ways from those in the first group. They are largely provincial rather than Dominion, they are designed to aid farmers and traders rather than manufacturers, and they prevent competition by intention instead of limiting it by indirection. They are also much more recent, being largely a product of the decade since 1929. These two groups of statutes are considered in turn in the next two chapters.

THE COMPANIES ACT

It is evident that without the use of the corporate form many of the firms which now dominate Canadian industry would have arisen much more slowly if at all. An individual or even a partnership would find it difficult to buy up sixty canning plants. The combination is easily made, however, by incorporating a new company and issuing stock of this company in return for the plants. The Companies Act has not only made mergers possible, but has encouraged them by allowing large profits to accrue to company promoters.[1] Most Canadian mergers seem to have been promoted by men with financial rather than industrial experience, and promoters' profits seem to have been the largest single incentive to combination.[2] This

[1] The promoter performs a variety of functions: he buys or secures options on the properties which are to be combined, he sees to the incorporation of the new company, he turns over to it (for a consideration) the properties or options, and he arranges for the marketing of its securities. Profits arise chiefly through the sale of properties or options to the new company at a price above that paid by the promoter, and through the commission obtained for marketing the new company's securities. Promoters' profits are usually taken in the form of common or preferred stock of the new company, which can be converted gradually into cash as the securities become established in the market.

[2] See in this connection the opinion of H. G. Stapells, The Consolidation Movement in Canadian Industry (unpublished thesis, University of Toronto), and the Royal Commission on Price Spreads: Report, pp. 29–31.

view is supported by the fact that the two bursts of merger activity occurred during periods of exceptional prosperity, when fresh stock issues were quickly absorbed by optimistic investors. The hope of achieving price control has been an incentive in some cases.[3] Economies in production, while figuring largely

---

An interesting case of promotion by financiers is that of Canada Power and Paper, one of the leading consolidations of the late twenties. The leading figures were Mr. J. H. Gundy and Sir Herbert Holt, who were associated in the investment banking firm of Holt, Gundy & Co. Mr. Gundy explained to a House of Commons committee: "What brought us into the paper business was the failure of the Bay Sulphite Co. of which we had sold the bonds. . . . We tried to get Price Bros. and the Abitibi crowd to take it and they would not, so we looked after it ourselves." The group then proceeded to acquire other paper companies — St. Maurice and Belgo-Canadian in 1925, Canada Paper and Anticosti Corporation in 1926, Laurentide in 1928. In 1928 Canada Power and Paper was set up as a holding company, with Holt as chairman of the board and Gundy as a director. Indeed, of 16 directors of Canada Power and Paper in 1930, only 3 were "pulp and paper men," while 5 were bankers. In 1929 Bay Sulphite, which had been reorganized as Port Alfred Paper Co., was bought from Mr. Gundy for some 250,000 shares of Canada Power and Paper common. Mr. Gundy made the mistake, however, of holding these shares until after the 1929 crash so that he actually lost by his promotional activities. (House of Commons: Select Standing Committee on Banking and Commerce, 1934. Minutes of Proceedings and Evidence, pp. 722–749.)

[3] This seems to have been a leading consideration in the formation of Canada Power and Paper. Mr. Gundy testified as follows before the Committee on Banking and Commerce (Evidence, pp. 728–729): "The underlying reason for promoting these mergers was to eliminate causes of friction in the industry which were destructive," and at p. 744: "The purpose was to organize the industry . . . for its own protection . . . to prevent destruction of the industry . . . to bring mills into harmonious groups." Mr. Chahoon, President of the Laurentide Co. and later of Canada Power and Paper, said (p. 783): "The underlying reasons were principally the idea of keeping the industry from flying into a thousand parts. We felt that if the paper industry could be organized into three groups — a Quebec group, an Ontario group, and the International Paper Co. — the thing would be run in an intelligent, economical manner."

Canadian Canners was formed for similar reasons. In 1893 nine canning companies formed a trade association, Canada Packers Assoc., for promotional work. A few years later a selling syndicate, "Dominion Syndicate," was formed. Competition of independent canners, however, hampered

in company prospectuses, do not seem to have been an important incentive. In many cases, indeed, it appears that net disadvantages have resulted from the merger. Of eighty-seven important consolidations between 1900 and 1920, nineteen were compelled to liquidate or reorganize within four years of their formation. Of 131 mergers of the period 1920–30, only 15 have shown improved earnings since consolidation.[4]

The most spectacular result of these mergers, and the one most often criticized, has been the large losses to buyers of securities. Tens of millions of dollars have been drained from the hands of investors into the pockets of promoters and investment dealers. The far-reaching effects on competition have been less frequently remarked. The most evident effect appears in those cases where the merger puts one company in a position to dominate an industry. Few of the leaders of Canadian industry reached their present positions by growth alone. Most of them are the result of a merger or a succession of mergers. The following companies, for example, are "mergers of mergers":

the syndicate's operations and in 1903 outright consolidation was decided on. Canadian Canners Consolidated was organized to buy out members of the syndicate and a considerable number of independents — some thirty companies in all. In 1910 seventeen more independents were absorbed and the name of the firm changed to Dominion Canners. Independents, however, continued to spring up and in 1915 it was necessary to form a new marketing agency, Canadian Canners Ltd., one half of whose shares were held by Dominion Canners. In 1923 this loose arrangement was consolidated by the incorporation of the present Canadian Canners, which bought out Dominion Canners and 29 independent firms. (Evidence before the Price Spreads Committee, Vol. VI, pp. 3015 *et seq.*) The present Canadian Canners, in short, has been built up by successive absorptions of independents, with the object of securing more effective market control than can be exercised by a selling syndicate.

[4] Price Spreads Report, pp. 31–32. The persistence of general depression since 1929 must, of course, be taken into account. Moreover, the fact of failure does not necessarily mean that productive efficiency was lowered by the merger. An alternative explanation is that the inflation of capital accounts incidental to the merger loaded an unduly heavy burden of fixed charges onto the new company.

Dominion Textile Co., Asbestos Corporation, Canadian Canners, Dominion Steel and Coal Corporation, Consolidated Power and Paper, Canadian Industries Limited. Canada Cement, Steel of Canada, Canada Bread, Canada Packers, National Breweries and Brewing Corporation, on the other hand, attained their present form by a single merger with (in some cases) subsequent purchases of properties. A few companies, including Imperial Oil, Imperial Tobacco, International Nickel, Aluminium Ltd., Algoma Steel, Canadian Celanese and Courtauld's (Canada) Ltd. have maintained their identity from the outset and have grown largely by internal expansion.

Where the merger does not ensure price control, there is an indirect effect on competition through the inflation of capital values. It is difficult to define "overcapitalization" with any exactness. Capitalization might be considered fair if it included the capitalized earning power of the constituent companies, averaged over a period of years, plus the expense of incorporating the new company, plus a "reasonable" return to the promoter for his services. In practice, however, the capitalization of a merger is likely to be considerably above this figure. The absorbed properties are frequently bought at unduly high prices.[5] The promoter, moreover, is rarely satisfied with a reasonable return.[6] The promoter's profit arises from the spread between the price paid for the merged properties and the capitalization of the new company. The higher the new capitalization, there-

[5] In some cases properties may be obtained for less than their true value. The directors of a concern, for example, may be willing to "sell out" the owners in return for a handsome bonus or an executive position in the new company. The opposite case, however, is also common. A prosperous concern which is not anxious to be absorbed and whose inclusion seems essential to the success of the merger may hold out for a price well above the capitalized value of its earnings.

[6] It must be considered, of course, that the business of promotion requires special talents and also involves some risk of failure. Making due allowance for these facts, however, promoters' profits seem in most cases to be entirely unreasonable.

fore, the greater is the possibility of profit. The upper limit to capitalization seems to be set by considerations of "what the traffic will bear," i.e., how great a quantity of securities can be marketed in view of the record of the merged companies and the mood of the investing public. If the issue is handled by a large investment dealer, however, he must consider that he will be appealing to investors in the future, and that if this issue turns out badly his reputation will suffer. A long-run view thus militates against extreme stock-watering. Some attention must be paid to the probable future earnings of the consolidation. During a period of prosperity, however, it is easy to take an over-optimistic view of future earnings, and the promoter may in good faith saddle the new concern with interest charges which it will be unable to bear.

A few examples of inflated capitalization are given below, not because they are in any way unusual, but because the information is available and the companies are relatively important.[7] The Canada Cement Co. was incorporated in 1909 to combine eleven cement companies throughout Canada. The owners of these companies were paid some $12,881,475 in cash and securities. The total securities issued by the new company, however, amounted to $19,756,966, leaving almost seven millions to cover expenses of organization and promoters' profits.[8] In 1927 the existing company was bought out and a new company organized, through the investment firm of Wood, Gundy and Co. It is impossible to state the exact amount paid for the common and preferred stock since this was accumulated gradually over a period of more than a year, but the figure has been estimated at $38,258,000. From the sale of new bonds and preferred stock $40,800,000 was obtained. In addition, the promoters appear to have retained 515,000 out of 600,000 shares of com-

[7] Additional examples will be found in Annex IV of the Price Spreads Report.

[8] Stapells, *op. cit.*, pp. 121–122, 144–145.

mon stock. There were heavy sales of common in 1928 at an average price of about $30.

The Dominion Textile Company was formed in 1905 by a syndicate of 16 men, including Sir Herbert Holt and Sir Charles Gordon, to take over four existing cotton companies. Members of the syndicate contributed $1,000,000 in cash. In return they received $500,000 of preferred stock and all of the common stock (par value $5,000,000). The remainder of the transaction was straightforward enough, consisting in a transfer of preferred stock and bonds of Dominion Textiles for stock of the four constituent companies. In 1922 a new company was incorporated. For each share of common in the old company, three no-par shares in the new company were issued, the total issue of new common having a book value of $15,000,000. A member of the original syndicate who continued to hold his common stock would thus have multiplied his investment by several thousand per cent in 17 years.[9]

Dominion Canners Ltd. (predecessor of the present Canadian Canners) was incorporated in 1910 to combine some 50 canning plants, nearly all in the province of Ontario. Several of these were purchased at much more than their actual value.[10] In addition, $320,000 of common stock was issued to Garnet P. Grant and others for their services in the promotion of the company. When the amalgamation was completed some $6,000,000 of stock had been issued. An expert appraisal, which one may suppose to have been favorable to the company, found that plant and equipment was worth only $3,725,000. The

[9] Royal Commission on Textiles: Brief of Counsel to the Commission, Mr. J. C. McRuer, pp. 143–162.

[10] The Lakeside Canning Co., for example, with issued stock of a par value of $30,500, was paid $42,156 in cash and $26,250 in preferred and common stock. The directors of the company, having knowledge of the proposed merger, were able to buy up almost all the stock of the company at par. They then resold to the promoters for more than double the amount they had paid.

remaining $2,275,000 was then set up on the books as "goodwill"! Professor W. T. Jackman observed of this merger: "With the vast amounts of stock which were given for the plants — which were taken over at values in some cases two, three, and in others almost four times their commercial value as going concerns — and the immense block of stock issues in payment of promotion expenses, there is no reason to doubt that this company's stock is watered to dilution." [11] When Dominion Canners became Canadian Canners in 1923, fixed assets were written up by an additional $2,950,000.

Canada Bread Co. Ltd. was formed in 1911. The five companies included had a total capitalization at that time of $575,000. They were all prosperous "family businesses" and in order to induce them to enter the consolidation it was necessary to pay $1,510,000 for the properties. The promoters received from the new company in cash and stock $1,975,250. After paying all expenses of the promotion, there must have been a clear profit of at least a quarter of a million, and the capitalization of the five plants had been increased almost fourfold.[12]

British Empire Steel Corporation was incorporated in 1920 to consolidate all of the steel and the coal interests of Nova Scotia, including Dominion Steel Corporation, Dominion Coal, Nova Scotia Steel, and Halifax Shipyards. The terms of the merger involved an increase in capitalization of $19,000,000. Moreover, the companies included were themselves the result of previous mergers, in the course of which their stock had been liberally watered. Professor Forsey has stated that "the promotion and bonus stock in Besco and its subsidiaries was at least $57,500,000 out of a total bond and share issue of approxi-

[11] W. T. Jackman, Report on the canning industry of Canada (prepared for the Board of Commerce, 1919.) See also Royal Commission on Price Spreads, Evidence, Vol. VI, pp. 3015 *et seq.*

[12] Stapells, *op. cit.*, pp. 94 *et seq.*; 117–119, 153–154.

mately $129,000,000."[13] The earnings record of the corporation was poor and it was reorganized in 1930 as the Dominion Steel and Coal Corporation.

Penman's Limited, the leading producer of knit goods, was incorporated in 1906 to take over a previous business of the same name. The promoters bought the stock of the previous company for $2,528,400, and proceeded to issue new stock and bonds amounting to $5,000,000. At the same time the book value of plant was increased by $422,830, and more than two million dollars was added to the goodwill account. Later in 1906 the assets of the Anchor Knitting Co., valued at $124,261, were acquired by issuing to the owners $225,000 of Penman's stock. The discrepancy was corrected by adding an additional $100,000 to "goodwill." The profits of the company since 1906 have been very substantial, and the auditor of the Textile Commission has estimated that "for no capital investment in the company at all, the promoters of the syndicate that organized the company in 1906 have realized $10,205,304" in dividends and accrued equities.[14]

The evidence before the Price Spreads Commission, the Textile Commission, and other bodies is filled with similar accounts, and one is forced to conclude that nearly every important merger in Canada has been accompanied by a considerable inflation of capital values. Perhaps equally important has been the tendency to increase the proportion of bonds and preferred stock and reduce the proportion of common stock. Since senior issues are more attractive to investors, they are commonly used to pay off the owners of the absorbed companies, while the common stock of the new company is retained by the promoters. To the extent that the capitalization of the absorbed companies consisted of common stock, this involves

[13] E. Forsey, Economic and Social Aspects of the Nova Scotia Coal Industry, McGill Studies in Economics, Number 5, Toronto, 1927.

[14] Royal Commission on Textiles, Exhibit 1070.

a substitution of senior for junior issues.[15] Between 1921 and 1933, $192,236,700 of securities was offered to the public as a result of consolidations. Of this total $93,989,000 consisted of bonds, $87,738,000 was preferred and "A" stock, while only $9,510,000 was common stock.[16]

The merger movement, then, has not only increased the demands made on industry for interest payments, but has given these demands greater legal force. The capital structure has been forced into such a form that failure to earn a prescribed rate of interest means insolvency. Control of industry, too, tends in the process to be transferred from men experienced in production to men experienced in finance, as owner-managers are superseded by boards of directors composed of promoters and bankers.

It is clear that this must have important effects on price policy. As the burden of fixed charges becomes more insistent price competition becomes more dangerous. Financially-minded directors tend to regard a corporation primarily as a source of interest payments and commissions. If competition threatens regular earnings, competition must be suppressed. Prices must

[15] A particularly flagrant case is that of the reorganization of the Burns meat packing company, a prosperous "family business," in 1928. The net value of fixed assets was written up by $3,160,144. At the same time the capital structure was altered as follows:

	Bonds	Preferred Stock	Common Stock	Total bond interest and preferred dividends
Before reorganization	$3,078,500	$3,906,200	$5,000,000	$473,536
After reorganization	7,000,000	6,900,000	99,997	799,000

The Dominion Securities Corporation, promoter of the reorganization, received approximately $1,000,000 for marketing the securities of the new company. The earnings of the business fell off seriously after 1929. Preferred dividends stopped in 1931 and bond interest in 1932. In 1934 a further reorganization was effected in which bond interest was reduced, preferred stockholders were reduced to common stockholders, and common stockholders were paid one new share for 20 old shares. (Price Spreads Report, Annex IV.)

[16] Price Spreads Report, p. 31.

be stabilized at a level which will yield a "fair" return on the inflated capital. If economists or public officials complain of price fixing, the directors reply that the company is only earning a moderate return on its investment,[17] and that to reduce prices would "discourage" industry. This seems on the surface to be an adequate answer, and the matter is usually not pursued. To discover how the capitalization of a company was built up and to determine whether it represents the "fair value" of the properties requires a staff of accountants and a large expense account. Moreover, by the time an investigation is made the damage has usually been done. The promoters have unloaded their bonus stock, and a forced reduction of interest payments would punish the unfortunate buyers whose only offence is their ignorance and optimism.

The Companies Act contains several provisions relating to promoters' profits. The 1917 amendments to the Act provided that any prospectus issued by a company must contain, among other things, (1) the names and addresses of the vendors of any property purchased or proposed to be purchased by the company, the amount payable in cash or shares to the vendor, and the amount of this which is payable for goodwill; (2) the amount paid or payable as commission for sale of the company's securities; (3) the amount paid or intended to be paid to any

[17] Consider, for example, the case of Canadian Canners. The Price Spreads Commission concluded ". . . of the $14,000,000 capital stock and bonds at present outstanding, at least $6,000,000 represents intangible values, appraisal fees, increases in the value of fixed assets, and bonuses paid over and above the appraised value of assets acquired." Their earnings on the inflated capital from 1923 through 1934 averaged less than 3 per cent (Report, pp. 361–362). The company contended before the Commission that the industry was unprofitable, and that these low earnings were evidence that it had not abused its dominant position. If earnings are calculated on the basis of "unwatered capital," however, they average almost six per cent, which was about the general level of manufacturing profits during this period. This illustration could be multiplied many times from the records of other Canadian companies.

promoter, and the consideration for such payment; (4) full particulars of the nature and extent of the interest of every director in the promotion of, or in the property proposed to be acquired by, the company, with a statement of all sums paid or agreed to be paid to him. A copy of the prospectus was to be filed with the Secretary of State, and a *per diem* penalty was imposed for delay in filing. In the event of any untrue statement appearing in the prospectus, all directors and other persons authorizing it were rendered liable to suit by purchasers of the securities for any losses sustained by them. Since a company was not obliged to prepare a prospectus, however, these provisions had scarcely any effect.

The 1934 amendments appear at first glance to strengthen this section of the act. "Prospectus" is defined broadly enough to include almost any sort of solicitation addressed to investors. Issuance of a prospectus, formerly voluntary, is now made obligatory in the case of any direct sale of securities to the public. A copy of the prospectus, moreover, must be sent to each applicant for shares at least 24 hours before the acceptance of his application. Neglect of these provisions renders the company and each of its officers liable to a penalty of $1,000, and the investor is allowed to withdraw his application at any time within 30 days of its acceptance.[18] The loophole in these provisions arises from the fact that few large companies offer their shares directly to the public. The general practice is to sell a new issue outright to an investment dealer, who then retails the securities to investors. Where this course is followed, however, the company need not prepare a prospectus, the dealer is not bound by the terms of the act, and the whole structure of legal safeguards falls to the ground.[19]

[18] Dominion Companies Act (1936 consolidation), sections 73–80.

[19] See in this connection the opinion of Professor Smails: "The new act . . . wastes one eighth of its physical bulk in specifying the information which must be contained in a document which no company need ever

The first explicit recognition of stock-watering appears in the 1935 amendments. Section 12(9) of the amended act provides that stock shall not be issued except for cash or "for a consideration payable in property or services which the directors may determine by express resolution to be in all the circumstances of the transaction the fair equivalent of cash to the total nominal value of the shares so issued." This does not in itself reduce the power of the directors (i.e., the promoters) to allocate stock on whatever basis they please. In a subsequent section (96B), however, they are rendered liable to suit by any shareholder, creditor or director of the company. If the court decides that the consideration received by the company was less than the value of the shares issued, the directors are jointly and severally liable to the company for the deficiency. It must also be shown, in the case of any director, that he had knowledge that the consideration received was inadequate or that he failed to take reasonable steps to find out. Any suit under this section must be brought within three years of the transaction.

These safeguards, while impressive on paper, are ineffective in practice for a number of reasons. Each of the penalty clauses, in the first place, contains exceptions which enable directors to evade responsibility with relative ease. A director may escape liability for an untrue statement appearing in a prospectus, for example, if he can show that "he had reasonable ground to believe and did . . . believe that the statement was true," or that it was a "fair copy of or extract from a report or valuation of an expert." [20] Promoters are thus able to take refuge in the intricate question of what constitutes good faith, or to place

---

trouble to prepare if it has the wit to sell its securities outright to an investment banker instead of offering them direct to the public. And no great amount of wit is required in following a course which has been almost universal practice for the past quarter century on this continent." Canadian Journal of Economics and Political Science, Vol. 1, p. 60.

[20] Dominion Companies Act (1936 consolidation), section 78(1)(iv).

the blame on the misguided optimism of an engineer or accountant. Similarly, the issue of shares for less than a fair consideration may be excused if the director has "taken reasonable steps to ascertain" whether the consideration was fair.

Failure to provide adequately for the enforcement of these provisions constitutes a more serious defect. Enforcement is at present left almost entirely to civil suits by injured investors. The ordinary stockholder, however, is unlikely to have the information on which a complaint might be based. He sees that the price of his stock has fallen, or that dividends have ceased, or that the company has gone into receivership. But there might be several reasons for this. How is he to know whether the promoters were at fault? To prove that the promoters' profits were excessive is a technical and costly matter. Few investors have a financial interest in any one company sufficient to warrant their spending the sums necessary for a successful suit.

Worse still, the consuming public may suffer even though all investors gain. If a merger results in effective price control, it may be possible to earn good profits even on an inflated capitalization. In this case no investor has cause to bring suit, yet consumers of the product have clearly been injured.

If stock watering is to be prevented, there is an evident need for some type of administrative control.[21] The Companies Branch of the State Department performs at present scarcely any regulatory function. Applications for letters patent are scrutinized to see that they contain all the information required by the Act — the purpose of the company, its head office, the amount and types of its stock, the provisional directors, etc. If the application has been properly completed, the charter is

[21] Several provinces already have securities commissions. The most important is that of Ontario, which has a larger and stronger staff than the Dominion Companies Branch. The Commission deals mainly with mining, oil and other unlisted securities, however, and is concerned chiefly with preventing the more flagrant types of fraud. It has not been much concerned with stock watering in industrial concerns.

issued as a matter of routine. There is no attempt to inquire into the physical assets behind the proposed stock issue or into promoters' profits. The Companies Branch takes the attitude that these are matters between the directors and the prospective stockholders. If the directors violate the Companies Act they are liable to prosecution and punishment, and their guilt or innocence is a matter for the courts to decide. This attitude reflects the strongly legalistic character of the Act itself, and the tolerance of promotional practices which has characterized Canadian governments. The Companies Branch can also say quite justly that its present facilities do not allow it to embark on regulatory work. A staff of thirty persons, of whom nearly all are stenographers and clerks, is scarcely sufficient to supervise the corporate hierarchy of the country.

The frequently-advanced proposal for a Dominion securities board raises many questions. The stiffening of the Companies Act in 1934 and 1935 led to increased incorporation in the provinces. Would additional regulation drive still more companies to seek provincial charters? Would companies chartered by a province come within the jurisdiction of a Dominion board? If not, could adequate provincial regulation be ensured? To discuss these questions here would go beyond our present purpose, which was simply to show that the Companies Act has permitted the inflation and freezing of capital structures, and that this has in turn intensified the desire of business men to substitute price control for price competition.

THE TARIFF ACT

Canadian manufacturers are sheltered from foreign competition by moderately high tariff rates. The average *ad valorem* rate on dutiable imports has fluctuated between 20 and 30 per cent during the past sixty years. The level tends to rise under Conservative governments and to fall under Liberal governments, but there has been no long-term trend in either direction.

It is impossible without extensive study to say very much concerning rates on particular products, since the rate depends on the country of origin,[22] physical characteristics of the product, and administrative rulings of the Department of National Revenue. Casual inspection of the tariff schedules and of the sources of imports, however, indicates that the rates are highest on refined sugar, woolen and silk fabrics, clothing of all sorts, hardware and hand tools, bath tubs and similar products, electrical equipment, medicinal and pharmaceutical products. The effective rate on these products is in most cases between 30 and 50 per cent. Finished iron and steel products, cotton cloth, men's shoes, gasoline, furniture, leather and tires enjoy protection ranging from 20 to 30 per cent. Primary iron and steel products, cotton yarn, most chemicals, agricultural machinery, automobiles and their parts have still lower rates. Goods not made in Canada and raw materials of all sorts enter duty free or at very low rates.

The Tariff Board of Canada, created in 1931 to assist in administering the British trade agreement of the following year,[23] now plays a considerable part in tariff making. It has general authority to hear appeals from rulings of customs officials concerning classification of products, valuation for duty purposes,

[22] The Canadian tariff contains British preferential, intermediate and general rates. The United States, which is much the largest source of Canadian imports, enjoys the intermediate rate less 10 per cent as a result of the trade agreement of 1935. Great Britain is the largest source of cotton yarn and fabrics, wool yarn and fabrics, rayon yarn and fabrics, household linen, men's shoes, whiskey, confectionery, tinplate, iron and steel sheets, cutlery, pottery, some acids and drugs, and a number of less important products. The British preferential rate is usually between one-half and two-thirds of the intermediate rate, though some British products enter duty free.

[23] The 1932 agreement provided that British manufacturers should have "full opportunity of reasonable competition" on the basis of relative costs of production. This made necessary some tribunal before which British producers could present data on relative costs and argue for tariff adjustments, and the Tariff Board was designed to meet this need.

and other technical matters. It may also, at the request of the Minister of Finance, examine the rates of duty on any product or group of products and recommend that these rates be increased, reduced or left unchanged.

While only a small proportion of all tariff changes are referred to the Board for investigation, these are usually the more important and complicated cases.[24] Upon receipt of a reference from the Minister, a preliminary notice is sent to the Canadian Manufacturers' Association, the British Trade Commissioner, and a selected list of persons who are especially interested in the product under consideration. When a date is fixed for hearings on the reference, notice of this date is sent to some five thousand persons on the Board's mailing list. At the hearings, which are ordinarily public, any person or group favoring or opposing the proposed change may present its views to the Board. Producers of the article usually present confidential information concerning costs, prices and profits. The Board's research staff gathers information concerning the article from published statistics, and examines the additional data presented by the producers. The final recommendation of the Board rests on a number of factors, including the comparative cost of production in Canada and other countries, competitive conditions in the Canadian market, comparative prices in Canada and elsewhere, and the importance of the industry as measured by

[24] The investigations of the Board to date have included, among other things, such important industries as automobiles, petroleum, iron and steel, cotton yarns and fabrics, woollen yarns and fabrics, radio, boots and shoes, furniture, and artificial silk fabrics.

There is probably some tendency to refer to the Board requests for tariff changes which are politically embarrassing. The Minister can in this way assure the interested parties that their request is being investigated and will be dealt with on its merits, without himself assuming direct responsibility for the decision. The Board thus serves as a buffer between the Minister and powerful business groups, and makes it somewhat easier to go against the wishes of a particular group when this seems advisable in the general interest.

employment afforded or value of products. A total of 68 reports had been rendered at the end of October, 1938. The Board recommended no change in 28 cases, a reduction of duties in 26 cases, and an increase of duties in 8 cases. In every case the recommendation of the Board has been accepted by the Minister of Finance. A mimeographed report is prepared on each case and is available to the public. A confidential report containing cost and profit data furnished by the companies is also prepared for the use of the Minister.

This procedure is clearly superior to tariff making by private political bargaining. That it leaves much to be desired is not the fault of the Tariff Board, but rather of the conditions under which it works. Those who have an interest in maintaining or increasing tariff rates usually act more quickly and more effectively than those who have an interest in reducing these rates. Trade associations regard the preparation of "tariff information" as one of their major functions, and are prepared on short notice to throw their entire strength behind proposals for rate increases.[25] Importers and manufacturers who stand to lose by these increases are usually unorganized, and the loss to any one company may be insufficient to cause it to take an active interest in the matter. If requests from British producers be excepted, applications for tariff increases have been much more frequent than applications for reductions.[26] Moreover, in spite of the

[25] Some indication of the manufacturers' viewpoint may be obtained from the evidence of Douglas Hallam, Secretary of the Primary Textiles Institute, before the Textile Commission of 1937. When asked about promotion of legislation by the Institute, he testified as follows: "*Q.* I suppose that would be the promotion of high tariffs? *A.* If you like to call it high. *Q.* That is how it is interpreted, anyhow, by the Association? *A.* I do not think the Association would admit there was such a thing as high tariffs." (Evidence, p. 7945.)

[26] Of references to the Board to date, 40 have involved requests for higher tariff rates, 33 have involved requests for lower rates, while 16 have been requests by the Minister for a complete review of certain tariff items or of an entire industry. Most of the requests for decreases have come

Board's efforts to notify all interested parties, the hearings frequently fail to produce an even balance of contending forces. The proponents of a tariff increase usually have the advantage of the initiative and of months spent in preparing their case. Those who stand to lose by a tariff are frequently not represented at all, and are usually inadequately represented. The general consumer interest is not represented in any systematic way, though briefs are occasionally filed by labor or consumer groups.

The criteria used in determining the proper level of tariff rates are also open to criticism. Chief of these is the principle that the tariff should equalize the cost of production in Canada and in other countries.[27] Domestic producers spend much of their time before the Board in stressing the great disadvantages under which they work, and the remarkably low production costs of other countries. The Board, whose staff is too small for extensive cost studies, is largely dependent on the producers for cost data. The producers, however, are not impartial witnesses, and may be expected to give themselves the benefit of any doubts in accounting. If domestic costs are of doubtful validity, foreign costs are frequently unobtainable, and the Board is

from British producers. Section 11 of the Canada-United Kingdom trade agreement of 1932 provided that "protective duties shall not exceed such a level as will give United Kingdom producers full opportunity of reasonable competition on the basis of the relative cost of economical and efficient production." Under this section British producers of boots and shoes, cotton and woollen textiles, jute yarns and twines, coke and other important products have applied to the Minister for tariff reductions, and these requests have been referred to the Board for hearings.

[27] This principle was written into the Tariff Board Act of 1931, and the Board is thus bound to give it due consideration. Section 4 instructs the Board to inquire into "(a) the price and cost of raw materials in Canada and elsewhere . . . ; (b) the cost of efficient production in Canada and elsewhere, and what increases or decreases in rates of duty are required to equalize differences in the cost of efficient production. . . ." As noted above, the same principle was inserted into the British trade agreement of 1932.

forced to rely on general comparisons of wage rates, raw material costs, and the like. Even if perfect cost data were obtainable, the principle of cost equalization would be an unsatisfactory criterion for tariff policy. If this principle were consistently applied, the greater the natural disadvantages of Canada for a particular product or the greater the inefficiency of Canadian producers, the larger should be the subsidy to the industry.

The Board has also come dangerously near at times to accepting the view that the "value" of an industry to Canada can be measured by the employment which it affords or the amounts spent by the industry in Canada.[28] This principle and that of cost equalization, of course, are taken as self-evident not only by business men but by the general public, and the Board is probably not free to depart very far from them. Business propaganda has so effectively confused the issues that few people realize that a protective duty is a subsidy to a particular business group, and that whether this subsidy should be larger or smaller is a matter of political expediency rather than of economics.

The fixing of a nominal rate of duty is only part of the process of tariff-making. The Department of National Revenue is able by administrative rulings to raise or lower the actual rate greatly with no change in the nominal rate. The Department is empowered to (1) determine the tariff item under which an article falls. (2) Determine whether it is "of a class

[28] In its Report on the automobile industry, for example, the Board points out (a) that Canadian consumers paid in 1930 fourteen million dollars more for their cars than they need have paid if these cars had been imported from the United States, (b) that the total amount spent in Canada by the automobile companies in this year was between forty and forty-seven million dollars. It then concludes that "the figures would indicate that it is 'good business' for Canada reasonably to encourage the maintenance and expansion of the Canadian automotive industry." (Report on Reference 91, 1936, pp. 230–231.)

or kind made or produced in Canada." [29] If it is not produced in Canada it will usually enter free, while in the opposite case it may incur a large duty. (3) Determine the value of the article for duty purposes. This is to be "the fair market value of such goods . . . as sold in the ordinary course of trade. . . . Provided that the value for duty of new or unused goods shall in no case be less than the actual cost of production of similar goods at date of shipment direct to Canada plus a reasonable advance for selling cost and profit, and the Minister shall be the sole judge of what shall constitute a reasonable advance in the circumstances and his decision thereon shall be final." [Customs Act, sec. 35–36] (4) Where an article is invoiced to Canada at less than the fair market value as determined above, a special dumping duty is imposed, equal to the difference between the invoice price and the fair market value. This duty, however, may not exceed 50 per cent. [Customs Tariff Act, sec. 6] (5) If the currency of the exporting country is substantially depreciated, an additional duty is levied to remove this advantage. [Customs Tariff Act, sec. 6]

While flexible administration is necessary in order to adapt the Act to rapidly changing circumstances, it is evident that this flexibility may easily be abused by over-zealous administrators. A customs official who considers his main function to be the shielding of Canadian industry can easily find means to exclude imports altogether, and in so doing may go far beyond the intention of Parliament.[30] There is evidence that these

[29] The procedure here is to send samples of the imported article to Canadian producers of similar goods, and to inquire whether they produce the article in question. If they answer affirmatively the article is classified as "made in Canada" and duty is imposed. Evidence before the Textile Commission disclosed that in some cases textile companies which were not at the time producing the imported article set to on receipt of samples and turned out a very small amount so that they could assure the Minister that the good was "made in Canada."

[30] The Vancouver customs office, for example, seems to have imposed a dumping duty on gasoline from the United States sufficient to prevent it

powers were used in the years 1930–35 to impose actual duties much higher than the nominal rates,[31] and that this served to shield Canadian manufacturers from the drastic fall of prices in other countries. Perhaps equally important is the uncertainty introduced into the tariff schedules by these provisions. Importers have testified that they were not able to obtain in advance any indication of the rate which would be imposed, and that this risk deterred them from importing.[32]

We are concerned here, not with the effect of the tariff on international trade, but with the related problem of its effect on competition within Canada. Has the tariff, as is frequently alleged, contributed to the growth of monopoly and price agreement? Would substantial lowering of the tariff restore competition in many industries? This sort of question can only be settled industry by industry, and any generalization would require substantiation by a separate monograph. In the absence of such a study one can only hazard a few general opinions.

At least five cases may be distinguished. In the first two of these there is no visible connection between tariff protection and the freedom of competition, while in the last three some connection is evident. (1) Some articles, such as sand and gravel, do not enter to any extent into international trade. A

---

from being imported and sold below the British Columbia retail price (fixed by the Imperial Oil Company!). Whether from ignorance or intent, they interpreted "fair market value" of gasoline as the value in *Canada* rather than in the United States. (Report of the British Columbia Coal and Petroleum Products Commission, vol. I, pp. 228–229.)

[31] The evidence before the Textile Commission indicated that this was done for all types of textile products. A duty of approximately 50% on grey cotton sheeting from the U. S., for example, was raised to almost 100% by special duties; a rate of 35% on bleached flannelette from the U. S. was raised to 66%; a rate of 22½% on knitted wool cloth from Great Britain was raised to 66%. (Report, pp. 79–80.)

[32] See testimony of gasoline importers before the B. C. Coal and Petroleum Products Commission (Report, vol. 1, pp. 229–230).

tariff on them is unnecessary and could have no effect on the extent of domestic competition.

(2) In some industries — notably automobiles, tires, electrical equipment, breakfast foods and toilet articles — the tariff has stimulated the building of branch factories in Canada.[33] While this movement involves a relocation of production in a higher-cost area, it does not necessarily bring any change in the number of competitors or in the relations among them. There seems no reason why the United States firms should be more (or less) willing to enter price agreements than they were before. Indeed, the market relations among the subsidiaries in Canada tend to be much the same as among the parent companies in the United States. In both countries, for example, the tire industry is marked by severe price competition, while in heavy electrical equipment price competition plays a negligible rôle.

Canadian producers in these industries have been caught in a dilemma. They have urged the necessity of high tariffs, but have tried at the same time to prevent the natural consequence of high tariffs, viz. the branch-factory movement. The textile trade associations, for example, have tried to discourage United States producers from building Canadian plants by sending gloomy accounts of business conditions to United States trade journals, by censoring favorable news, and by direct persuasion of individual firms.[34] United States producers, on their side,

[33] See K. W. Taylor, F. A. Southard, and H. Marshall: Canadian-American Industry, New Haven, 1936.

[34] Royal Commission on Textiles: Brief of J. C. McRuer. See particularly at p. 281 a letter from Douglas Hallam, secretary of the Primary Textiles Institute, to the trade press in the United States, in which he states that the Canadian silk industry is very much overbuilt and that Canada is not a promising field for investment. In 1933 a favorable news item was allowed through some oversight to reach the press. The President of the Silk Association wrote to Mr. Hallam to inquire who had released this item, and remarked "it might be as well to make inquiries, with a

have at times threatened to build branch plants in order to dissuade Canadian producers from requesting higher tariff rates.[35]

(3) In some industries, foreign producers continue to ship over the tariff wall. British producers of textiles, clothing, shoes and rolled steel, for example, ship large quantities of these goods to Canada in spite of the tariff. While competition is not necessarily reduced in these cases, it seems likely that this will occur. Some foreign producers may be prevented from exporting by relatively high costs. The larger profits made possible by the tariff, too, may strengthen existing Canadian producers and enable them to expand so rapidly that new firms are unable to arise. The number of competitors, then, is likely to be smaller than it would be if the tariff were lower. Moreover, Canadian producers may be able, by threatening to press for a tariff increase, to induce foreign producers to agree on a division of the market and a fixed price.

(4) Where the tariff is made prohibitively high, and where foreign producers do not choose to establish branch plants in Canada, the number of competitors in the Canadian market has evidently been reduced. Instances of this sort, however, are probably rather rare.

(5) In many cases, finally, there is no importation of goods into Canada because of an international agreement. In many industries the principal Canadian producer is owned by a British or American company. Du Pont and Imperial Chemicals are not likely to ship chemicals to Canada in competition with their joint subsidiary, Canadian Industries Limited. Nor are Courtauld's Limited and Celanese Corporation likely to com-

---

view to stopping this kind of news, which in my opinion would be best left unpublished."

[35] United States Steel, for example, owns a large tract of land just across the river from Detroit, and has threatened to construct a large plant there unless Canadian producers are "reasonable" in their tariff demands. (Advisory Board on Tariffs and Taxation: Hearing on Reference No. 2 — Iron and Steel, Nov. 27–29, 1928.)

pete with their Canadian subsidiaries. There is evidence that Imperial Oil has been able by informal methods to prevent shipment of gasoline from the United States to price-cutting distributors in Canada, even though this gasoline could profitably have been imported over the tariff wall.[36] In other cases, indigenous Canadian producers have secured agreements with companies in other countries whereby the latter agree not to export to Canada,[37] or to export only at agreed prices. There is no evidence as to the frequency of such agreements, but they must be rather common.

While in these cases competition would be restrained even in the absence of any tariff barrier, the tariff is not entirely without effect. It is frequently used by Canadian producers as an excuse for charging prices considerably above those which prevail in Britain or the United States. It was pointed out above that the price of copper, zinc and lead in Canada is the London price, plus freight to Canada, plus the customs duty, though the metal may be delivered directly from the smelter to a factory next door. Similarly, the price of gasoline is deter-

[36] See the evidence of Mr. C. E. Thompson, manager of the Independent Gasoline Co., before the British Columbia Commission on Coal and Petroleum Products: ". . . our suppliers told us in Seattle that they had been approached to discontinue our supply . . . if we did not conform to the regulations here. . . . We agreed to that [a price of 29 cents per gallon] believing it was the best arrangement we could make at that time." Report of the Commission, vol. 1, p. 75.

[37] Page-Hersey Tubes Ltd., for example, applied to the Tariff Board for a duty on seamless steel tubes. The application was refused on the ground, among others, that they were already sufficiently protected by a selling agreement. "Page-Hersey Tubes Ltd., the only manufacturer of boiler and similar pressure tubes in Canada, is a party to a selling agreement whereby Page-Hersey Tubes Ltd. sells in Canada boiler and similar pressure tubes only in sizes from 2½ inches to 4 inches outside diameter, while manufacturers in other countries who are parties to this agreement do not export tubes in such sizes to the Canadian market without the permission of Page-Hersey Tubes Ltd." (Report of the Tariff Board on Reference 17 — Boiler Tubes.)

mined by taking the price at refinery door in the mid-continent field, adding freight to the Canadian destination, customs duty, sales and excise taxes, and handling charges. Actually, of course, it is crude oil rather than gasoline which is shipped, and crude oil not only moves at lower freight rates but enters Canada duty free.[38]

The relative frequency of these five types cannot be determined without additional investigation. It is clear, however, that in some cases — perhaps in many cases — the existence of the tariff has reduced the number of competitors in the Canadian market and tended to stimulate price agreement. Moreover, where price control has arisen for other reasons, the tariff makes possible higher prices and larger profits, and thus serves to fortify the position of the combine. There is a strong tendency, particularly in the consumer goods industries, for organized producer groups to take full advantage of the tariff. So well recognized is this tendency that the government, in granting the sharp tariff increases of 1930, felt constrained to plead with producers not to raise their prices. As the period was one of recession, producers were quite willing to promise that prices would not be increased.[39] Many prices, however, were stabilized during the depression at a level which was undesirably high and which probably could not have been maintained had tariff rates been lower.[40]

[38] See Report of the B. C. Commission on Coal and Petroleum Products, vol. 1, pp. 79–82; Tariff Board of Canada, Report on Reference 84 — Petroleum and its Derivatives; House of Commons Standing Committee on Banking and Commerce, Inquiry into the petroleum industry, 1932, Exhibit 229.

[39] These promises, however, were usually so phrased as to be meaningless. The agricultural implement makers, for example, promised that "they will not increase prices of implements to consumers, *provided the factors entering into manufacturing costs are not increased*." (House of Commons: Special Committee on Farm Implement Prices, 1937, Minutes of Proceedings, p. 1280.)

[40] The most thorough study which has been made in this field is that of

The Combines Act provides that a report by the Commissioner that a combine exists shall be *prima facie* ground for reduction of customs duties on the product. It is evident from the above discussion that this remedy will be more effective in some industries than in others. In industries where an international understanding exists, such as rayon, chemicals and explosives, gasoline, and non-ferrous metals, a tariff reduction would probably not lead to increased imports. It might, however, lead to a reduction of prices in Canada, since it would be more difficult to justify the existing level of prices before government investigators and the public.

Where price control has been established within Canada but international ties are weak, as in cement, sugar, hardware, farm implements, and most iron and steel products, tariff reductions might be expected to weaken the effectiveness of domestic price

---

the Textile Commission. They found the following movement of textile fabric prices between 1929 and 1937.

INDEX NUMBERS OF WHOLESALE PRICES OF TEXTILE PRODUCTS
(EXPRESSED IN CANADIAN FUNDS)
1921 = 100

Year	Cotton Fabrics Can.	Cotton Fabrics U. S.	Cotton Fabrics U. K.	Wool Fabrics Can.	Wool Fabrics U. S.	Wool Fabrics U. K.	Silk Fabrics Can.	Silk Fabrics U. S.
1929	100.0	100.0	100.0	100.0	100.0	100.1	100.0	100.0
30	90.4	85.7	82.0	85.7	90.2	80.0	86.4	84.7
31	79.5	69.8	67.6	77.2	72.7	64.6	78.2	64.3
32	75.1	60.9	58.2	73.1	67.0	53.9	76.5	52.5
33	79.2	78.9	63.1	77.1	77.6	61.6	68.5	58.2
34	83.1	86.7	76.5	83.1	80.7	78.5	67.9	55.1
35	80.9	84.8	72.7	76.1	78.2	75.0	67.8	56.8
36	76.9	80.9	74.3	81.7	84.9	84.2	67.8	55.2
37 (Oct.)	79.3	73.5	78.7	86.4	92.1	83.0	67.3	60.6

The Commissioner concludes: "I think that the effect of customs duties and appraisals may be measured by saying that, without these charges, prices of textile products in Canada would probably have fallen from 40 to 50 per cent by 1932 from the 1929 level, instead of only 25 to 30 per cent, on the whole." (Report, pp. 102–104.)

control. Imports would tend to increase and prices to fall. Canadian producers would probably try to replace the tariff with a new selling agreement including the foreign producers, but their efforts would not always be successful. Complicated differences of interest arise in the formation of international cartels, and frequently make a binding agreement impossible. Low-cost foreign producers would probably not consent to enter an agreement unless they were given substantial quotas and allowed to sell at a lower price than that which prevailed before the tariff was reduced. While competition might be only temporarily restored by the tariff cut, there would probably be a permanent reduction in the level of prices.

Where competition prevails in the domestic market, as in furniture, boots and shoes, clothing, and many textile products, tariff reductions would increase the number of competitors and the severity of competition. Canadian prices would be brought nearer to foreign prices, and the less efficient domestic producers would be eliminated. Since in these industries the number of producers is large and entrance is easy, international agreements restricting competition would be very difficult, and the new situation would probably be permanent.

While the effects of tariff reduction will differ from industry to industry, then, they will almost always be beneficial to the consuming public. Where competition still exists, it will be intensified. Where price control has been established, a tariff cut may lead either to a renewal of competition or to an international agreement on prices and output. Even in the latter event, however, the level of prices will probably be lower than before.

THE PATENT ACT

The purpose of the Patent Act is to encourage the making and publication of inventions by granting to the inventor an exclusive right to exploit his process for a stated period of time.

In order to obtain a patent, an applicant must furnish models, drawings or specimens of his invention, must demonstrate to the satisfaction of the Commissioner of Patents that he has employed a new principle not covered by any existing patent, and must pay two fees totalling $35. The patent itself consists of a diagram and a series of claims, "stating distinctly and in explicit terms the things or combinations which the applicant regards as new and in which he claims an exclusive property or privilege." [41] Considerable skill is required to draw these claims so that they will cover the maximum possible territory, and for this among other reasons it is desirable to have the advice of a patent attorney. Legal fees and incidental expenses usually raise the cost of patenting a simple invention to $150 or $200, while a complicated patent will cost considerably more. Companies of any size usually have patent departments as well as research staffs, and the majority of patents are now obtained by corporations. In very few cases does a private inventor secure sufficient financial support to exploit the invention himself.

A patent is a grant of monopoly, and the Patent Act contains provisions designed to prevent the patentor from abusing his monopoly position. In the first place, a patent expires at the end of seventeen years, after which anyone is free to make use of the invention. This provision, however, is less significant today than in earlier times. At the present time technical change is so rapid that the economic usefulness of an invention may be fully exploited within the patent period.[42] The expiration of the patent in this case means little, since a new process has now been patented and serves to extend the monopoly for an additional seventeen years. The other principal safeguard in the

[41] The Patent Act, Sec. 35(2).

[42] A good example of this is the case of radio tubes. Tubes patented in the early twenties are now obsolete, and there is every likelihood that the tubes in use today will be obsolete before their patents have expired.

Act is the provision that "any person interested may at any time after the expiration of three years from the date of the grant of a patent apply to the Commissioner alleging . . . that there has been an abuse of the exclusive rights thereunder and asking for relief." Abuse of the patent is deemed to exist "if the patented invention is not being worked within Canada on a commercial scale, and no satisfactory reason can be given for such non-working," or "if the demand for the patented article in Canada is not being met to an adequate extent and on reasonable terms," or "if any trade or industry in Canada . . . is unfairly prejudiced by the conditions attached by the patentee . . . to the purchase, hire, licence, or use of the patented article." The relief granted may consist in revocation of the patent or in compulsory licencing of the patented article on terms determined by the Commissioner.[43]

These provisions, however, are less formidable than they appear on paper. In the first place, "any person interested" means in practice a business man requiring the patented article for the conduct of his business. Secondly, it is easy enough to prove, by judicious arrangement of cost and profit figures, that demand is being met on "reasonable terms," and that the patentee is producing all that can be profitably sold. Only where production is being severely restricted and prices maintained at a clearly exorbitant level can one be certain of obtaining relief. The whole procedure, finally, involves considerable expense, particularly if either party exercises his right of appeal to the Exchequer Court. Applications can only be expected, therefore, from business groups which have a vital interest in a patented article and which at the same time have considerable financial resources.

The public, then, has little real protection against the free use by patent holders of their monopoly power. Indirectly, too, the Patent Act serves to fortify positions of monopoly. The

[43] The Patent Act, Sections 65–66.

precise ground covered by a patent is a highly technical matter and leaves room for almost endless legal debate. It is thus possible for a large company or an association to frighten away new producers by claiming that they are infringing a patent and threatening to bring suit for damages. The small producer may have a good case, but the cost of establishing this case in the courts and of fighting successive appeals is prohibitive. He can thus be forced to close down, and if the combine is charitable it may offer to buy his plant — on its own terms.

The "patent pool" is primarily a matter of convenience for firms engaged in similar lines of production. Where one firm has a patent on an essential process while others have exclusive control of related processes, the labor of cross-licensing can be reduced by setting up a holding company to own all the patents and license all members of the group. There is no doubt, however, that such a company can serve other and less desirable purposes. It may act as watch dog for the industry, warning away "intruders" and putting the joint resources of existing producers behind infringement suits. It may also provide a convenient vehicle for output control, division of the market, and price regulation.[44]

Whether these considerations outweigh the stimulus to invention which patents provide, whether the existing Act should

[44] Canadian producers of radio tubes have a patent pool, which is allegedly used to control prices and output and to frighten away new producers.

be amended and if so in what directions, are matters which cannot be settled here. Enough has been said to indicate that the patent machinery, whatever its benefits, results in the creation and support of monopolies against which the public has no adequate protection.[45]

[45] Since trade marking plays a considerable part in the differentiation of products, it should be noted that exclusive use of trade names and brands is guaranteed by the Trade Mark and Design Act (R. S., c. 201) and the Unfair Competition Act (ch. 38, statutes of 1932). The Commissioner of patents is authorized by these acts to keep a register of trade marks, in which any mark may be entered on payment of a fee of $25, provided only that it is not the same as or similar to any existing mark and that it is not of a type forbidden by the Act (use of the royal arms, the Canadian flag, etc.). Use of a registered trade mark by anyone except the owner or his assignees is forbidden, as is also the use of a mark so similar to a registered mark as to be misleading to buyers. Distribution of any unlawfully branded goods may be restrained by injunction, and the court may also order the destruction of all infringing labels or dies.

VIII

PUBLIC POLICY TOWARD COMPETITION: PREVENTION

THE ACTS DISCUSSED ABOVE were not designed primarily to limit competition. By conferring broad powers with few genuine restrictions on the exercise of these powers, however, they have materially assisted business men in limiting competition and raising prices. Since 1929 there has been a growing demand that government should take the additional step of expressly prohibiting competition. This demand has come mainly from farmers, retail merchants, small-scale manufacturers, and other groups which find voluntary price control difficult. Since the regulatory powers of the Dominion government have been narrowly limited by court decisions, pressure has been directed increasingly to the provincial governments. The result has been a flood of provincial legislation interfering with competition in a great variety of ways.

These statutes may be divided into four main groups. The "industrial standards" acts of Quebec, Ontario, Saskatchewan and Alberta, while designed primarily to ensure uniform wages to all workers in a given trade, serve indirectly to encourage price fixing. Acts regulating the sale of gasoline exist in Nova Scotia, New Brunswick and British Columbia, while British Columbia and Saskatchewan regulate the sale of coal. Legislation designed to limit retail price cutting has been passed in British Columbia and Alberta. Eight of the nine provinces regulate the sale of fluid milk, while Ontario, British Columbia and New Brunswick control the marketing of certain other natural products.[1]

[1] The titles of these acts are listed below. The year given is that in which the act was first passed. Most of these acts, however, have been

The discussion below is based on the texts of the acts, the regulations issued under them, and correspondence with administrative officials. Some of the inferences drawn are doubtless mistaken, for a statute which seems on its face to mean a great deal may in practice mean nothing at all, or may be turned in an unexpected direction by its administrators. It seemed better, however, to make an imperfect survey of this important and rapidly growing field than to leave it entirely untouched.

INDUSTRIAL STANDARDS ACTS

The most far-reaching of these statutes is the Quebec Collective Labour Agreements' Act. The Act provides that whenever an association of workers has entered into a collective agreement with one or more employers, the parties may petition the Minister of Labour to make the agreement binding upon all

---

amended at least once since their first passage. Discussion below is based on the acts as amended to June, 1938.

(1) Industrial Standards and Related Acts: Collective Labour Agreements' Act (Quebec, 1937), Industrial Standards Act (Ontario, 1935), Industrial Standards Act (Saskatchewan, 1937), Industrial Standards Act (Alberta, 1936), Tradesmen's Qualifications Act (Alberta, 1934), Department of Trade and Industry Act (Alberta, 1934), Licensing of Trades and Businesses Act (Alberta, 1936).

(2) Regulation of the Coal and Gasoline Industries: Gasoline Licensing Act (Nova Scotia, 1934), Gasoline Licensing Act (New Brunswick, 1935), Coal Mines Act (Saskatchewan, 1935), Coal and Petroleum Products Control Act (British Columbia, 1937).

(3) Resale Price Maintenance Acts: Sale of Goods Act Amendment Act (Alberta, 1936; repealed, 1939), Sale of Commodities by Retail Act (British Columbia, 1937), Minimum Loss for Food Products Act (British Columbia, 1937).

(4) Regulation of Agricultural Marketing: Dairy Arbitration Act (Nova Scotia, 1938), Dairy Products Act (New Brunswick, 1935), Milk Control Act (Ontario, 1934), Milk Control Act (Manitoba, 1937), Milk Control Act (Saskatchewan, 1935), Public Utilities Act Amendment Act (Alberta, 1933), Natural Products Marketing Act (British Columbia, 1934), Natural Products Control Act (New Brunswick, 1937), Farm Products Control Act (Ontario, 1937).

employers and employees in a stated region of the province. The Minister, after giving notice in the public press and hearing objections, may approve the petition with any changes which are deemed expedient. The decree approving the petition is binding on all engaged in the industry in the stated region from the date of its publication in the Official Gazette, and may be amended or revoked at any time by a similar notice. The terms of the decree constitute minimum standards for the industry and do not prevent an employer from offering higher wages or more favorable conditions of work.

Employers and employees are obliged to form a joint committee to supervise the operation of the decree. This committee, by publishing its by-laws in the Official Gazette, becomes a corporation with the ordinary powers, rights and privileges of corporations. It is specifically empowered to (1) compel employers to keep adequate payroll records, (2) examine these records at any time, (3) take evidence from any employer or employee under oath, (4) levy upon employers alone or upon employers and employees the sums necessary for administration of the decree, (5) create a board of examiners to determine the competency of employees, (6) institute suits on behalf of workers who have been paid less than the stipulated wage, and recover not only the arrears of wages but twenty per cent additional as liquidated damages. The Act also contains fines for intimidation of employees by threats, dismissal or blacklisting, for the use of closed shop agreements, for refusal or neglect of an employer to follow the instructions of a joint committee, for payment of wages below those specified in the decree, and related offences.

In June, 1938, some sixty decrees were in effect, of which fifteen related to the barber trade, twelve to the building trades, and the remainder to a long list of miscellaneous occupations. The great majority cover only a single town or county. Montreal, for example, has decrees covering the following industries:

printing, shoe repairing, baking, millinery, barbering and hair-dressing, automobile repairing and stevedoring. In these industries competition is primarily local, and local agreements are therefore sufficient. The following decrees, however, cover the entire province: men's and boys' clothing, furniture, ladies' cloak and suit, shoe, working glove, paint, men's and boys' hat and glove, building material, and lithographing. The printing and clothing agreements, which were negotiated by strong and experienced trade unions, are lengthy documents covering hourly wage rates, wage differentials between Montreal and the remainder of the province, piece-work, hours, overtime, apprenticeship, division of work and other matters. Most of the other decrees are much simpler, dealing mainly with minimum wages and maximum hours of work, and it is apparent that the associations involved have come into existence recently in order to take advantage of the Act.[2]

While the primary purpose of this legislation is to set a minimum standard of working conditions, it is bound also to have important effects on competition among employers. In industries where competition extends over the whole province or over several provinces, there may be some effect on the location of production. It is too early to say whether the Act will reduce the wage differentials between Montreal and rural Quebec and between Quebec and Ontario, but if this should occur there might be a considerable relocation of industry. Probably more important is the organization of industry on corporative lines, with associations of workers and employers dealing together

[2] The Act seems, indeed, to be part of a comprehensive plan to head off the growth of trade unionism. This supposition is strengthened by the provision against the closed shop (sec. 39) and the definition of an "association" as "a group of employees or employers . . . having as object the study, defence and development of the economic, social and moral interests of its members *with respect for law and constituted authority*" (Sec. 1). This provision makes it possible for the government to deny the advantages of the Act to any union of which it disapproves.

under government supervision. It will be strange if employers, having learned the advantages of coöperation in dealing with labor, do not also learn the advantages of coöperation in setting prices. In service industries where labor is the principal cost the authorities have already adopted the principle that wage protection involves price protection. The decrees relating to barbering and hairdressing, shoe repairing, automobile repairing and taxicab service, in addition to prescribing minimum wages, also prescribe minimum prices for the services performed. A barber in Quebec City who cuts hair on the eve of a holiday for less than 40 cents is liable to a fine. A taxi driver in Sorel must charge $4.00 for a wedding party, though one can go to a funeral for $2.50 or to a christening for only $2.00.

The provisions relating to competency of employees may also prove to be important. In any town with a population of more than five thousand, the joint committee of an industry may declare a certificate of competence obligatory for all employees. It may set up a board of examiners to conduct examinations and issue certificates of competence, or it may allow the employees' association to issue certificates to its members. These provisions may serve a legitimate purpose in trades which require considerable skill and which involve public health or safety. It is clearly possible, however, that they may be used to restrict entrance to the trade, create a guild of privileged workers, and introduce a monopoly element into the price of the product.

The Ontario Industrial Standards Act differs from the Quebec Act mainly in its more centralized administration.[3] Schedules of wages and hours are drafted under government supervision,

[3] From the trade union standpoint there is a further significant difference in the definition of "association of employees." The Ontario definition excludes company unions, which the Quebec definition does not, while the phrase requiring "respect for law and constituted authority" does not appear in the Ontario definition.

and their enforcement, which in Quebec is left to the interested parties, in Ontario is entrusted to an Industrial Standards Officer acting under the Industry and Labour Board. The element of public regulation is thus more evident in Ontario, while the element of industrial self-government is less pronounced. A schedule is initiated by a petition of employers or employees to the Minister of Labour. A preliminary conference of employers and employees is then convened, and the details of the proposed schedule are debated. In many cases no agreement can be reached. Where an agreement is arrived at, it is usual to call a full conference of the industry in order to hear all objections and to make final alterations. If the Minister considers that there is a sufficient measure of agreement, he may then declare the schedule binding on all members of the industry in a prescribed zone. All employers covered by a schedule are required to keep full payroll records and to produce them on request. The Industrial Standards Officer is empowered to conduct public inquiries and to examine witnesses under oath. Prosecutions may be instituted only by the Industry and Labour Board. An employer convicted of breach of a schedule is liable to fine or imprisonment, and in addition must pay to the Board any wages owing to employees. Enforcement activities have thus far been handicapped by the lack of an adequate staff of inspectors and by the unsympathetic attitude of the courts. Since an unsuccessful prosecution may seriously weaken the effectiveness of a schedule, the Board has confined itself so far as possible to education and mediation. Despite frequent complaints of infraction, most of the schedules have been sufficiently well observed to maintain their effectiveness.

The Act provides for an advisory committee of not more than five members, nominally appointed by the Minister but actually suggested by the employer and employee groups. The committee may fix special wage rates for handicapped workers or for persons engaged in more than one industry. In industries which have been designated by the Board as interprovincially competitive, it may with the approval of the Board collect assessments up to one per cent of the payroll. It may issue interpretations of the schedule and hear complaints of infraction. It has no power, however, to compel the attendance of witnesses or to punish offenders. It serves as an informal investigating body, educating employers and employees in the meaning of the Act and turning over confirmed offenders to the Board for punishment. An appeal may be taken to the Board from any decision of an advisory committee.

Two-thirds of the seventy schedules in effect at the end of June, 1938, were in the barbering trade. The Ontario Act makes definite provision for price fixing,[4] which in Quebec is carried on under the guise of wage regulation. The barbers of St. Thomas grasped the possibilities of the Act in January, 1937, and drew up a schedule setting minimum prices for barbering operations as well as minimum wages for barbers. By July the good news had spread to Toronto, and within a year nearly every town and city in the province had its schedule. The building trades unions were also quick to take advantage of the Act, and in 1936 had thirty schedules in effect. At the present time only fourteen schedules exist in the building trades and nine of these are in two cities, Windsor and Ottawa. In other centers the unions have either lost faith in the Act or, with the resumption of building activity, have felt able to maintain wages without its support. Five schedules cover the entire province: hard furniture, soft furniture, ladies' cloak and suit, men's and boys' clothing, and brewing. The clothing and furniture industries were for some time reluctant to accept a schedule

[4] The schedule may "fix the minimum charge which may be paid, accepted or contracted for with respect to the labour content of any service, work, operation or art and with the approval of the Board fix the minimum charge which an employer or employee may contract for or accept for any service, work, operation or art." (Section 7J.)

because of fear of Quebec competition. When Quebec manufacturers in these industries signed agreements under the Quebec Act, however, Ontario manufacturers fell in line. Wage rates in the clothing schedules are almost exactly the same in Ontario and Quebec, probably because of the strength of trade union organization. In the unorganized furniture industry the Quebec minima appear to be somewhat below the Ontario rates.

The Saskatchewan Act is almost identical with that of Ontario. Most of the schedules are in the barbering and building trades, though the taxicab, creamery, and draying industries also have schedules in effect. Price fixing is permitted with the approval of the Commissioner of Labour and Public Welfare, and the barbers and taxicab operators have taken advantage of this provision. The importance of the Act is not great because of the overwhelmingly agricultural complexion of the province. Administration of the Act is in the hands of only two men, and enforcement is probably rather loose.

A series of recent Alberta acts give the provincial government very wide powers of economic regulation. The Department of Trade and Industry, created in 1934, is empowered to convene conferences of persons engaged in any business in order to formulate a code of ethics, check detrimental competitive practices, and establish minimum prices and wages.[5] The cabinet, upon being satisfied that the code has been approved either by a majority of the persons or a majority of the capital engaged in the trade, may declare it binding on all. Where members of a trade are unable to agree, the Minister may draft

[5] In the words of the Act, the conferences are held ". . . for the purpose of formulating . . . codes and setting up standards of ethics, methods, practices and systems applicable to the trade . . . calculated to effect stability in the conditions thereof, with the object of putting an end to competitive practices which are in their nature detrimental . . . and with the object of establishing and fixing the minimum and maximum prices chargeable . . . and minimum standards as to hours of employment and wages." (Section 5.)

a code, which becomes binding when approved by the cabinet. Enforcement of the codes is facilitated by the Licensing of Trades and Businesses Act. The Minister of Trade and Industry is empowered to require all those engaged in any trade or business to secure a provincial license, to prescribe the conditions on which a license may be issued, to suspend or cancel the license of any person who has on more than one occasion departed from the prescribed prices or wage rates, and to refuse an application for the issuance or renewal of a license "if he is satisfied that it is in the public interest so to do."

The control actually exercised has been less than the text of these laws would imply. Codes were quickly adopted for retailers, wholesalers, dry cleaners, barbers, printers, photo finishers and automotive dealers. Opposition arose, however, from consumers who found prices increased, and from trades which had no code protection. Evasion of the codes was common and often open. The price provisions were accordingly deleted, and the codes now relate entirely to business practices. Enforcement is carried out by threatening to revoke the offender's license rather than by prosecution. The most important code is probably that regulating retail trade, which is discussed below.

The Tradesmen's Qualifications Act provides that members of certain trades [6] may be required to obtain certificates of proficiency, and that persons without certificates may be prohibited from engaging in the trade. This Act has been used to regulate entry to almost all of the specified trades. In order to enter one of these trades an applicant must have had considerable experience, usually from three to five years, and this ap-

[6] Construction and repair of automobile engines, steam engines, boilers, internal combustion engines, radios, refrigerators, and the trades of plumber, steam fitter, gas fitter, electrician, electric welder, acetylene welder, barber, and any other trade in which 66 per cent of the persons engaged in the trade have petitioned the government to be included.

prenticeship period must have been served under the direct supervision of a certificated tradesman. He must also pass a written and practical examination, the passing grade varying from 50 to 75 per cent. In some trades two or three classes of certificates are issued, depending on the mark obtained by the candidate. There is a possibility of abuse in these provisions if the apprenticeship period is prolonged and the examinations made very severe with a view to protecting those already engaged in the trade. Whether this has been done in practice could only be determined by closer investigation.

COAL AND GASOLINE

The coal mining and gasoline distributing industries have been subjected to provincial regulation for different reasons. Pressure for control of the gasoline trade has come mainly from consumers and public authorities, and the regulations have been designed to check the multiplication of service stations, prevent the domination of retailers by refiners, and reduce the price of gasoline. Coal regulation, however, has been proposed by those engaged in the industry with the object of controlling production and maintaining prices.

The New Brunswick Gasoline Sales Act of 1935 requires all wholesalers and retailers of gasoline to obtain annual licenses from the Department of Public Works. No outlet not in existence on March 4, 1935, is to be licensed unless "public convenience and necessity" so require, and the license of any pump may be cancelled unless at least 500 gallons are sold from it annually. Wholesalers may not "furnish, sell, lease, loan or give" any equipment to any retailer, nor lend money to a retailer, nor obtain a lease of land and sublet it to a retailer. A company-owned service station, however, may be leased to an operator. The Minister is empowered to establish grades of gasoline,[7] to

[7] On May 1st, 1935, regulations were issued defining minimum standards for commercial gasoline and setting up four grades. Grade 1 must have an

fix the maximum price at which any grade may be sold in any part of the province at wholesale or retail, and to prescribe the conditions to be observed by licensees. Both wholesalers and retailers are required to keep their prices plainly posted and to observe these prices until changed. Retailers are expressly forbidden to give premiums, conduct lotteries, or grant other rebates. These provisions, if effectively enforced, may effect some reduction in the number of service stations and in the unit cost of retailing. They do not directly attack the price leadership of Imperial Oil, however, nor do they prevent the use of refinery profits in competitive selling. The oil companies, if prevented from subsidizing and controlling "independent" retailers, may turn increasingly toward company-owned stations. For these reasons the Act will probably not cause a significant reduction in the retail price of gasoline.

The Nova Scotia Gasoline Licensing Act contains the basic provisions of the New Brunswick act together with additional features which increase its severity. The Act is administered by the Board of Commissioners of Public Utilities, which is empowered to conduct investigations, compel evidence, and assess the cost of examining a company's books against the company. Several provisions aim to end the control of refiners over retailers. All previous contracts relating to the purchase of gasoline by a retailer are declared null and void. Contracts which compel the retailer to buy all or a stated proportion of his gasoline from a particular wholesaler are forbidden. Equipment installed before Dec. 31, 1931, is declared to be the property of the retailer, and equipment installed since that date may be purchased by the retailer if he so desires. If the retailer and wholesaler are unable to agree on a price for the equipment, application may be made to the Board, which will set a price.

---

octane number not less than 75, Grade 2 not less than 66, Grade 3 not less than 56, Grade 4 below 56.

The Board may fix gasoline prices in any part of Nova Scotia when this is deemed expedient. The prices in force on January 1, 1937, may not be increased without the Board's consent. The Act contains a general prohibition of any practice which might tend to increase the price unduly.

The powers granted by the British Columbia Coal and Petroleum Products Control Board Act of December, 1937, are even wider. The Control Board has authority over refining as well as distribution and over other petroleum products as well as gasoline. The powers of the Board are stated in rather general terms. It may "regulate and control" the industry within the province, prohibit any practice which might tend to increase unduly the price of the product, license all those engaged in the industry and prescribe the conditions for licenses, conduct investigations with powers equal to those of the Supreme Court of the province, establish grades and standards, and lay down detailed price schedules.[8] Several important regulations have already been issued under this Act. All producers, wholesalers and retailers of coal and petroleum products must obtain annual licenses from the Board. Wholesalers and retailers must make monthly returns showing the quantities and prices of goods bought and sold. Regulation number 7 establishes quality standards and maximum retail prices for gasoline. Gasoline may be sold in only two grades: "regular," which must have an octane number of not less than 68, and "premium," which must have an octane number not less than 78 and must meet certain other specifications. The province is divided into fifteen price zones. The maximum retail price for "regular" gasoline ranges from 24 cents per gallon at Vancouver to 33 cents per gallon at

[8] The Board may "fix the price or prices, maximum price or prices, minimum price or prices . . . at wholesale or retail . . . and may: (a) fix different prices for different parts of the Province; (b) fix different prices for licensees notwithstanding that they are in the same class of occupation; (c) fix schedules of prices for different qualities, quantities, standards, grades, and kinds. . . ." (Sec. 14.)

Prince George. "Premium" gasoline may be sold for not more than 2 cents more than the regular price.[9]

The overexpansion of coal mining in Alberta and Saskatchewan and the inability of producers to control prices have led them to request aid from the provincial governments. Regulations issued under the Saskatchewan Coal Mining Industry Act of 1925 require each mine operator to secure a provincial license. In order to obtain a license he must submit a schedule of his wages, which may be altered by the Minister of Natural Resources. He must promise not to sell below the price schedule issued by the Minister, not to make secret rebates, and not to engage in misrepresentation or other unfair practices. Breach of any regulation renders an operator liable to revocation of his license, fine or imprisonment, and an injunction forbidding him to mine coal. The price schedules specify a price for each size of coal and for each of the leading brands. These are minimum prices only, and the regulations expressly provide that "any association or group of licensees . . . (may enter) into an agreement setting minehead prices for coal mined by such licensees for sale in any specified area . . . provided such prices are higher than the minimum prices." There is no provision, however, for output control, and without a large staff of inspectors to detect violations it is doubtful whether price regulation alone can be of much effect. The extent to which Saskatchewan prices can be raised is also limited by the competi-

[9] Shortly after Regulation 7 was issued the oil companies secured an injunction from the Supreme Court of British Columbia restraining the Board from putting this regulation into effect. At the same time action was commenced in the Supreme Court with a view to having the price fixing section of the Act declared *ultra vires* of the province. The Supreme Court of British Columbia gave a verdict for the plaintiff, but this was reversed by the Appeal Court of British Columbia, which held that the province had power to control the prices of petroleum products. The oil companies will probably carry the matter to a higher court. In the meantime the Board is marking time, making no attempt to issue further regulations until the extent of its authority has been determined.

tion of Alberta coal. Alberta, despite an express grant of powers in the Trade and Industry Act of 1934,[10] and a royal commission report in 1935 recommending price and production control, has taken no action in this direction. Since Alberta is much the largest producer in Western Canada, and regularly provides 50 per cent of the coal used in Saskatchewan, Saskatchewan minehead prices cannot exceed Alberta minehead prices by more than the freight differential.

The British Columbia operators are in a much better position. Three large firms produce most of the coal and have been able, in spite of competition from fuel oil and Alberta coal, to earn good profits. The Coal and Petroleum Products Commission decided that the price of coal was too high, not only because of the price policy of producers but also because of an inefficient distributive system.[11] The powers granted to the Control Board with respect to petroleum products apply also to coal, and extensive intervention in both the producing and distributing ends of the industry seems likely if the Act is sustained in the courts.

RESALE PRICE MAINTENANCE

The acute rivalry between chain and independent stores was discussed in Chapter V. The main weapon of the chains in this struggle has been their ability to undersell the independents, often by a large margin. The independents, organized in the Retail Merchants' Association, are naturally eager to secure legislation which will curtail or remove this advantage. The tactics of the Association are simple and effective. It prepares a draft bill. A committee visits cabinet members and persuades

[10] Part III of the Act empowers the Minister of Trade and Industry to convene conferences of coal operators and distributors for the purpose of establishing a common selling agency, limiting total production and allocating production quotas, and eliminating the less efficient mines from production.

[11] British Columbia: Report of the Royal Commission on Coal and Petroleum Products, Volume II, pp. 249–301.

them that it will be politically advantageous not to oppose the bill. The bill is introduced by a sympathetic member of the legislature. There is no organized opposition, and the measure is passed with virtually no alterations. These tactics have already been successful in Alberta and British Columbia, and it is possible that price maintenance legislation may spread across Canada in the same way that it has already spread throughout the United States.

Two sorts of legislation are sponsored by the Association, corresponding closely with the two types now in force in most of the United States. The first of these is directed against the use of price leaders. The British Columbia Act, which applies only to food products, prohibits their sale at a price less than five per cent above cost to the retailer, under penalty of a five hundred dollar fine.[12] In Alberta, a code of fair competition for retail trade has been set up under the Department of Trade and Industry. This code, which covers all retail sales in the province, specifically prohibits the use of "loss leaders." This term is defined to mean any sale at less than 5 per cent above retailers' cost. All retailers have been licensed under the Licensing of Trades and Businesses Act, and are forced to comply with the code by the threat that their licenses may be revoked. The retailer, who cannot afford to have his store closed during a trial, almost invariably complies with the Department's wishes.

In their present form these laws probably do little harm. The average margin of grocery stores in 1930 was 16 per cent, and of all retail stores 24 per cent. A retailer can therefore still sell considerably below the "normal" mark-up without violating the law. Price leaders are not prevented, but cannot be made so attractive as before, and this may force mass distributors to spread their price concessions over a larger number of items. The only danger is that the law may be amended in time so as to require a minimum mark-up of (say) 10 or 15 per cent. If

[12] An Act Respecting a Minimum Loss for Food Products, Ch. 51, 1937.

the margin were set high enough, the result would be to fix all retail prices.

The second type of law is designed to legalize fixed retail prices for trade-marked goods. The Alberta act,[13] which was repealed in 1939, provided simply that no contract relating to the sale of a trade-marked product which was in fair and open competition with other products of the same general class should be deemed illegal by virtue of any price maintenance provisions which it might contain. The British Columbia act [14] goes much farther. A producer or wholesaler may fix the retail price of an article by notifying the retailer at the time the goods are sold to him, or by publishing the price in a newspaper or price-list, or by notifying the provincial office of the Retail Merchants' Association. When a price has been fixed, retailers are forbidden to sell the article below this price or to grant an indirect reduction by selling the article in combination with another commodity. Offenders are liable to a penalty not exceeding five hundred dollars. The Alberta act merely permitted the fixing of resale prices through a contract, leaving enforcement to the parties. The British Columbia act makes price fixing much simpler, and at the same time attaches a criminal penalty to violations of the fixed price. Since no enforcement agency is provided, however, the effectiveness of the Act will depend largely on the energy of the Retail Merchants' Association in hunting down offenders and initiating prosecutions. No information is available concerning the number of manufacturers who have taken advantage of these laws or the effectiveness of enforcement.

So long as only a few brands of a product are sold at fixed prices, price maintenance probably does little harm. Retailers still have the alternative of selling other brands at lower prices, and consumers have the opportunity of buying them. If, how-

[13] An Act to Amend the Sale of Goods Act, Ch. 29, 1936.

[14] An Act respecting the Sale of Commodities by Retail, Ch. 9, 1937.

ever, prices should be fixed for all brands of a product, or worse still for a whole category of products such as drugs, we should be in exactly the situation which the Proprietary Articles Trade Association tried to establish in 1926. The immediate effect would be an increase in retail prices, an increase in dealers' margins, and a freezing of the entire price structure from manufacturer to consumer.[15] From a long-run standpoint, fixed dealer margins would tend to slow up the displacement of less efficient by more efficient retailers. This process would not be entirely prevented, for chain stores could fight back to some extent through private brands. Their lower costs would also enable them to earn larger profits, and they could take their revenge by investing these profits in more and larger stores.

The other important long-run tendency would be a steady upward pressure on dealers' margins. If margins are set initially at an attractive level new stores may be built, reducing the business of existing retailers, raising their unit costs and making increased margins seem essential. Moreover, dealers no longer able to compete with each other on prices are likely to turn to non-price competition. Competition in service and salesmanship, however, is expensive, and for this reason too there will probably be a demand for higher margins.[16] There is even the

[15] This is confirmed by the experience of California after the passage of the "fair trade act" in 1933. Los Angeles drug prices were increased by roughly one-third when the price maintenance contracts came into effect. In smaller centers where prices had never been so drastically cut the increase was smaller. In Stockton, for example, the increase was about one-quarter, in Martinez about one-fifth. (E. T. Grether: Solidarity in the Distributive Trades in Relation to the Control of Price Competition, in *Law and Contemporary Problems*, June, 1937, p. 381.)

[16] The British P. A. T. A., for example, allowed wholesale druggists a margin of 12½ per cent. This proved satisfactory in the beginning. But before long wholesalers, in their rivalry for sales, began to telephone retailers twice a day and make deliveries three or four times per day. This raised costs and led to a demand for a larger margin. (E. T. Grether:

possibility that manufacturers may compete with each other by granting larger margins in order to induce dealers to "push" their particular brands.

The newest and most powerful weapon against the large retailer is taxation. This usually takes the form of a progressive tax, the rate increasing with the number of stores operated or with the gross volume of sales.[17] This tax is evidently intended to bear more heavily on large retailers than on small retailers, and to discourage the addition of new stores to a chain. It is evident that the chain store systems could be eliminated entirely by graduating the tax very steeply. While these measures are not common as yet, their rapid spread in the United States suggests the possibility of a similar development in Canada.

AGRICULTURAL MARKETING: DOMINION LEGISLATION

The Natural Products Marketing Act of 1934 had an active life of only two years, terminated by a Supreme Court decision in June, 1936. Most of the marketing schemes initiated under it, however, have since been continued under provincial marketing acts patterned on the Dominion measure. The operation and prospects of these acts can best be understood by viewing them against the background of experience accumulated under the Natural Products Marketing Act. Moreover, as the limitations of provincial regulation become apparent, there will prob-

---

Resale Price Maintenance in Great Britain, University of California Publications in Economics, Volume 11, No. 3, Berkeley, 1935, p. 319.)

[17] Nova Scotia, for example, amended the Provincial Revenue Act in 1934 so as to impose a tax of $15 on each of the first five stores of a chain, a tax of $40 on the sixth to the tenth store, and a tax of $100 on each store in excess of ten. Department stores are taken care of by a provision that a store with an annual gross revenue of $150,000 shall be counted as three stores; each additional $150,000 of gross revenue counts as one store until a total of $750,000 is reached; above this, each $250,000 of gross revenue counts as an additional store. (Acts of 1934, c. 16, s. 27.)

ably be a renewed demand for Dominion legislation. For both of these reasons it is desirable to survey what was attempted and accomplished under the Dominion Act.

The pressure behind the Act came from farmers who had seen the price of their produce cut in half between 1929 and 1932, while the margins of processors and distributors fell only slightly. The object of the Act was to increase farmers' incomes by improving the technique of marketing, correcting inequalities of bargaining power between farmers and dealers, and controlling the quantities marketed. A Dominion Marketing Board was created under the Minister of Agriculture, to regulate the marketing of any "natural product," including lumber and fish, and any article of food or drink wholly or partially manufactured from a natural product. The Board was empowered "to regulate the time and place at which, and to designate the agency through which the regulated product shall be marketed, and to determine the manner of distribution, the quantity and quality, grade or class of the regulated product that shall be marketed by any person at any time, and to prohibit the marketing of any of the regulated product of any grade, quality or class." It could also license all producers or distributors of the regulated product, cancel licenses for violations of the Act, and levy tolls and charges on the marketing of the product to cover administrative expenses. To strengthen the constitutional position of the Act, it was provided that these powers could be exercised only where the principal market for the product was outside of the province of production, or where some part of the product might be exported. The provinces were willing to coöperate, however, and almost immediately passed acts designed to regulate intra-provincial marketing of products for which a Dominion scheme was in operation.

Marketing schemes might be initiated either by the Minister of Agriculture or by petition of "a representative number of persons engaged in the production or marketing" of the product.[18] The Board required four things of any scheme coming before it for approval: (1) It must satisfy the legal requirements of the Act by relating to a natural product, a considerable part of which was marketed outside of the province of production. (2) It must be "economically sound." The Board, following the underlying assumptions of the Act, took as its criterion of soundness whether or not the scheme would raise the income of growers. The consumer interest was not represented before the Board and received little consideration. (3) It must be administratively feasible. (4) The local board must have been properly elected and must represent the bulk of the producers. Where doubt existed on this point, a poll of producers was taken by the Board. Many proposals were rejected on one or other of these grounds. Of thirty schemes considered during the fiscal year 1935–36, twelve were approved, eight were rejected, and ten were still under consideration when operations were suspended.

Administration of an approved scheme was ordinarily [19] left to a local board, composed of growers' representatives with, in some cases, a few representatives of the dealers. The Dominion Board was allowed to delegate to the local board any powers necessary for the operation of the scheme. Local boards were usually given the essential powers of the Dominion board — to regulate quantity and quality of goods marketed, to designate a marketing agency,[20] to license producers and shippers, and to

[18] Of 22 schemes approved under the Act, 16 were suggested by producers, 2 by processors, and in 4 cases the Minister of Agriculture took the initiative.

[19] The four schemes initiated by the Minister of Agriculture, however, were supervised directly by the Dominion Board. These schemes were the Processed Berry Marketing, Butter Export Stabilization, Dairy Products Equalization, and B. C. Red Cedar Shingles Export.

[20] The "marketing agency," which determined the details of prices, quantities shipped, and marketing technique, was in some cases the local board itself, in some cases a separate person or committee appointed by

levy tolls and charges to cover administrative expenses. Although price fixing was not mentioned in the Act, certain local boards took it upon themselves to maintain fixed prices, with results which will be discussed below.

Nineteen schemes were approved by the Board, of which seventeen actually came into operation.[21] Petitions were received most rapidly from producers of fruits, vegetables, and tobacco, not because they were more impoverished than other farmers, but simply because they were better organized. In more than half of the cases the growers already had some sort of coöperative organization. Persistent price cutting by non-members, however, had seriously weakened most of the co-operatives, and the prospect of a compulsory scheme was eagerly welcomed. It is no accident that almost half of the approved schemes came from British Columbia, where coöperative marketing was particularly well developed.[22]

Rarely was there complete unanimity among producers and dealers, and most of the schemes therefore involved an element of compulsion. The large herring producers opposed the Grand Manan Herring scheme by political pressure and non-coöperation, largely on the ground that small producers were allowed

---

the local board. This, however, is a technical detail. For practical purposes, all acts under a scheme may be taken as acts of the local board.

[21] These are listed below in the order of their approval by the Governor-in-Council: British Columbia Tree Fruit (Aug. 25, 1934), Fruit Export Marketing (September, 1934), B. C. Red Cedar Shingles Export (Oct. 16, 1934), B. C. Dry Salt Herring and Salmon (Oct. 22, 1934), Ontario Flue-cured Tobacco (Oct. 26, 1934), Eastern Canada Potato Marketing (Jan. 18, 1935), Western Ontario Bean Marketing (Jan. 31, 1935), B. C. Interior Vegetable Marketing (Mar. 4, 1935), Jam Marketing (Apr. 10, 1935), B. C. Halibut Marketing (June 10, 1935), Ontario Cheese Patrons (June 25, 1935), Processed Berry Marketing (June 29, 1935), Dairy Products Equalization (July 20, 1935), Nova Scotia Apples (Aug 15, 1935), Grand Manan Herring (Aug. 15, 1935), Ontario Burley Tobacco (Sept. 3, 1935), Butter Export Stabilization (Sept. 18, 1935).

[22] See p. 37 above for a brief history of coöperative marketing of tree fruits in British Columbia.

unduly large market quotas by the democratically elected local board. The B. C. Tree Fruit Board was opposed by Doukhobor growers who feared that their product would not meet the Board's quality specifications. Small jam producers with little "consumer preference" broke away from the jam marketing scheme because with a uniform price their orders fell off greatly. The Cedar Shingles scheme had to overcome dissension over the proper basis for export quotas. Most of the B. C. schemes encountered opposition from grower-shippers, who were forbidden to pass on any of the savings of direct distribution by offering lower prices. The tobacco schemes, the Western Ontario Bean scheme, and the Lower Mainland Milk scheme also had groups of dissenters, differing in most cases on grounds of economic interest.

The main enforcement weapon of the local board was revocation of the offender's license. This was usually sufficient to bring about compliance, but most boards were obliged on one or more occasions to resort to the courts. Some cases were lost because of the inexperience of local board members in legal matters. Cases were launched on insufficient evidence and technical errors were made. Local magistrates took a critical attitude toward the Act, and frequently refused to convict on technical grounds. In spite of these difficulties, most local boards won enough cases to maintain control of the situation. The schemes which broke down did so because they were ill-conceived, and adverse court decisions merely hastened their end. The dependence of all of the schemes on legal sanctions, however, was made clear after the reference of the Marketing Act to the Supreme Court in October, 1935.[23] The doubt thus

[23] The Act had been passed in 1934 by a Conservative government over strong Liberal opposition. When the Liberals were returned to power in September, 1935, one of the new government's first acts was to refer the Marketing Act and several other acts to the Supreme Court for an opinion as to their constitutionality. From that time on the Dominion Board de-

cast on the constitutionality of the Act made it impossible to obtain convictions in the lower courts, and without this sanction most of the schemes rapidly disintegrated. Even the strong B. C. Interior Vegetable Board was obliged to give up all control of prices in the spring of 1936.

From an economic standpoint, the plans may be divided into four groups: (1) Emergency plans involving subsidies by the Dominion: Processed Berry Marketing, Dairy Products Equalization (a bonus of 1.5 cents per pound to cheese producers), and Butter Export Stabilization (subsidized export of butter, the maximum subsidy being set at 1.5 cents per pound). (2) Plans intended to divide an export market equitably among a number of producers: B. C. Red Cedar Shingles Export, B. C. Dry Salt Herring and Salmon, Grand Manan Herring. (3) Plans designed to improve the technique of marketing: Fruit Export, B. C. Halibut, Ontario Flue-cured Tobacco, Ontario Burley Tobacco, Ontario Cheese Patrons. (4) Plans intended to control price and quantities marketed: Nova Scotia Apple, B. C. Tree Fruit, B. C. Interior Vegetable, Eastern Canada Potato, Western Ontario Bean, Jam Marketing. The last two groups are probably of greatest significance for future policy, and discussion will be confined to them.

While almost all of the plans involved changes in marketing methods,[24] those included in group three above were preëminently measures of market reform. The object of the Fruit

clined to approve new schemes, and existing schemes were weakened by the virtual cessation of convictions under the Act. In June, 1936, the Supreme Court held that the Marketing Act was beyond the powers of the Dominion.

[24] Consignment selling was frequently prohibited on the ground that it facilitates false returns to producers and that hurried unloading of produce by commission men may cause sharp breaks in prices. Prohibition of the sale of inferior produce, regularization of the flow of produce to market from day to day and week to week, requiring of full returns from shippers and growers regarding sales and inventories, diffusion of market information — all were employed in one or more schemes.

Export Board was to prevent flooding of the British market with Canadian apples until after the British apple crop had been marketed, and to regulate the quality of apples exported. The British Columbia Halibut scheme attempted to reduce the seasonal variation of prices by spreading the catch over a longer fishing season. The Ontario Cheese Patrons' scheme, by compelling the buying of cheese at public auctions in each county instead of private buying from farmers by wholesalers' agents, reëstablished a competitive market in this industry. Ontario Tobacco growers, thoroughly dissatisfied with their treatment by Imperial Tobacco, had in 1934 already formed three coöperative sales agencies. Advantage was immediately taken of the Marketing Act, and a Flue-cured Tobacco Board was set up. Imperial Tobacco, disturbed by the hearings of the Price Spreads Commission and an investigation under the Combines Act, agreed to deal with the Board, and the 1934 crop was marketed at a price agreed on by a joint committee of three growers and three buyers.[25] So successful was this experience that a Burley Tobacco Board was set up in 1935, and both boards continued to operate after the invalidation of the Marketing Act.

It will be sufficient to describe two of the plans which attempted to control prices and quantities marketed, the British Columbia Tree Fruit and the Western Ontario Bean Marketing.

[25] The method of procedure is as follows: (1) The Board makes an inventory of the entire crop, and classifies it by grades. (2) Relative values are assigned to the various grades. (3) An average price per pound for the entire crop is negotiated by the Joint Appraisal Committee. (4) The price of each grade is then obtained by applying the scale of relative values previously determined. (5) The Board sends to each grower a statement of how his crop has graded and what he should receive for it; this naturally strengthens the grower's hand in dealing with the buyers. (6) Buyers are allowed to buy wherever they wish and at any price they can obtain. If, however, at the end of the season, any buyer has paid less for his tobacco than he would have paid if it had all been bought at the agreed price, he must remit the difference to the Board.

Fruit moving from British Columbia to the prairies usually passes through the hands of shippers who sell to the prairie jobbers. At the beginning of the 1934 season, the Tree Fruit Board attempted to control prices by simply licensing all shippers and directing them to observe a common f.o.b. price to all prairie markets. This sort of control broke down in about three weeks, for a shipper could gain greatly in volume by a small amount of secret price cutting. The next step was to set up a system of quotas with percentage releases. Each shipper was allotted a quota of (say) apples, based on his average shipments in previous years. At the beginning of the season he would be permitted to ship perhaps ten per cent of his quota, after a few weeks he would be notified that another twenty-five per cent might be shipped, and so on. When a shipper had exhausted his quota, orders received by him were turned over to the local Board, which placed them with shippers who were behind. This system enabled the flow of produce to market to be checked or accelerated at will, and also removed the incentive to price competition among shippers. The system was never completely perfected, but worked more efficiently in the 1935 season than in 1934. The technique of the B. C. Coast Vegetable, B. C. Interior Vegetable, and B. C. Hothouse Tomato and Cucumber [26] Boards was almost exactly the same, and worked with a similar high degree of success. The B. C. Hothouse scheme was particularly efficient, as all of the produce was marketed through a single selling agency, and price competition was thus made impossible.

The Western Ontario Bean scheme operated in a similar way. In preparation for the marketing of the 1935 crop, the local

[26] The B. C. Coast Vegetable board and the B. C. Hothouse Tomato and Cucumber board, together with the Lower Mainland Dairy Products board, operated entirely within British Columbia and derived their authority from a provincial Natural Products Marketing Act. They also, however, maintained close contact with the Dominion Marketing Board.

board licensed all bean dealers, fixed the price at which they might buy from growers at $1.50 per bushel, and the price at which they might sell to jobbers at $1.74 per bushel. The dealers' net spread, after allowing for bagging and brokerage charges, was to be 15 cents per bushel. All orders from jobbers for beans were to be referred to the Board, which distributed them to the various dealers on a quota basis. Growers were allowed to sell one-third of their crop at the outset, and were directed to hold the remainder for percentage releases as directed by the Board. The other price-maintenance schemes in Eastern Canada, while less elaborate, were cut on the same pattern.

These schemes had several consequences: (a) Prices were increased in nearly all cases, and in some cases the increase was very sharp. Beans, which in 1934 had sold from $1.00 to $1.25 per bushel, sold in 1935 at $1.74. Returns to potato producers were advanced in some cases as much as 100% during the duration of the Eastern Canada Potato Marketing Scheme. The Nova Scotia Apple Board and all of the British Columbia Boards succeeded in advancing prices to jobbers. (b) Where prices had been raised very sharply, as in the Ontario Bean and Eastern Canada Potato schemes, sales fell off and large carryovers were built up, contributing to the subsequent downfall of the schemes. (c) Higher prices served as a stimulus to increased plantings. The flue-cured tobacco growers met this danger by establishing an acreage allotment committee. Anyone who wished to increase his acreage, or any new grower desiring an allotment, was obliged to secure the consent of this committee. Growers planting more than the acreage allotted to them found that for some reason or other no buyers appeared to purchase their crops. Other boards relied mainly on exhortation.[27] If the Act had remained in effect, it is

[27] The Interior Vegetable Board, for example, issued on April 11, 1936, an "Information Circular," which read in part as follows: "The Board

likely that mere appeals would have been found insufficient, and that control of production would have been incorporated in many of the schemes.

Even before the adverse decision of the Supreme Court in June, 1936, several plans had collapsed under rather interesting circumstances. In anticipation of higher prices, Ontario bean growers increased their spring plantings, which together with an unusually high yield caused a record crop in 1935. In the face of this, the attempt of the local board to raise prices by roughly fifty per cent was clearly unwise. Sales of beans in December were fifty per cent below the average of previous years, while January sales were forty per cent below normal. Farmers grew restive and began to sell their crop secretly at cut prices. Dealers dissatisfied with the quota arrangement were only too ready to buy and to resell for less than the official price of $1.74 per bushel. The Board confessed its error by belatedly lowering prices to $1.07 per bushel. In February, 1936, control was withdrawn altogether, and prices to growers fell to between sixty and seventy-five cents.

The Eastern Potato Marketing Scheme, embracing Ontario, Quebec, New Brunswick and Nova Scotia, failed for similar reasons. A relatively high official price and a very good crop resulted in the piling up of a large unsold surplus. Producers became nervous and willing to sell at almost any price. Dealers began to buy and sell below the established price, and their large numbers and wide geographical distribution made it impossible to control them. In Ontario, where most of the potato crop is trucked to market, control was particularly difficult.

---

wishes to point out to all producers the danger of increasing vegetable production and strongly urges that acreage be limited to a figure closely corresponding to that planted last year. . . . Producers who intend increasing their acreage of any of the regulated products are advised that should a surplus of any commodity be apparent, steps may be taken to see that those responsible for the increase are made to hold that increase so that all producers may get their share of the market."

The scheme was finally abandoned in August, 1935, after a life of only seven months.

The other major failure was that of the Jam Marketing plan. The jam manufacturers, who had for some years been engaged in intermittent price warfare, turned to the Marketing Act as a possible avenue of escape, and petitioned for a marketing scheme. The Dominion Board, on securing a promise that part of the gains from price maintenance would be passed back to the fruit growers, approved the scheme. A central marketing agency was set up, all of the 98 producers in Canada were licensed, uniform list prices, discounts, and freight allowances were established. Prices to be paid to growers were negotiated by a Coördinating Committee. Wholesalers, however, when faced with uniform prices, showed a marked preference for the established brands of jam and marmalade. Smaller and less widely known producers found themselves with few orders, and realized that they could only secure business by lower prices. They accordingly began to make reductions, and the scheme was abandoned in January, 1936, nine months after its adoption.

The results of the Act cannot be summarized in any simple formula. It was used to give direct subsidies to certain groups of producers. It helped other groups to exploit foreign markets more effectively. Several plans increased the effectiveness of competition by diffusing information, checking abuses and redressing inequalities of bargaining power. Other plans, however, attempted to prevent competition and maintain prices. These plans resembled price-fixing agreements among manufacturers both in their structure and their effects, and were equally undesirable from the consumer's standpoint. The Dominion Board, moreover, tended to encourage rather than discourage such plans by taking as its criterion of "success" the raising of producers' incomes.

The experience of the price-fixing plans confirms well-known principles of cartel organization: that success depends on experienced administration, a moderate price policy, and the ability to reconcile conflicting interests of different producers, and that control of price must be supported by control of output. In spite of several notable failures, these plans were sufficiently successful in raising farmers' incomes that some of them have been continued under provincial auspices.

AGRICULTURAL MARKETING: PROVINCIAL LEGISLATION

Provincial legislation in this field has been concerned largely with the sale of fluid milk. A generation ago most towns and cities bought their milk from farmers living in the neighborhood and marketing their own produce. Since milk could be turned to either fluid or manufactured uses, the price of fluid milk tended to follow closely the movements of butter prices. A higher price for milk in the fluid market led to diversion of milk from butter to fluid sales, and vice versa.[28] The growing size of cities and the increasing stringency of health requirements have drastically changed the organization of the fluid milk market in recent years. As a city expands and draws its milk from greater and greater distances it becomes impossible for most farmers to bring their milk to market and the large distributor makes his appearance. In most cities the distribution of milk is now in the hands of a few firms, two or three of which usually have the bulk of the business. While producer-distributors linger on in the smaller centers, they have been eliminated in the large cities by the requirement that all milk must be pasteurized. Other health requirements — that herds must be tuberculin free, that buildings must pass a sanitary inspection, that milk must be handled in a prescribed way — have raised the cost of producing fluid milk above that of producing milk for butter and other manufactured uses. The result

[28] For a good discussion of the pricing of milk under competitive conditions see J. M. Cassels: A Study of Fluid Milk Prices, Cambridge, 1937.

has been to create a specialized class of fluid milk producers, which can be entered only by making a considerable capital expenditure and securing the consent of the health authorities, and which expects to receive a premium price for its milk.

Milk dealers quickly learned the advantage of coöperation in setting both the price charged to consumers and the price paid to producers. Where producers are unorganized dealers can pay any price they choose above the minimum set by the competition of butter and cheese factories.[29] Where a producers' association exists bargaining strength is more nearly equal, but the dealers still have an advantage. The dealer grades the farmer's milk, transports it to market and charges the farmer a certain amount for this service, and usually pays for the milk on a utilization basis.[30] Any increase in the nominal price obtained by the producers can thus be whittled away because of their inability to control these other terms in the bargain. It is very difficult, too, for an association to maintain complete control of supply. By offering a price slightly above the association price a dealer can usually induce farmers to remain "independent." If the association should be successful in securing good prices, it will be difficult to prevent new producers from entering the market. Only where there are legal limitations on entry and where the producers' association is all-

[29] For a short period, distributors need probably pay no more than the farmers could obtain by selling their milk for butter or cheese. Over a longer period, however, they must pay something above this in order to induce farmers to incur the greater costs of fluid milk production.

[30] The dealer usually receives a considerable surplus of milk above his fluid requirements, and this surplus is turned into manufactured products which yield a lower return. Since it is impracticable to trace a particular farmer's milk to its destination, a convenient fiction is adopted. If in a particular month a dealer sells 80 per cent of his receipts in fluid form, it is assumed that 80 per cent of Farmer A's milk was used in this way. For this 80 per cent the farmer is paid the basic price, for the remaining 20 per cent a lower "surplus" price. For the honesty of these calculations the farmer is obliged to trust the dealer.

inclusive can the farmers meet the dealers on equal terms.

Both producers and dealers seem to have enjoyed good returns during the twenties. In the mid-twenties, indeed, a shortage of milk was threatened in some markets and dealers were obliged to persuade farmers to enter the industry. During the depression, however, the prices paid to producers fell sharply. A falling demand and the complaints of consumers led dealers to reduce retail prices. The full force of these reductions was passed back to producers, while dealers' margins were maintained or even increased.[31] The price of butter and cheese, however, fell still faster, so that the fluid milk market looked relatively attractive. More and more milk was shipped to dealers, the proportion of surplus milk mounted, and returns to producers fell off still further. Producers' organizations appealed more and more urgently for government assistance.[32] Nor were the distributors averse to a certain amount of judicious price fixing. In some markets, farmers turned during the depression to peddling their own milk at prices below the estab-

[31] The situation in the Montreal market, for example, was as follows:

	Retail price (per quart)	Reported price to producers	Distributors' margin
1929	0.128	0.070	0.058
30	0.128	0.064	0.064
31	0.114	0.049	0.065
2 (June)	0.098	0.035	0.063

(Report prepared by M. C. Bond for the Quebec Provincial Dairy Commission, 1932, p. 40.)

Eleven Montreal and Quebec distributors studied by Dr. Bond made profits of 0.0115 per quart on their milk and cream operations during 1931. (*Ibid.*, p. 43.)

[32] This faith in the efficacy of public regulation is expressed in the following extract from a petition of the Alberta milk producers to the public utility commission of the province: "It is a common thing for the Distributor to use surplus production as the reason for the producers' low price. They still claim that price is governed by the law of supply and demand which in the light of present day knowledge is considered to be a myth and we realize that there is not anything that cannot be controlled." (Stated case of the Edmonton and Calgary milk producers, 1933, p. 8.)

lished level. Chain stores using milk as a price leader also cut into dealers' sales. While dealers' margins had been well maintained, falling sales meant rising unit costs and reduced profits. Although they were in a much better position than producers to escape the incidence of the depression, they were sufficiently damaged to welcome public assistance.

The milk control laws passed during the depression differ more in form than in substance. Alberta and Manitoba recognized milk as a public utility and placed its regulation under the public utility commission. Nova Scotia, New Brunswick, Quebec, Ontario and Saskatchewan set up special milk control boards. The Vancouver market in British Columbia was regulated by a local board of producers' representatives operating at first under the Dominion Natural Products Marketing Act and later under the provincial marketing act. The powers granted to these different bodies were very similar: to conduct investigations and compel the production of evidence; to require bonds from dealers in order to ensure payments of sums owing to producers; to approve and enforce agreements between producers and dealers; to license all transporters, processors and sellers of milk; [33] to fix schedules of prices; to make regulations concerning the purchase, transportation, handling, conversion and sale of milk; to suspend and revoke licenses, and to prosecute offenders. The powers granted, in short, were those deemed necessary to check retail price cutting, to control the prices received by producers, and to ensure fair treatment of producers in other respects. Only in British Columbia is there any direct provision for control of production.[34]

[33] Producers may also be licensed in Alberta and British Columbia.

[34] The British Columbia scheme is more drastic in its terms than any of the others. The board may license producers, compel all milk to be sold through a single marketing agency, control the quantities supplied to any market including manufactured as well as fluid uses.

The Ontario and Nova Scotia acts also contain several interesting provisions in addition to those noted above. They provide that the board

Prices to producers are now regulated in almost every important market. In some cases producers are paid a flat rate, in some cases the price varies with the butter-fat content of the milk, in other cases there are two price levels — one for milk sold in fluid form, the other for surplus milk converted into manufactured forms. The actual prices paid, of course, differ somewhat from the nominal prices because of the dealer's control over grading, hauling, and other services. Prices to producers are considerably higher than at the time when milk control was introduced. In any event, however, prices would have risen during the recovery period 1933–37, and further study would be necessary to estimate how much of the rise can be attributed to the milk control boards.

In most markets detailed schedules of selling prices are issued, covering sales of bottled milk and cream to consumers and stores, and bulk sales to hotels, hospitals and public institutions. A contentious question has been whether stores should be allowed to sell milk for less than the price from the dealers' wagon. Chain stores argue that they provide fewer services and that their customers are entitled to benefit from the saving, while the dealers contend strenuously for a uniform retail price. In all provinces except Alberta and Manitoba this question has been decided in favor of the dealers. Stores are allowed to buy at a discount of one cent per quart and are obliged to sell at the dealers' price. The price regulations are enforced by revoking the licenses of offenders and then prosecuting them for dealing without a license. This is simpler than a prosecution for price cutting, which would involve a considerable burden of proof. Enforcement has been adequate in most markets, probably

---

may arbitrate, adjust and settle disputes arising within the industry, may prohibit distributors from compelling producers to invest in a dairy plant, and may prohibit milk distributors from terminating the purchase of milk from a producer without just cause unless fifteen days' notice has been given.

because of a judicious selection of cases to be prosecuted.[35] The problem of controlling interstate flow of milk, which has troubled many state control boards in the United States, does not arise in Canada. With the possible exception of Montreal, no large center draws its milk from more than one province.

It is very difficult to arrive at a systematic basis for price fixing. There is no indisputable "cost of production" for milk. Out-of-pocket costs are a minor part of the total. The farmer's labor and that of his family, the investment in dairy herd and buildings, are overhead items. What they are worth depends on what he can get, or what some control board thinks he should get. The direct cost of producing milk is very low, particularly in a depression period. Producers' associations, however, by using sound business principles and translating their desires into the forms of accountancy, are able to turn out much higher cost figures. The control board, left without definite guide posts, is faced essentially with the problem of deciding how much it is wise to tax consumers in order to raise farmers' incomes.

Questions of equal difficulty arise in determining a "fair" margin for dealers. Dealers are always able to present cost statements which justify maintenance or increase of the existing margin, but these statements cannot be taken at face value. Fluid milk is only one product of a dairy plant, and may be bearing an unduly large part of overhead costs. Certain selling costs are results rather than causes of high price, and would probably be reduced if pressure were applied through a compulsory reduction of margins. Capitalization may have been inflated to the point where normal earnings appear subnormal. Only in Alberta has a careful audit been made of dealers' accounts. In other provinces the tendency has been to accept dealers' statements of their costs and profits, and to allow them

[35] An official of the Ontario board remarked: "We have not prosecuted nearly as many cases as the trade would have liked. They'd like us to go after every little price cutter all over the place."

a margin sufficient to cover these costs. Increased prices to producers have been accompanied by corresponding advances in consumer prices.

Only in Alberta and Manitoba have steps been taken to control production. The Alberta public utilities commission has declined to license any new producers or distributors "until such time as the public need or convenience requires." Each producer has been allotted a quota of fluid milk, and the quotas of producers leaving the field are divided among the remaining producers. A gradual decline in the number of producers, an enlargement of quotas for those remaining, a decrease of surplus milk, and a rise in producers' returns has taken place over the past four years.[36] These arrangements are reënforced by an informal understanding with the health authorities that only farms within a zone of 15 miles around Edmonton and 25 miles around Calgary will be inspected. The Manitoba utilities commissioners have allotted production quotas in the Winnipeg milk-shed. In the other provinces, the boards have not undertaken to control production, though producers' coöperatives frequently set quotas for their members. Unless the coöperative is very powerful, however, this type of production control is not very effective. It may prevent existing producers from expanding, but cannot prevent new producers from entering with a consequent increase of surplus and fall in producers' returns. As this is more clearly realized there will undoubtedly be increased pressure in all provinces for licensing of producers, fixing of quotas, and other control measures.

The most serious weakness of the legislation is its preoccupation with the needs of producers and dealers. The boards

[36] The following figures indicate the situation in the Calgary milk-shed:

	No. of shippers	Surplus milk (per cent)	Average price received by producers (per 100 lbs.)
1935	225	39.6	$1.44
36	207	36.3	1.66
37	201	28.6	1.96

have tended to assume that their function is to protect existing investments in the industry. The possibility of reducing prices to consumers through more efficient methods of distribution has been almost completely overlooked. Most boards, it is true, have been reluctant to license new dealers and this has checked the growth of distributing capacity. They have done very little, however, to eliminate the duplication of facilities and the high distribution costs which constitute the chief economic problem of the industry. The tendency has been rather to stabilize inefficiency and to guarantee a return on overexpanded plant and watered capital.

Three provinces have provided for regulated marketing of other agricultural products. When the Dominion marketing act was invalidated in 1936 a dozen marketing schemes, located mainly in Ontario and British Columbia, were left without legal sanctions. To enable these schemes to continue in operation, Ontario and British Columbia passed marketing acts in 1936 and New Brunswick followed in 1937. The powers of the provincial marketing boards constituted by these acts are very similar to those formerly exercised by the Dominion Marketing Board. They may conduct investigations into the processing and distribution of any natural product, control the marketing of any such product, require all persons engaged in processing or marketing a natural product to secure licenses, designate the agency through which marketing shall be carried on, fix minimum prices, and levy tolls to cover administrative expenses. In practice the administration of an approved marketing scheme is delegated to a "local board" elected by the producers. The provincial board is occupied mainly with studying proposed schemes and drafting them into suitable form, watching over the activities of local boards, hearing appeals and complaints, and prosecuting violations of approved schemes.

Under existing court decisions a province may not regulate inter-provincial trade, and this at once removes from the boards' jurisdiction most of the trade in grain, livestock, butter and cheese, eggs and poultry, lumber and fish. The milk trade is regulated by special milk control boards. The marketing boards are thus left with little more than the fruit and vegetable trade, and exports which go directly from the province to the importing country. Nearly all of the schemes operating at present were in existence under the Dominion Act: the Grand Manan herring, Ontario cheese producers, B. C. tree fruit, B. C. coast vegetable, B. C. interior vegetable, B. C. hothouse tomato and cucumber, B. C. halibut, and B. C. salt fish. In Ontario, however, two new schemes are in operation covering the sale of peaches and asparagus to processors. All processors and buyers are required to be licensed, and all produce must be sold through the local board. The price for the entire crop is determined by a Negotiating Committee of three growers and three processors or, if they fail of agreement, by a specially constituted Board of Arbitration. This type of marketing, first devised by the tobacco growers as a means of securing bargaining equality with Imperial Tobacco, has also proved satisfactory in these two cases. Additional schemes of this sort are under consideration for tomatoes, strawberries, cherries, pears and plums.

SUMMARY

In spite of differences in their subject-matter, the acts discussed above have a strong family resemblance. Nearly all of them set up an administrative agency with power to conduct investigations, to regulate wages or prices, to license producers and dealers, and to enforce its regulations by revocation of licenses and prosecution. More important is the similarity of their objectives. Most of them were designed to check competition and raise prices, and at the same time to strengthen the bargaining position of workers' and farmers' associations so that they might receive a fair share of the increased sums taken from consumers. This mixed motivation makes it difficult either to approve or to reject most of these measures. There is no doubt that workers and farmers have long been inferior in bargaining power, and that they have frequently been exploited by business men. The policy of collective bargaining under public supervision, however, while it tends to improve the position of these groups, contains serious dangers in another direction. The possibility now arises of two strong organizations — milk producers and dealers, tomato growers and canners, trade unions and manufacturers — uniting to exploit the consumer. The pressure on prices under legislation of this sort is entirely in one direction. Nor are the control boards in a position to impose effective checks on price raising. Their popularity depends on their serviceability to the groups which requested their creation, and a board which insisted on efficiency and low prices would probably be legislated out of existence. The root of the difficulty lies in the political activity of organized minorities and the political impotence of the consumer interest. The idea that increasing the income of a particular group increases the national income, and that all groups in the system can attain prosperity by preying on each other, is one of the hardiest and most widespread of economic fallacies.

A few exceptions must be made to this discouraging conclusion. The Nova Scotia and New Brunswick gasoline licensing acts, and the British Columbia Coal and Petroleum Products Control Act are instances of well-conceived legislation directed toward the protection and service of consumers. The results of these acts should be watched with a view to their imitation in other provinces and other industries.

IX

LEGAL AND POLITICAL LIMITS OF ECONOMIC POLICY

It is relatively easy to criticize the past actions of governments and to advocate changes in policy. The practical difficulties of implementing these recommendations, however, must not be overlooked. Before an idea can be made effective in governmental action it must run a long gauntlet. It must be considered politically expedient by the government of the day. The statute must be so drawn as to fall within the authority of the enacting body. Some agency must be charged with enforcement of the statute, and the structure of this agency must be adequate to its intended functions. At any of these points an economically sound proposal may come to grief.

The object of this chapter is to indicate some of the basic conditions which determine what Canadian governments can and cannot do. Judicial interpretations of the constitution form an evident check on government action. Less obvious are the limits imposed by the balance of political forces in the country and by the nature of the administrative process. It is not suggested that economists should confine their proposals within the bounds of the immediately practicable. The limits on governmental action are themselves subject to change. It is extremely important, however, to realize clearly what policies are possible within the existing legal and political framework, and at what point basic institutional changes become necessary before economic reforms can be effected.

CONSTITUTIONAL LIMITS

The British North America Act resembles the Constitution of the United States in that it is a written document intended, among other things, to demarcate the legislative authority of the Dominion from that of the provinces. There are important differences, however, in the powers granted to the federal government under the two systems. The B. N. A. Act, in the first place, contains no bill of rights and no reservation of residual power to the people. The Dominion and the provinces thus possess between them complete legislative authority,[1] and legislation cannot be held "unconstitutional" on the ground that it invades private rights. Canadian constitutional cases turn rather on the question of whether the legislation has been enacted by the competent authority, whether a province has invaded a field reserved by the Act to the Dominion, or *vice versa*. Where there is a conflict between validly enacted provincial and Dominion statutes, the Dominion statute prevails, and the Dominion also has residual authority over matters of national importance. On the surface, then, the legislative authority of the Canadian government is much wider. In practice, as will appear below, court decisions have narrowed the federal power even more effectively in Canada than in the United States.

Section 91 of the Act empowers the Dominion "to make laws for the peace, order and good government of Canada, in relation to all matters not coming within the classes of subjects by the Act assigned exclusively to the Legislatures of the Provinces." It is also given specific and exclusive authority over a list of subjects, the most important of which from our standpoint are "the regulation of trade and commerce," "the raising of money by any mode or system of taxation," and "the criminal law." The provincial legislatures are granted by section 92 exclusive authority over other subjects, including "direct taxation within the province," "shop, saloon, tavern, auctioneer and

[1] There are a few exceptions to this statement. Thus neither the Dominion nor the provinces may impose provincial customs tariffs or levy taxes on Crown property.

other licenses in order to the raising of a revenue for provincial, local, or municipal purposes," "property and civil rights in the Province," and "generally all matters of a merely local or private nature in the Province." No matter coming under an enumerated head of section 91, however, is to be considered "merely of a local or private nature."

The ambiguous and overlapping character of this arrangement is evident. Almost any type of economic regulation will affect both "trade and commerce" and "property and civil rights." Does it thereby fall under Dominion or under provincial jurisdiction? There is no evidence that problems of this sort were debated by the drafters of the Act. The conferences and debates which preceded the union were concerned mainly with the distribution of revenue between Dominion and provinces, with the scheme of representation in the central parliament, and with safeguarding the civil rights of the French-Canadian minority. In an economy based almost entirely upon agriculture and other extractive industries, the problems which were to arise from the growth of manufacturing and trade could scarcely be foreseen. The result has been to throw upon the courts, and particularly upon the Privy Council, the entire burden of deciding whether the increasingly important regulatory functions of government are to be exercised by the provinces or by the Dominion.

The Privy Council has laid down certain general rules for the construction of the Act. The usual procedure is to inquire first whether a disputed statute falls under an enumerated head of section 92. If it does not, the matter is evidently within the jurisdiction of the Dominion. If the statute does come within the ambit of section 92 the further question arises: does it also come within an enumerated head of section 91? If it does, the authority of the Dominion overrides that of the Province and the matter is still within Dominion jurisdiction.[2] If

[2] "The legislation of the Parliament of the Dominion, so long as it

the matter comes under section 92, and does not come under an enumerated head of section 91, it is within provincial jurisdiction, and any Dominion legislation concerning it is invalid. Only in the event of a national emergency may the Dominion encroach upon provincial powers to the extent necessary for the "peace, order and good government of Canada."

These rules appear to offer definite guidance for the determination of particular cases, but their apparent clarity is highly deceptive. Once it has been decided under which head or heads of sections 91 and 92 a particular statute falls, the argument becomes relatively simple. But this is in most cases precisely the issue. In almost every case counsel for the Dominion parade the federal authority to "regulate trade and commerce." With equal regularity counsel for the provinces bring forth "property and civil rights in the provinces." Decision between these two ancient rivals rests with the court. It is accordingly necessary to inquire in what way these terms and others have been construed by the Privy Council.

Upon first glancing over the powers assigned to the Dominion one is impressed by their wide scope: "the regulation of trade and commerce," the power to decide what acts shall be criminal offenses, the power to make laws "for the peace, order and good

strictly relates to subjects of legislation expressly enumerated in section 91, is of paramount authority, even though it trenches upon matters assigned to the provincial legislatures." (Attorney-General for Canada v. Attorney-General for British Columbia, 1930 A. C. 111.) This does not mean, however, that the provinces are debarred from legislating on a particular subject merely because the Dominion has legislated or may legislate upon it, and *vice versa*. The jurisdictional distinction is based upon the scope and intention of the legislation as well as upon its subject-matter. Dual legislation on any subject is possible so long as each parliament is operating within its constitutional powers. The most famous illustration is the power of the provinces, despite the Canada Temperance Act, to enact local regulations concerning the sale of liquor. Hodge v. the Queen, (1883) 9 A. C. 117; A. G. for Ontario v. A. G. for Canada, (1896) A. C. 348; A. G. of Manitoba v. Manitoba License Holders' Association, (1902) A. C. 73.

government of Canada." What legislation could not be brought under one or other of these heads? The sweeping character of these clauses was early observed by the Privy Council, and it was felt necessary so to interpret them that they should not entirely swallow up the legislative jurisdiction of the provinces. This process of limitation must now be examined.

Most striking has been the fate of the residual legislative power of the Dominion. In successive decisions the exercise of this power has been restricted to: i. Cases in which the subject involved falls under none of the enumerated heads of section 92. This view, stated in the Liquor case of 1896,[3] was reasserted more forcibly in the Insurance case of 1916.[4] Since there are few cases which cannot be brought under some head

[3] Attorney-General for Ontario v. Attorney-General for Canada, (1896) A. C. 348. Lord Watson said in part: "The exercise of legislative power by the Parliament of Canada, in regard to all matters not enumerated in section 91, ought to be strictly confined to such matters as are unquestionably of Canadian interest and importance, and ought not to trench upon provincial legislation with respect to any of the classes of subjects enumerated in section 92. To attach any other construction . . . would practically destroy the autonomy of the provinces. If it were once conceded that the Parliament of Canada has authority to make laws applicable to the whole Dominion, in relation to matters which in each province are substantially of local or private interest, upon the assumption that these matters also concern the peace, order, and good government of the Dominion, there is hardly a subject enumerated in section 92 upon which it might not legislate, to the exclusion of the provincial legislatures."

[4] Attorney-General for Canada v. Attorney-General for Alberta, (1916) A. C. 588. Viscount Haldane said in part: "It must now be taken that the general authority to make laws for the peace, order and good government of Canada, which the initial part of section 91 of the British North America Act confers, does not, unless the subject-matter of legislation falls within some one of the enumerated heads which follow, enable the Dominion Parliament to trench on the subject-matters entrusted to the provincial legislatures by the enumeration in section 92. There is only one case, outside the heads enumerated in section 91, in which the Dominion Parliament can legislate effectively as regards a province, and that is where the subject-matter lies outside all of the subject-matters enumeratively entrusted to the provinces under section 92."

of section 92, and in particular under "property and civil rights," the effect of this interpretation in itself is practically to annihilate the federal residual power. The Supreme Court of Canada in a 1925 case took the extreme view that inability of the provinces to legislate effectively does not in itself justify Dominion action.[5] From this would follow the strange conclusion that situations may arise in which no legislative action is possible. ii. Situations of national emergency. Government regulation of the prices and movement of commodities during the War was upheld on this ground. Care was taken, however, to point out that such measures would be indefensible in "normal circumstances." [6] The fate of the "New Deal" legislation of 1935 seems to indicate that severe depression is not considered to be a national emergency and does not justify the exercise of extraordinary powers by the Dominion.

The Dominion power to regulate trade and commerce has suffered a similar process of attrition. The classical definition of this clause was laid down in the Parsons case, where it was held that the power to regulate trade and commerce "does not comprehend the power to regulate by legislation the contracts of a particular business or trade, such as the business of fire insurance

[5] The King v. Eastern Terminal Elevator Co., (1925) S. C. R. 434.

[6] Fort Frances Pulp and Paper Co. v. Winnipeg Free Press, (1923) A. C. 695. It was held that under the B. N. A. Act the Dominion Parliament has an implied power, for the safety of the Dominion as a whole, to deal with a sufficiently great emergency, such as that arising from war, although in so doing it trenches upon property and civil rights in the Provinces, from which subjects it is excluded in normal circumstances. The enumeration in s. 92 is not repealed in such an emergency, but "a new aspect of the business of government emerges." The Dominion Government must be granted considerable freedom to judge whether a sufficiently great emergency exists to justify an exercise of the power, and also to decide when the emergency is at an end. "It is clear that in normal circumstances the Dominion Parliament could not have so legislated as to set up the machinery of control over the paper manufacturers which is now in question." But in an emergency, measures may be necessary which can only be taken by the central government.

in a single province." [7] This judgment, however, is liberal compared with the uncompromising dictum of Viscount Haldane in the Board of Commerce references: "The authority of the Dominion Parliament to legislate for the regulation of trade and commerce does not, by itself, enable interference with particular trades in which Canadians would, apart from any right of interference contained in these words, be free to engage in the provinces." [8] In the Snider case, Viscount Haldane went the extreme length of denying to this power any independent validity, holding that it could be exerted only in support of some other power possessed by the Dominion independently of it.[9]

[7] Citizens' Insurance Co. v. Parsons, (1881) 7 App. Cas. 96. Sir Montague Smith, after pointing out that the clause if taken in an unlimited sense would permit any regulation, from the most general to the most minute, went on to say: "Construing therefore the words 'regulation of trade and commerce' by the various aids to their interpretation above suggested, they would include political arrangements in regard to trade requiring the sanction of parliament, regulation of trade in matters of inter-provincial concern, and it may be that they would include general regulation of trade affecting the whole Dominion. Their Lordships abstain on the present occasion from any attempt to define the limits of the authority of the Dominion Parliament in this direction. It is enough for the decision of the present case to say that in their view, its authority to legislate for the regulation of trade and commerce does not comprehend the power to regulate by legislation the contracts of a particular business or trade, such as the business of fire insurance in a single province."

[8] In re The Board of Commerce Act, (1922) 1 A. C. 191.

[9] Toronto Electric Commissioner v. Snider, (1925) A. C. 396. Viscount Haldane said in part: "The contracts of a particular trade or business cannot be dealt with by Dominion legislation so as to conflict with the powers assigned to the Provinces over property and civil rights. . . . The Dominion power has a really definite effect when applied in aid of what the Dominion Government are specifically enabled to do independently of the general regulation of trade and commerce, for instance, in the creation of Dominion Companies with power to trade throughout the whole of Canada. (Wharton case cited.) . . . It is, in their Lordships' opinion, now clear that, excepting so far as the power can be invoked in aid of a capacity conferred independently under other words in s. 91, the power to regulate trade and commerce cannot be relied on as enabling the Dominion Parliament to regulate civil rights in the Provinces."

This decision marks the nadir of federal authority. It was criticized by Chief Justice Anglin in the Eastern Terminal Elevators case, and has since been specifically repudiated by the Privy Council.[10] This latter judgment to some extent rescues "regulation of trade and commerce" from its previous obscure position, and it is possible that in future decisions it will experience a genuine renaissance. Up to the present, however, it has been successfully applied in only one major case.[11] It is also worth noting that the power of regulation has been held not to include the power of prohibition.[12]

The other major power which concerns us here is that over the criminal law. It is evident that this power, if unqualified, is very sweeping. Any commercial policy displeasing to the

[10] In re Combines Investigation Act, (1931) A. C. 310. The Act was sustained as coming under the head of "criminal law." It was therefore unnecessary to consider whether it could be upheld under "regulation of trade and commerce." Lord Atkin went on to say, however: "Their Lordships merely propose to dissociate themselves from the construction suggested in argument of a passage in the judgment in the Board of Commerce case under which it was contended that the power to regulate trade and commerce could be invoked only in furtherance of a general power which Parliament possessed independently of it. No such restriction is properly to be inferred from that judgment. The words of the statute must receive their proper construction where they stand as giving an independent authority to Parliament over the particular subject-matter. But their Lordships in the present case forbear from defining the extent of that authority. They desire, however, to guard themselves from being supposed to lay down that the present legislation could not be supported on that ground."

[11] In the Wharton case, 1914, it was held that the power to regulate trade and commerce enables Parliament to prescribe the extent and limits of the powers of Dominion-wide companies, and that the status and powers of a Dominion company as such cannot be destroyed by a provincial legislature. John Deere Plow Co. v. Wharton, (1914) A. C. 330.

[12] City of Toronto v. Vigo, (1896) A. C. 88. Lord Davey said in part: "Their Lordships think there is a marked distinction to be drawn between the prohibition or prevention of a trade and the regulation or governance of it, and indeed a power to regulate and govern seems to imply the continued existence of that which is to be regulated or governed." See also the Liquor case, 1896, referred to above.

Dominion government might simply be declared a criminal offense and the provinces could have no recourse. The clause has accordingly been qualified by judicial decisions. It is now well established that the Dominion cannot justify regulatory legislation merely by attaching to it penal provisions.[13] An attempt was made by Viscount Haldane to limit the Dominion's authority still more rigidly to cases "where the subject-matter is one which by its very nature belongs to the domain of criminal jurisprudence." [14] This rigid definition, however, was held impracticable in the more recent Combines Investigation case.[15]

[13] Attorney-General for Ontario v. Reciprocal Insurers, (1924) A. C. 328. Mr. Justice Duff said in part: "Their Lordships think it is no longer open to dispute that the Parliament of Canada cannot, by purporting to create penal sanctions under section 91, head 27, appropriate to itself exclusively a field of jurisdiction in which, apart from such procedure, it could exert no legal authority, and that if, when examined as a whole, legislation in form criminal is found, in aspects and for purposes exclusively within the provincial sphere, to deal with matters committed to the Provinces, it cannot be upheld as valid."

[14] In the Board of Commerce case, Lord Haldane said in part: "It is one thing to construe the words 'the criminal law . . .' as enabling the Dominion Parliament to exercise exclusive legislative power where the subject-matter is one which by its very nature belongs to the domain of criminal jurisprudence. . . . It is quite another thing, first to attempt to interfere with a class of subject committed exclusively to the Provincial Legislature, and then to justify this by enacting ancillary provisions, designated as new phases of Dominion criminal law." (1922) 1 A. C. 191.

[15] Lord Atkin said in part: "The substance of the Act is by s. 2 to define, and by s. 32 to make criminal combines which the Legislature in the public interest intends to prohibit . . . if Parliament genuinely determines that commercial activities which can be so described are to be suppressed in the public interest, their Lordships see no reason why Parliament should not make them crimes. 'Criminal law' means 'the criminal law in its widest sense' (Hamilton Street Railway case, 1903 A. C. 524.) . . . The power must extend to legislation to make new crimes. . . . It appears to their Lordships to be of little value to seek to confine crimes to a category of acts which by their very nature belong to the domain of 'criminal jurisprudence'; for the domain of criminal jurisprudence can only be ascertained by examining what acts at any particular period are declared by the State to be crimes, and the only common nature they will be found to

The present position, then, is that parliament may declare to be a crime any economic practice which it genuinely believes to be so. Parliament may not, however, use the criminal law as a subterfuge to disguise a purely regulatory intention. The test, in short, is the object of the legislation, not the nature of the subject-matter.[16]

The Dominion is empowered by the B. N. A. Act to give effect by legislation to treaties entered into by Canada as part of the British Empire.[17] The Privy Council has held, however, that where Canada concludes treaties independently, the legislation necessary for the performance of the treaty obligations must be passed by the appropriate jurisdiction within Canada. The Dominion may legislate only on matters which fall within section 91 of the B. N. A. Act.[18] This interpretation seems effectively to prevent any enlargement of the Dominion's authority by use of the treaty-making power, and may also in some cases hamper or prevent the negotiation of treaties.

Most of the invalidated Dominion acts have been rejected

---

possess is that they are prohibited by the State and that those who commit them are punished." (1931, A. C. 310.)

[16] On this point see C. W. Jenks: "The Dominion Jurisdiction in Respect of Criminal Law," *Canadian Bar Review*, May, 1935.

[17] The Dominion is empowered by Section 132 of the B. N. A. Act to pass legislation "necessary or proper for performing the obligations of Canada or any province thereof as part of the British Empire towards foreign countries arising under treaties between the Empire and foreign countries." An act regulating aeronautics, passed in pursuance of a convention entered into by Canada at the 1919 Peace Conference, was upheld on this ground. In re Regulation and Control of Aeronautics in Canada, (1932) A. C. 54.

[18] A. G. of Canada v. A. G. of Ontario and others, (1937) A. C. 326. The statutes in question here were the Minimum Wages Act, the Limitation of Hours of Work Act, and the Weekly Rest in Industrial Undertakings Act, passed in 1935 in adherence to conventions of the International Labor Organization. The court held that these subjects fell within the scope of "property and civil rights in the provinces," and that the Dominion could not use its treaty-making power to invade provincial jurisdiction.

as encroachments on "property and civil rights in the provinces." The authors of this phrase seem to have been concerned mainly with assuring to the French-Canadian minority freedom of education, religion, and the practice of its own civil law. The term has been interpreted by the courts, however, in quite a different fashion. As early as 1881 it was held to include contractual rights as well as personal rights.[19] But granted this, it becomes possible to regard any act which touches the sale of goods, services or labor as an interference with "property and civil rights." This additional step was taken by Lord Haldane in several notable cases. In the Board of Commerce case he asserted: "It can, therefore, be only under necessity in highly exceptional circumstances, such as cannot be presumed to exist in the present case, that the liberty of the inhabitants of the provinces may be restricted by the Parliament of Canada." And again, in the Snider case: "The contracts of a particular trade or business cannot be dealt with by Dominion legislation so as to conflict with the powers assigned to the provinces over property and civil rights."

"Property and civil rights" has thus become a weapon which can be used at will to destroy almost any piece of economic legislation. The result is to leave the judges free to decide the fate of each statute on its merits. The decision seems to a lay observer to turn on whether the statute in question pleases or offends the judges' view of the functions of government, the wisdom of interference with private enterprise, and similar matters. On whichever side the decision falls, it is easily rationalized in terms of previous interpretations. If the court wishes to uphold a Dominion statute it usually begins by pointing out that the enactment falls under criminal law, or regulation of trade and commerce, or some other enumerated power. At the end, it

[19] "The words are sufficiently large to embrace, in their fair and ordinary meaning, rights arising from contract." Citizens Insurance Co. v. Parsons, (1881) 7 A. C. 96.

is conceded in a paragraph that civil rights are indeed affected. But since the act falls under an enumerated head of section 91 this is beside the point, and civil rights must give way. The strongest assertions of this point of view are perhaps to be found in the Russell case [20] and the Combines Investigation Act case.[21]

If it is desired to reject a Dominion statute, the argument takes a different course. It is first pointed out that the statute touches on property and civil rights — this is the easiest step of the argument. Next it is shown that the statute cannot be justified under the head of "criminal law," since the penalty provisions are merely incidental and cloak a regulatory purpose. Nor can it be justified under "regulation of trade and commerce." This is a difficult step, which Lord Haldane eventually surmounted simply by denying any independent validity to this Dominion power. Nor can the act be justified under the residual power, since this power only comes into play when the subject falls under no enumerated head, i. e., when it does not affect "property and civil rights." This again is an easy and obvious step, and leads to the conclusion that the act is invalid. The judgments in the 1916 insurance case, the Board of Commerce case, the Snider case, and many lesser cases conform closely to this pattern, which has tended to become more and more common since 1900.

[20] "What Parliament is dealing with in legislation of this kind is not a matter in relation to property and its rights, but one relating to public order and safety. That is the primary matter dealt with, and though incidentally the free use of things in which men may have property is interfered with, that incidental interference does not alter the character of the law." (1882) 7 App. Cas. 829.

[21] "If then the legislation in question is authorized under one or other of the heads specifically enumerated in s. 91, it is not to the purpose to say that it affects property and civil rights in the Provinces. Most of the specific subjects in s. 91 do affect property and civil rights but so far as the legislation of Parliament in pith and substance is operating within the enumerated powers there is constitutional authority to interfere with property and civil rights." (1931, A. C. 310.)

The contention is not that Privy Council judgments have been consciously partisan. In a field where wide differences of opinion exist, judges cannot avoid shaping their decisions in the light of their own political preferences. These preferences have been inimical to economic regulation and to centralized authority, and have resulted in a virtual transfer of residual power from the Dominion to the provinces. The close parallel with conditions in the United States is apparent. In both countries phrases intended for the protection of cultural minorities have been used by the courts to protect business men against public regulation. It may be said that this is not true in Canada, since the provinces may legislate in the fields from which the Dominion has been excluded. But it is a commonplace that provincial regulation frequently means no regulation, either because provinces are afraid to fall behind their neighbors in the race for competitive advantage, or because the problem transcends provincial boundaries. The limitation of federal powers, while it has made for some increase in provincial legislation, has tended primarily to stifle governmental control of any sort. Nor is there any evidence of a shift of judicial opinion similar to that which occurred in the United States in 1937.

It is impossible to say whether the situation would have been different had the final decision in constitutional cases been left to the Supreme Court of Canada. The decisions of the Supreme Court have been at least as unfavorable to the Dominion as have those of the Privy Council,[22] and it may be argued that this indicates an equally strong bias in favor of "property and civil rights" on the part of Canadian judges. This argument, however, is far from conclusive. The Supreme Court is inferior

[22] Of 26 cases for which complete records were found, 13 were decided for the Dominion by the Privy Council, while the Supreme Court gave decisions for the Dominion in only 9. In half of the cases, the decision of the Supreme Court was reversed by the Privy Council, but the reversals were about evenly divided.

in rank and must necessarily follow the Privy Council once that body has given a lead. If left to itself, it is quite possible that the Supreme Court would have interpreted more liberally the trade and commerce clause and the residual power of the Dominion.

The decisions outlined above would appear to confine future Dominion legislation within narrow bounds. While labor legislation lies outside the scope of this volume, it should be pointed out that the Dominion has been almost entirely excluded from this field. Laws providing for unemployment insurance, minimum wages, maximum hours, and a weekly day of rest have all been invalidated. It also seems clear that any act similar to the National Labor Relations Act in the United States would be invalid. The provinces are entirely free to legislate in these fields, but have been slow to pass laws and still slower to enforce them.

Still more complicated and unsatisfactory is the position of agricultural marketing. Here a series of decisions appears to leave both the Dominion and the provinces with no substantial authority. British Columbia passed a marketing act in 1926–27, under which large quantities of produce were shipped to the prairie provinces. This act was held invalid by the Supreme Court in 1931, on the ground that it interfered with the exclusive power of the Dominion to regulate trade and commerce, and that the levies imposed on producers constituted indirect taxation.[23] A similar view was taken by the Privy Council in the Crystal Dairy Case.[24] The power of the Dominion, however, far from being strengthened, has been annihilated by another series of decisions. The Live Stock and Live Stock Products Act has been held not to apply to transactions oc-

[23] Lawson v. Interior Tree Fruit and Vegetable Committee of Direction, (1931) S. C. R. 357.

[24] Lower Mainland Dairy Products Sales Adjustment Committee v. Crystal Dairy Ltd., (1933) A. C. 168.

curring entirely within one province,[25] even though the province has passed legislation intended to validate the Dominion Act within its boundaries.[26] The Canada Grain Act was held invalid on the ground that it regulated transactions occurring within a province along with inter-provincial and export trade.[27] The Natural Products Marketing Act of 1934 was rejected on similar grounds by both the Supreme Court of Canada and the Privy Council.[28]

[25] Rex v. Zaslavsky, Saskatchewan Court of Appeal, (1935) 2 W. W. R. 34; The King v. Brodsky et al., Manitoba Court of King's Bench (unreported).

[26] This is a rather surprising device, developed in recent years to evade constitutional obstacles to marketing regulation. The province says in effect to the Dominion: "If it turns out that the regulations you have laid down were beyond your constitutional power to make, we hereby declare that they shall be law in our province in any event." For example, section 2 of the Saskatchewan Live Stock Act read as follows: "If and insofar as any provision of an Act of the Parliament of Canada entitled the Live Stock and Live Stock Products Act, and the amendments thereof and the regulations thereunder heretofore enacted or made, is within the legislative authority of the province and outside that of the Dominion of Canada, such provision shall have the force of law in Saskatchewan, and unless otherwise enacted by the legislature of Saskatchewan, shall be and remain in full force and effect therein to all intents and purposes whatsoever." Such abdication of authority by the province was in Rex v. Zaslavsky held impossible under the B. N. A. Act. Despite this decision, however, such acts are still passed in large numbers. When the Dominion passed the Natural Products Marketing Act in 1934, all of the provinces "coöperated" by passing supplementary acts of this character.

[27] The King v. Eastern Terminal Elevator Co., (1925) S. C. R. 434. Justice Duff said in part: "There are two fallacies in the argument advanced on behalf of the Crown: first, that, because in large part the grain trade is an export trade, you can regulate it locally in order to give effect to your policy in relation to the regulation of that part of it which is export. Obviously that is not a principle the application of which can be ruled by percentages. If it is operative when the export trade is seventy per cent of the whole, it must be equally operative when that percentage is only thirty; and such a principle in truth must postulate authority in the Dominion to assume the regulation of almost any trade in the country."

[28] 1936 S. C. R. 398; 1937 A. C. 377. Chief Justice Duff in delivering the opinion of the Supreme Court said in part: "The power of regulation

Almost every decision in the field of marketing has been negative in tone, a denial of authority now to the provinces now to the Dominion. The Dominion has power to regulate interprovincial and export trade, but to frame regulations which will accomplish this without at the same time affecting purely local transactions is a nice problem in administration. The provinces may legislate only with reference to intra-provincial trade, but trade in nearly all of the important agricultural products flows across provincial boundaries. Court decisions have implied that the situation might be met by carefully framed dual legislation, under which the provinces would control that part of (say) the live stock trade which is local in character while the Dominion would control that part which is inter-provincial and export. But such a division can be made more easily in law than in practice. At the present time, then, effective regulation is difficult or impossible for most agricultural products. The only exceptions are products, such as fluid milk, which are sold entirely in local markets.[29]

The Dominion is in a somewhat better position to control industrial practices. Sections 498 and 498A of the Criminal Code, which prohibit price discrimination, predatory price cutting, and the formation of combines, have been upheld under the Dominion power over criminal law.[30] It is now well established that Parliament may declare criminal any competitive

vested in the commissioners extends to external trade and matters connected therewith and to trade in matters of interprovincial concern; but also to trade which is entirely local and of purely local concern. Regulation of individual trades, or trade in individual commodities, in this sweeping fashion is not competent to the Parliament of Canada." The Privy Council simply affirmed this position.

[29] Regulation of fluid milk marketing by the province of British Columbia was recently held valid by the Privy Council. Shannon v. Lower Mainland Dairy Products Board, (1938) A. C. 708. The court took care to point out that the transactions regulated took place entirely within the province.

[30] For section 498 see (1931) A. C. 310; for section 498A see (1937) A. C. 368.

practice or any restraint or competition which it considers harmful. The only requirements are that the prohibited act must be clearly defined and that the criminal law must not be used merely as a cloak for positive regulation. It is also clear that the Dominion may set up special investigating bodies to assist in the detection of offenders. The Combines Investigation Act was upheld in 1931 on the ground that its primary object is to make the formation of a combine a criminal offence, and that the investigatory powers of the Registrar are reasonably ancillary to this object. The power of the Dominion Trade and Industry Commission to investigate alleged unfair trade practices has also been upheld.[31] Both bodies have full power to secure oral and documentary evidence, and cannot be restrained by injunction. The legal obstacles to investigation of private businesses which have so seriously hampered the work of the Federal Trade Commission and similar bodies in the United States do not arise in Canada.

It is extremely doubtful, however, whether the Dominion can go beyond prohibition and investigation to positive regulation. Any attempt to control prices, output, investment and other policies of particular industries would almost certainly be wrecked on the rock of "property and civil rights in the provinces." It would be almost impossible to regulate industries on a national scale without also regulating local transactions, and it would therefore be easy to find the statute invalid. There is in theory a field of inter-provincial trade which the Dominion can regulate, but this power is practically useless given the present disposition of the courts to uphold provincial rights at every turn.

The courts have been very jealous, too, of any attempt to delegate judicial powers to administrative bodies. While the Board of Commerce Act and section 14 of the Dominion Trade and Industry Commission Act were rejected by use of the usual

[31] (1937) A. C. 405.

formula of "property and civil rights," the judges seem to have been mainly concerned with the power of the Board of Commerce to determine guilt and assess penalties, and with the power of the Dominion Trade and Industry Commission to prevent prosecution of the parties to an approved price and production agreement.[32] In the Combines Investigation Act case, on the other hand, the judges noted with approval that no penal consequences follow from the Registrar's report and that resort must be had to the courts for determination of guilt.[33] Any attempt to set up regulatory boards of the sort suggested by the Price Spreads Commission [34] would thus be almost certain to encounter judicial disapproval.

POLITICAL LIMITS

The political factors which condition the type of legislation enacted are best seen by a survey of the legislative process. In the first place, new legislation must be proposed by someone. Measures which are in the general interest but do not yield great benefits to any one economic group are apt to be brought forward rather slowly. Most proposals of economists are of this sort, and it is not strange that they are slow to find sponsors. Legislation in the field with which we are concerned comes usually from one of two sources. Organized interest groups are

[32] See in this connection the Report of Argument before the Supreme Court in the Dominion Trade and Industry Commission case, especially Vol. III, pp. 320–330 and Vol. IV, p. 405 *et seq.*

[33] "None of these powers (possessed by the Board of Commerce) exists in the provisions now under discussion. There is a general definition, and a general condemnation; and if penal consequences follow, they can follow only from the determination by existing Courts of an issue of fact defined in express words by the statute. . . . It is noteworthy that no penal consequences follow directly from a report of either commissioner or registrar that a combine exists." (1931) A. C. 310.

[34] The Price Spreads Commission recommended, among other things, a Securities Board, a Federal Trade and Industry Commission, a Live Stock Board, and a Fisheries Control Board. (Report xviii–xxv.)

always at work preparing milk marketing laws, labor legislation, resale price maintenance laws, tariff changes, and the like. While these measures are not necessarily against the public interest, they are designed to yield their greatest benefits to the sponsoring group. The Royal Commission method of developing legislation is now being used with increasing frequency. The Board of Commerce Act, the Dominion Trade and Industry Commission Act, Sections 498 and 498A of the Criminal Code, the British Columbia Coal and Petroleum Products Control Act, the coal regulations of Alberta and Saskatchewan, to mention only a few, were based on Commission reports. While this sort of legislation is less likely to be strongly biased in favor of a particular group, it is not always free of bias. A Royal Commission inquiry tends to become a trial by combat between different economic groups, whose representatives appear and plead their case. The Commissioners thus tend inevitably to think in terms of group interests rather than of economic welfare, to sympathize with those groups which seem to have suffered under existing arrangements, and to frame their recommendations with an eye to redressing injuries. The recommendations may contribute to economic efficiency, but this will be more by accident than by conscious intention.

Provided the government has a clear majority, approval of a measure by the government means approval by Parliament. Lobbying activity, instead of being concentrated on committees of the legislature, as in the United States, tends to be focused on Cabinet members. Sponsors of a measure try to secure the support of Cabinet members, and particularly of the Prime Minister, through visits, letters, petitions and other means. When news leaks out that such a measure is under consideration, there will be visits and counter-representations by opposing groups. The decision to adopt or reject a proposal probably depends on the relative political strength of the groups favoring and opposing it, and on a forecast of the public reaction. If the

Opposition, by playing on accepted stereotypes, will be able to arouse widespread public resentment against the bill, it may be too dangerous to touch even though its supporters are strong. If the bill is too complicated to arouse public interest, however, the pressure of the groups directly concerned may determine its fate.

While it is difficult to find out much about what goes on in Ministers' offices, two hypotheses may be advanced. It seems likely that proponents of a measure have a strategic advantage over opponents. They are more intimately acquainted with the probable effects of the measure, since they have usually helped to draft it. They have the first chance to influence the Minister. Opponents will probably not learn of the proposal for some time, and by this time it may be too late to alter the Minister's opinion. The supporters, finally, usually stand to gain large and direct benefits, and will therefore put forth their best efforts. The opponents frequently have a relatively small interest in the matter, and may not consider it worthwhile to make a determined fight. A manufacturer seeking a tariff advance, for example, has every incentive to press his case vigorously. Consumers, importers and other manufacturers who stand to lose only slightly by the change will probably not provide equally vigorous opposition. Tariffs thus move upward more easily than downward.

It may be suggested, secondly, that business interests are able to exert much stronger pressure than other interests. Business men are well organized in trade associations and in larger bodies such as the Chamber of Commerce and the Canadian Manufacturers' Association. Consumers, on the other hand, are completely unorganized, labor organizations include only a very small part of all workers, and even the farmers do not present a strong and unified front. The financial resources of business associations enable them to hire the best lawyers and accountants, to maintain permanent secretariats in Ottawa,

Montreal and Toronto, and to spend large sums for "educational" purposes. Contributions to party campaign funds help to pave the way to the inner council chambers. Large newspapers almost invariably reflect business views and, while editorials probably carry little weight at present, the more effective propaganda of the news columns is feared by governments.

The greatest advantage of business, however, is the prestige which it still retains. Most members of Parliament are still convinced of the superiority of business leadership and that "what is good for business is good for Canada." Cabinet members do not need to be bribed to accept the business viewpoint. They already think like business men. For all of these reasons measures beneficial to business groups have a great initial advantage, while measures opposed by business stand a much smaller chance of acceptance. The emasculation of section 498 of the Criminal Code before its passage, and the rejection of most of the Price Spreads Commission's recommendations were noted in Chapter VI, and many other examples could be given. Occasionally a measure such as the Combines Investigation Act is passed in spite of business opposition. The Combines Act, however, was a favorite project of the Prime Minister, while the opposition to it was divided. The Retail Merchants' Association was split on the question and took no action, and even the manufacturers were not unanimously opposed.

A bill accepted by the Cabinet is assured of passage through the House, though amendments may be conceded if opposition is particularly strong. The Senate offers a stronger barrier to economic legislation. Senators are usually old, frequently wealthy, and almost always conservative. They show a strong tendency to overlook party lines in order to set aside measures which curtail the "liberties" of business men. Party discipline and public opinion usually prevent them from rejecting such measures altogether, but crippling amendments may render the final statute ineffective.

The final political barrier which all legislation must pass is that of the Supreme Court and the Privy Council. It has been shown above that the law is sufficiently flexible to allow free play to the opinions of the judges who constitute the court at a particular time. These opinions have on the whole been distinctly conservative, though differences of degree can be detected. Under a Sankey economic control by the Dominion is possible; under a Duff it is very difficult; under a Haldane it is out of the question.

There runs through the entire legislative process a distinct bias against certain types of legislation and in favor of others. Legislation which protects or advances business interests tends to be approved, while legislation which seeks to regulate business activities in the interest of unorganized groups or of the general public tends to be disapproved. Association secretaries are paid for coining and promoting proposals of the first type. These proposals receive a favorable hearing from Ministers predisposed toward anything which will "improve business." They are supported by all available channels of propaganda. Opposition is usually poorly organized and inarticulate. Nor are they likely to be challenged by the Senate or the Courts, since the rights which they impose upon — the right of consumers to obtain goods at the lowest possible prices, for example, or the right of labor to organize and to be paid a just wage — are not recognized by law or by conservative opinion. Regulatory legislation, on the other hand, is slow to be developed and proposed, encounters violent business opposition, is vulnerable to attack by Senators and judges as a restriction on property rights. For these reasons even the mildest reforms must fight for their lives, while really effective measures for the promotion of economic efficiency are quite outside the field of practical politics.

ADMINISTRATIVE LIMITS

An act approved by Parliament and by the courts may still fail of its intended effect. In the first place, the circumstances may make successful administration impossible. It is true that legal restrictions on the actions of administrative bodies are less burdensome in Canada than in the United States. The provincial acts described in Chapter VIII, for example, are nearly all drawn in general terms which the administrators are allowed to interpret. The argument that this constitutes undue delegation of legislative power has rarely if ever been used by the courts in rejecting a statute. Canadian administrators have wide powers in compelling oral and written evidence, while use of the well-established licensing power makes possible enforcement of their rulings with little or no resort to the courts.

A board which is legally free to regulate an industry, however, may find practical limits imposed on its activities. If a considerable part of the industry is opposed to regulation, as has been true for some agricultural marketing schemes, the task of policing may prove too great and regulation may break down. In other cases two or more groups with divergent interests may exist, each determined to control the regulating body. The long-standing feud between the Fraser Valley Milk Producers' Association and independent milk producers in the Vancouver area, for example, has made the regulation of milk marketing very difficult and at times impossible.[35] A plan of regulation may also be impracticable because it requires information

[35] Most of the independent shippers are located nearer to Vancouver than the Fraser Valley producers. The independents also have larger dairies on the average and produce milk of a lower bacteria count. The independents tend to receive more for their milk because of its better quality and the shorter haul to the market. Fraser Valley producers have tried for years to secure an equalization scheme under which all producers would receive the same return per 100 lbs. They are in a strong strategic position, since they have a very large volume of milk, own their own dairy in Vancouver, and could hurt the independents very seriously by a price war.

which is unobtainable or which could be obtained only at prohibitive cost.

An act may fail, secondly, because the administrative machinery provided is inadequate. Even where the act simply prohibits certain trade practices and attaches penalties to them, provision must be made for the detection of offenders and the determination of guilt. These functions are ordinarily performed by local law enforcement officers and by the criminal courts. Where social legislation is concerned, however, this system works clumsily or not at all. Breaches of the law are difficult to detect. In cases of theft or murder it is usually clear that a crime has been committed, and the problem is to detect the guilty party. But in economic matters the question whether a crime has been committed is itself the central problem. Definite proof that a worker has been paid less than a stated minimum wage is much more difficult than one would think. To establish the existence of a price-fixing agreement may require hundreds of interviews and the examination of thousands of documents. If questions of cost or profit are involved, months of labor by skilled accountants may be necessary.

Under these conditions individuals cannot be expected to possess evidence of law violations. Even where an individual does possess adequate evidence, he may be unwilling to lay a complaint. Though the injury to wage-earners or consumers as a whole may be great, the injury to a particular person is usually too small to warrant his spending time and money in redressing it. The possibility that he may be punished through economic discrimination for having complained is an additional deterrent. For these reasons enforcement of social legislation usually requires a special administrative body to investigate alleged violations and initiate prosecutions. Without this a statute which seems impressive may be invoked rarely or not at all.[36]

[36] This lesson seems to be very slowly learned, for most regulatory laws

This view is supported by the history of combines legislation in Canada. The enforcement of Section 498 Cr. Code was from 1890 to 1923 left to the ordinary law enforcement authorities. During this period there were only six reported prosecutions, and only three of these were successful. It is clear from Chapter I that this cannot have been due to a scarcity of combines, but rather to a failure of the ordinary legal machinery to detect them. It is significant that the few cases which did arise resulted from the envy of those excluded from the agreement rather than from complaints by consumers. The American Tobacco Company was prosecuted as a result of a complaint by a rival manufacturer. Several dealers who had been refused licenses complained against the Alberta Retail Lumber Dealers' Association. An excluded wholesaler supplied the information in the Stinson Reeb case. Only where the freebooters fell out was the law called in. With the passing of the Combines Investigation Act a marked change is noticeable. The decade 1925–35 saw seven main groups of prosecutions — more than in the preceding thirty-five years — and six of these were successful. It seems clear that the Commissioner's investigations detected a number of combines which would otherwise have continued unmolested. These results support the contention that special administrative machinery is necessary for the enforcement of any act of this sort.

Not only must administrative machinery exist, but it must be adequate to its functions. An obvious requisite is that the staff and the funds of the agency should correspond to the tasks imposed upon it. The more complicated the statute, the more laborious the necessary investigations, the larger must be the agency's budget. A survey of Canadian regulatory legislation

still suffer an initial period of sterility before adequate enforcement is provided. This oversight is probably not always innocent. Enactment of strongly worded regulatory measures without any teeth is an excellent way to gain a reputation for liberalism without disturbing the *status quo*.

indicates that this requirement has been uniformly disregarded. The Combines Investigation Commission has only two full-time investigators in addition to the Commissioner. The Companies Branch of the State Department has only three or four men above the rank of clerk. The Tariff Board's research department comprises one trained economist with a few assistants. These three agencies have the responsibility of protecting the public interest at several crucial points, yet their combined staffs are smaller than the clerical force of a minor manufacturing company. This fact alone is almost sufficient to explain the wide divergence between their nominal powers and their actual influence. An increase of several hundred per cent in the technical staffs of these agencies will be necessary before they can even approach the influence which they should wield.

A second requirement is freedom from direct political control. While any administrative body must be ultimately accountable to a cabinet member, the Minister should not be allowed to prevent investigations or otherwise intervene in the everyday operations of the agency. The danger that innocent persons may suffer through arbitrary administrative action has been greatly exaggerated by those who wish to hinder public regulation. Far more serious is the danger that business groups may be able to prevent any investigation of their activities by putting pressure on the Minister. It is extremely difficult to generalize about the extent of political intervention in the administrative process at present, since this varies from one department to the next, changes with changing governments, and is influenced by the existence of general prosperity or depression. Political intervention is certainly not uncommon, and its reduction is much to be desired.

Much depends, finally, on the personal qualities of the top administrators, and on the capacity and morale of those who work under them. To serve the public interest consistently and at the same time earn the respect of the business men who are being regulated, an administrator must possess courage, tact, integrity, and a broad conception of his function. The ordinary staff member should at least have intelligence, a good technical training, and a sense of professional responsibility. The scarcity of these qualities in government service is probably due mainly to an unfortunate reluctance to pay salaries large enough to attract men of first-rate ability. Too often government agencies are obliged to pit second-rate lawyers and accountants against first-rate lawyers and accountants hired by corporations. The struggle is thus made needlessly unequal, and the public probably loses far more than would be required to hire men in the first rank of ability. Increased investment in this field would be good social economy.

X

LEGISLATION IN THE PUBLIC INTEREST

INFORMATION CONCERNING the extent of competition in earlier times is relatively scarce. It seems a reasonable hypothesis, however, that monopoly or agreement among sellers is the typical market situation in most periods. From time to time new developments, such as the great reduction in transport costs during the past century, increase the number of competitors in the market and break down existing controls. This intensified competition is felt by producers as a threat to their security and their incomes, and attempts are made to limit it by new agreements and by building legal barriers around the market. Competition thus appears to be self-destructive rather than self-perpetuating, an unstable transition period between two periods of price control. The increased price control of the past fifty years, while it may be viewed as a deviation from the competitive norm of economic theory, is perhaps better regarded as a return to the historical norm of market relations.

In the Canada of a century ago, those lines of production which were carried on outside the home seem to have been largely in the hands of local monopolists. The village grist mill, the village smithy, the village harness maker were protected by transport costs from the competition of producers in other localities. The coming of the railroad and the highway threw these local producers into competition with each other over a much wider area, and at the same time produced a desire to keep this competition within bounds. The earliest investigations reveal full-blown cartels already in existence. These conflicting tendencies have continued to the present time. In some industries competition has been further intensified by the growth of motor transport, by the versatility of research workers in developing substitute products, and by other dynamic impulses. At the same time producers have exerted every effort to bring competition under control through mergers, agreements and informal understandings. This has been particularly true since 1929, for competition which may be exhilarating in a rapidly expanding industry becomes unpleasant when stagnation or decline commences. A thorough historical study of the past century (which the writer does not pretend to have made) would probably reveal a cyclical movement from local price control through a stage of intensified competition and back toward price control on a regional or national basis.

The interesting question is why the abnormal state of competition still exists in many Canadian industries. It was suggested in Chapter I that competition has persisted where voluntary agreements are difficult to organize and enforce, either because the number of producers is very large, or because there are sharp cleavages of interest among producers, or because some condition (such as unused capacity) makes it particularly profitable for individual producers to break any agreement which may be reached. It does not follow, however, that these conditions will cause competition to continue indefinitely. Where voluntary organization breaks down legal compulsion is still available. It is safe to predict that during the next decade or two many competitive industries will appeal for government aid in controlling prices. The milk producers and distributors, the retail merchants and others have shown the way, and other groups will not be slow to follow. To the extent that they are successful in winning government support, the sphere of competition will continue to shrink.

The traditional proofs that free private enterprise must necessarily result in economic efficiency assume the general prevalence of perfect competition, and are therefore largely irrelevant to the sort of economic system which actually exists. It cannot be assumed that the existing system is at all efficient in maximizing the satisfactions of its members. It would, indeed, be very surprising if this were the case, since the motive power of the system is a *bellum omnium contra omnes* — an attempt by each group of producers to maximize its income at the expense of the rest. Rough criteria of economic efficiency were suggested at the beginning of Chapter III. We are concerned here chiefly with the requirements that goods should be sold at cost (including a "normal" profit), and that unit cost should be as low as is technically possible. In order for costs to be minimized, plants must be operated at capacity, they must be efficiently managed, and expenses which add nothing to the usefulness of the product must be avoided.

Judged by these standards — and overlooking entirely the tremendous wastefulness of depression unemployment — the Canadian economy operates much below maximum efficiency. In many industries prices are maintained at a level much in excess of costs. Unused capacity, at least partially attributable to price and production control, is a pervasive feature of the system. Large numbers of people are engaged in selling activities which raise prices without contributing anything to the welfare of consumers. Under monopoly or price agreement there can be no certainty of efficient management and economical production. Where costs are too high for any of these reasons, prices are also too high even though they yield only moderate profits.

A survey of Canadian policy during the past fifty years reveals few attempts to cope with this complex of problems. The nature of the problems has been imperfectly understood even by students, while the public has had only a confused impression of their existence. The spectacular expansion of the Canadian economy since Confederation has tended to divert attention from inefficiencies in its operation, and even now the view that government must intervene actively in order to secure economic efficiency is accepted by only a small minority.

More fundamental is the difficulty that the government is not a neutral arbiter in economic matters, but tends to reflect the aims of those groups which are in the best position to influence governmental decisions. Few would deny that the policies of Canadian governments since Confederation have been predominantly shaped by business men. Investigation would probably show that business men and lawyers have had a continuous majority in Parliament, and particularly in the Senate. Business interests, too, have been willing and able to spend large sums of money in advancing their claims. Permanent lobbies in Ottawa, innumerable special delegations, the unifying influence of conventions and trade journals, the molding of public opinion through newspapers and other media, contributions to party funds — all these investments have yielded an abundant return. Business men have been fortunate, finally, in the existence of vast unused resources whose exploitations could be made to seem a patriotic duty. To a limited extent the public interest in the development of natural resources coincided during this period with the business desire for profits. Adroit propaganda has been able to convert this partial coincidence into a complete identity.

A major object of business policy has been the control of competition through tariffs, patents, mergers, formal and informal agreements, and the development of brands and advertising. The attainment of this object did not until recently require the use of government as a tool,[1] but simply the sterilization of government by determined opposition to all regulatory

[1] This is not wholly true. Tariff protection, for example, requires positive legislation. The main effort of business, however, has not been directed toward obtaining legislation, but rather toward taking full advantage of "free enterprise" while at the same time fighting a rear-guard action against attempts of other groups to use government for the purpose of regulating business.

measures. The persistent depression of the past decade has rendered the control of competition more difficult and at the same time — from a business standpoint — more desirable. Manufacturers have therefore tended to look with increasing favor on the use of government as an instrument for controlling prices and output. Pressure for price control has come also from new sources — truck and dairy farming, milk distribution, retail trade, and other small-scale industries. The stream of control legislation during the years 1930–35 is an indication of the flood which another major decline in business activity would produce.

Against this general trend toward price control the Combines Investigation Act stands out almost alone. While the Act forbids only combines which operate "against the public interest," Canadian courts have tended to regard the fact of price control as *prima facie* evidence of such operation. The Act has been applied to a considerable number of price-fixing combinations with a fair measure of success. Its influence has been limited, however, by the small appropriations for its administration, and at times by the unsympathetic or indifferent attitude of the government. A more serious limitation lies in the highly concentrated structure of Canadian industry. A monopoly can be fined for operating against the public interest, but it does not cease to be a monopoly and the problem is not really solved. Many Canadian monopolies could not be dissolved for technical reasons, and even where dissolution is possible it is very doubtful whether the successor companies could be forced to compete.

In industries dominated by a few large firms the enforcement of competition is extremely difficult. Written agreements are scarcely ever used in these industries. The methods of control are so subtle, the understandings so informal, that their existence is very difficult to prove. The fact that the prices charged by different companies are identical proves nothing, for the price of a standardized article will necessarily be uniform under either agreement or competition. The maintenance of prices unchanged over a period of fluctuating demand is a more reliable indication of joint action, but the evidence is still circumstantial rather than direct. It is conceivable, though perhaps not likely, that the stability of prices is due simply to a strong tradition in the industry against price-cutting.[2] Even where joint action exists it may take some conventional form, such as price leadership, which does not require frequent consultation among producers.

Even if collusion can be demonstrated to the satisfaction of a court, the imposition of fines on the guilty companies does not constitute a permanent remedy. The companies have presumably been ordered to "compete." But what does this mean? It would seem to mean that each company must formulate its price and production policy quite independently of other producers. By an effort of the imagination, it must act as though other producers did not exist, or at least must assume that their policies will be uninfluenced by its own actions. But this can only lead to price cutting which will reduce profits and may even involve losses. Rather than face such a prospect most producers will prefer to run the risk of litigation, and to pay legal expenses and occasional fines. Business men, in other words, can probably not be forced by criminal legislation to act in a way which seems to them unnatural and which may result in losses or even failure.

In still other cases, the restoration of competition would not

[2] Even where prices are very rigid, as in the steel industry, producers will usually deny that this is due to agreement. All producers, it is claimed, knowing the demand situation and seeking a profit, come to identical decisions as to what the price should be. But is this explanation convincing? In the absence of any consultation, one would think that producers might reach different conclusions about the correct price because of differences in their costs and in their estimates of demand. Through reductions first by one producer then by another the price structure would gradually be higgled downwards. The avoidance of such reductions over months or even years of declining demand must indicate some sort of joint action.

be desirable even if it could be accomplished. In the milk distributing and coal mining industries, for example, rivalry for sales leads to such obvious wastes that a convincing defense of it is impossible.

It is clear, then, that no one technique of regulation can be applied to the whole of industry. The very complexity of the problems prevents any single policy from being universally applicable. It is necessary rather to classify industries on the basis of significant common characteristics, and to apply to each group a policy adapted to its needs. This pluralistic approach undoubtedly raises grave legal and administrative problems. From an economic standpoint, however, it seems entirely reasonable to suppose that the maintenance of efficiency may in some industries require one type of policy, in other industries a different and apparently contradictory policy.

In one group may be placed nearly all of the industries in which competition still prevails, together with some in which unstable agreements exist and which might perhaps be restored to the competitive column. For these industries competition, enforced through the Combines Act, is probably the best regulatory device available at the present time. At the opposite pole lies a group of industries in which monopoly is either unavoidable or could be avoided only at exorbitant cost — cement, nickel, aluminum, heavy electrical equipment, explosives, many iron and steel products, many chemicals. In this group may be included also industries, such as milk distribution, in which the possible savings through unified operation are very great. It is argued below that public supervision or operation is desirable for industries in this group, and that public operation is likely to be the more efficient of these methods.

When these two groups have been separated out we are left with a miscellaneous list of industries, conducted on a large scale by relatively few firms, and controlled by informal agreement: cottons, gasoline, sugar, tobacco, agricultural implements, and the rest. These industries constitute in a sense the core of the problem, yet our knowledge of their operation is painfully inadequate. For reasons already indicated, competition as a regulator tends to break down in these cases, and the choice is essentially between an unregulated private cartel and some type of public supervision. Is the inefficiency of these industries sufficiently great that public intervention could bring large gains? And what type of intervention is indicated? Our present knowledge does not permit even a rough answer to these questions. The only recommendation which can safely be made concerning these industries is that they should be closely studied. Regular collection of data concerning their operations should prove an invaluable aid in determining which industries may wisely be left alone, which should be supervised, and what types of supervision are likely to prove effective.

An attempt is made below to translate this general approach to the problem into concrete terms. The proposals are not intended to constitute a blue-print for a completely efficient economy. They are first steps only, advanced in the belief that it is possible to take first steps without quarrelling about eventual destinations. They assume that the object of public policy is the economic welfare of the citizens. If the object of policy is something else — national self-sufficiency, military strength, or the preservation of existing economic forms — much of what is said below may be quite irrelevant. The knowledge on which the proposals are based is far from perfect, and it goes without saying that additional data and additional analysis are urgently needed.

It is necessary to assume also a determined attack on the problem of depression. The criteria of economic efficiency set forth above rest on the assumption of full employment, and lose much of their force if this condition is not met. It is clearly desirable to free labor and capital by a more efficient organization of industry if there is an active demand for both. The desirability of such a policy is much less certain if the "freed" men must remain unemployed because of general depression. From a political standpoint, too, alleviation of depressions would enable the problems of industrial organization to be solved much more readily. Continued depression, with continued insistence on price control by producers whose incomes are threatened, may make a reasoned and constructive approach to these problems quite impossible.

COLLECTION OF INFORMATION

A thorough economic study of even a single industry is a difficult and costly matter, for which most university economists have neither the time nor the funds. More important, the necessary information is in the hands of companies and trade associations which will usually not release it voluntarily. Work in this field must therefore be done mainly by government agencies with adequate budgets and power to compel the production of information.

Most of the information now available has been gathered in two ways: through occasional investigations of particular industries by committees of Parliament, Royal Commissions and the Combines Investigation office, and through the regular statistical services of the government. Of the special investigations, those made under the Combines Act are the most informative, while those made by parliamentary committees are least informative. The parliamentary inquiries tend to degenerate into a succession of pot-shots at the witnesses by committee members, few of whom have expert knowledge of the subject. The discussions lack systematic order, irrelevancies are introduced by the score, and hundreds of pages of the evidence are virtually waste paper. Royal Commission reports, while more systematic and informative, tend to be compendiums of facts with a minimum of analysis and no clear sense of direction. This situation could be remedied in part by increased use of economic advisers, and by focusing the inquiries more definitely around problems of economic efficiency. The approach of Mr. Justice Macdonald may be suggested as a model in this regard. Throughout his long report[3] the following questions are kept steadily in the foreground: "Is the price of coal and gasoline to British Columbia consumers too high? By what methods, and by how much, could the price be reduced?" The excellence of the reports rendered under the Combines Act is also due to the Commissioner's steady concern for the public interest, his wide economic knowledge, and his use of able consultants.

The regular statistical services of the government are largely centralized in the Dominion Bureau of Statistics, which prepares annual and in some cases monthly reports on investment, employment, production, sales and prices in a large number of industries. These aggregate figures, while essential as background information, do not enable one to analyze the operations of particular industries in detail. Much of the material which would be necessary for such an analysis is not collected by the Bureau, while the material which is collected is not analyzed from this point of view. The reason is doubtless that there has been little demand for this sort of work, and that a considerable outlay would be required for staff and equipment.

It is suggested, therefore, that a new bureau be created, which might perhaps be called "The Division of Industrial Economics," and which might be attached either to the Dominion Bureau of Statistics or to the Department of Labour.[4] This

[3] Report of the Royal Commission on Coal and Petroleum Products, British Columbia, 1936. While the general approach of this Report seems entirely correct, it is much too long. Its usefulness would have been much improved by more thorough digesting of the material, and a briefer and more attractive presentation of the results.

[4] The Department of Labour is more concerned than most other departments with safeguarding the interests of the unorganized public, and probably comes nearest to taking the consumer point of view on economic

Division might function in either, or both, of two ways. It might require regular returns from all producers in selected industries, showing employment, wage rates, utilization of plant capacity, the main elements entering into unit cost, prices, profits, and related matters. This approach, of course, would require a large permanent staff. There is also a danger that tabulation and presentation of this material would become purely a matter of routine, and that producers would learn in time to submit data which would present their operations in the most favorable light. There is therefore much to be said for selecting each year one or a few industries for intensive analysis, making a thorough survey of their operations, and passing on to other industries in the following year. The weakness of this method is that a year is too brief a period to give much indication of the trends of development in an industry. Even a cross-section view can be very illuminating, however, provided that the right questions are asked and the data arranged so as to provide the nearest possible approach to an answer.

The objective of the Division would be to analyze the information collected with a view to explaining the level of costs, prices and profits in particular industries. It would not be the business of the Division to approve or indict particular industries or firms. The analyses provided, however, should enable economists and informed laymen to draw conclusions concerning the adequacy with which particular industries are serving the public interest. It will be objected by some that this is an unwarranted intrusion into private affairs. The efficiency of industry, however, is surely a matter of public concern, and a corporation which holds a charter to do business from the gov-

---

questions. Placing the proposed Division in the Department of Labour would make it clear that its function was not merely to collect information, but also to aid in evaluating the efficiency of industrial operations. On the other hand, such an arrangement might lead to the duplication of some of the work now done by the Bureau of Statistics.

ernment can fairly be required to give an account of its actions. Such an agency could accumulate more pertinent industrial data in a few years than economists have done in a generation, and should make possible great strides in public policy.

THE COMBINES INVESTIGATION ACT

The valuable work which has been done under this Act was described in Chapter VI. Amendment of the Act and a considerable increase in personnel would enable this work to be performed even more effectively. Most of the changes requested by the Minister of Labour in 1937 seem clearly desirable. Where the public interest seems to require immediate action, the Commissioner should be permitted to proceed with an investigation on his own initiative. The obstructive provision that the Commissioner must secure an order from a judge before he can compel the giving of evidence should be repealed. The maximum penalties for breach of the Act, now absurdly small, should be increased. There is much to be said for eliminating the expense of a full-dress trial before a jury which can have little knowledge of the technical issues involved. The trial at present consists almost entirely of a re-hearing of evidence already secured during the Commissioner's investigation. This might be avoided by giving the Commissioner's findings the legal status of a jury verdict, to be set aside by the court only if clearly contrary to the weight of the evidence,[5] and with the safeguard of appeal to a higher court. Finally, the Dominion Trade and Industry Commission Act, now reduced in stature and virtually unused, should be formally repealed.

The staff of the Commission should be considerably increased. A permanent nucleus of economists, accountants and lawyers

[5] This proposal was made by Professor Jacob Finkelman in a paper before the Canadian Political Science Association (Proceedings of the C. P. S. A., 1932), and the writer would agree with the arguments advanced there.

should be built up. In addition, the budget of the Commission should be large enough to permit the hiring of special assistants for as many investigations as seem clearly desirable. With resources of this magnitude and with a moderately favorable government, the Commission might hope to preserve competition over a considerable sector of the economy. The trading and service occupations, to which the Act has been applied most successfully in the past, might be policed fairly effectively. Some of the price-fixing associations in the textile, paper, hardware, and other industries could perhaps be broken up. The resultant savings to consumers would much more than repay the cost of administering the Act.

PUBLIC OPERATION OF INDUSTRY

In some industries monopoly is inevitable, while in others efficient operation can be secured only under unified control. The harmful results of unregulated private monopoly were discussed in Chapter III. Are these inefficiencies sufficiently serious to justify extensive government intervention? The answer to this question must remain for the present largely a matter of opinion, particularly since political, administrative and other considerations must be taken into account. The argument advanced below expresses merely the judgment of the writer, based to some extent on non-economic grounds.[6]

If one believes that the operations of monopolized industries should be controlled by government, two main alternatives are available: public *operation* of the industries in question, and public *supervision* of the sort exemplified by public utility commissions and milk control boards. The policy of supervision, while attractive in principle, has proved very unsatisfactory in practice. The decisions of regulatory commissions have in general been very favorable to producers, and the commission has

[6] For a competent and fair summary of the economic arguments on either side see A. C. Pigou: Capitalism versus Socialism, London, 1937.

tended to become merely a means of giving legal sanction to producers' desires. There are two main reasons for this situation. The Commission, in the first place, is dependent on the companies for data concerning profits, costs and other matters. Unless it is able to afford a large staff of accountants, it must accept these data on faith. When milk distributors say that the cost of distribution is six cents per quart, the control board has no alternative but to agree. Secondly, producer groups maintain constant pressure on the Commission for higher prices. The consumers who have an interest in lower prices are almost always unorganized, and are unable to exert an equal pressure in the other direction. It is thus natural for the consumer interest to be neglected and for producers to have their way about prices.

The purpose of control boards is usually conceived as the prevention of exorbitant profits. It has already been shown, however, that prices to consumers may be too high even though profits are only moderate. Costs may be too high because of inefficient management, unused capacity, selling expenses, and the like. The board has usually no power to compel increased efficiency or reorganization of the industry to make possible lower costs. It thus serves merely as a legal shelter for existing investments, enabling producers to recover a good profit in addition to their inflated costs. The milk control boards are a notable illustration of this tendency.

Really adequate control would be very expensive, since it would involve detailed analysis of costs and receipts, and extensive intervention in the day-to-day operations of management. The basic dilemma of this sort of control thus becomes apparent. A commission with limited resources will remain dependent on producers for the reasons given above, and will largely serve their purposes. A commission which wishes to enforce efficiency, on the other hand, must develop such a large staff, accumulate so much data, take over so many functions that it becomes a super-management capable of operating the industry.[7] The maintenance of two managements, one private and one public, overlapping and interfering with each other, is clearly inefficient, and outright public operation appears preferable. In short, commission control is either doomed to futility or, if it is made effective, private management becomes redundant. There is no comfortable half-way house between competition and public enterprise.

Wherever competition is impossible or involves great inefficiency, then, it would seem wise to introduce public operation as rapidly as is consistent with efficient management. A beginning could be made with the two sorts of industry noted above: industries which are already in the hands of a single firm — nickel, aluminum, cement, explosives and a number of others — and which could therefore be transferred from private to public operation with a minimum of friction; and secondly, industries such as the distribution of milk in which the inefficiencies of private operation are particularly glaring.[8] With the experience gained in these industries, public operation could be extended gradually to other fields. It is not necessary or indeed possible to say at this time where the line between private and public operation should eventually be drawn.

The words "public ownership" still rouse so many vague fears that it is necessary to state more precisely what is intended. The structure of public industries in Canada might well be similar to that of the London Passenger Transport Board. The Board acquired virtually all of the surface and underground transport facilities in the London metropolitan area, formerly

[7] The recently created Bituminous Coal Commission in the United States, for example, proposes to secure a duplicate invoice for each sale of coal by each producer in the country, and to record the details of these sales on tabulating cards. The enormous duplication of effort involved in such an attempt is apparent.

[8] We are concerned here only with manufacturing industry, but the argument applies *a fortiori* to railroads and public utilities.

owned by several private companies, by issuing its own shares to shareholders of these companies.[9] The Board's shares carry guaranteed rates of interest but no right of control. Directors of the Board are appointed by the Minister of Transport for a fixed term. While they are responsible to the Minister in matters of general policy, they have complete autonomy in the day-to-day management of the business. Employees are hired on the basis of their ability, and are paid market rates of wages. The experience of the Board and of other public corporations has demonstrated that public operation need not mean political management.

Nor does public operation necessarily mean operation by the Dominion. For many industries the province or the city is probably the appropriate unit. Milk distribution is a particularly good test case for municipal operation. The present organization of the industry is so inefficient that a municipal distributing system could probably reduce the retail price of milk by several cents.[10] Moreover, the experiment could be made in one city at a time. The results would probably lead to a rapid extension of the system throughout the country.

Publicly operated industries would undoubtedly encounter grave difficulties. There is space here to mention only three problems: the level of managerial ability, the danger of bureaucratic inefficiency, and the pressure of interested producer

[9] The problem of determining the price which should be paid to the private owners is admittedly very difficult. If the price is set too high, the new public corporation will be saddled with an unduly heavy burden of interest payments. The persistent deficits of the Canadian National Railways, so often urged as an argument against public ownership, have been due primarily to the gross overpayment of the former private owners, and the consequent exorbitant interest charges.

[10] A recent study in Milwaukee concluded that the unit cost of processing and delivering fluid milk in that market could be cut in half by a unified system. (Agricultural Adjustment Administration: Study of the Milwaukee Milk Market, 1933.)

groups. The manager of a public corporation should combine the energy and initiative of a captain of industry with a devotion to public service. There are undoubtedly men of this sort now engaged in private business whose services might be secured, and as the public corporations became firmly established there would be no lack of suitable candidates. In order to attract the highest level of ability, it would probably be necessary to pay salaries larger than those now paid to top civil servants but not so large as those prevailing in private industry. Initiative would also be stimulated by allowing these public managers fullest autonomy in the conduct of their concerns, by freeing them from minor political intervention, and by providing suitable public recognition for outstandingly successful administrators.

Centralized administration of a large industry, whether under private or public control, is apt to involve inefficiencies: inadequate supervision of subordinates, the dulling of initiative in the lower ranks of the administrative hierarchy, timidity, nepotism, petty theft and even large-scale plundering. One can hope only to minimize them by the development of adequate and recognized criteria for promotion, regular independent audits of the corporation's activities, inculcation of the spirit of public service, and other measures. The important thing is to realize that these types of inefficiency arise whenever the pressure of competition is removed, that they are prevalent in business as well as in government, and that they can probably be attacked more effectively in a public enterprise than in a private monopoly.

The directors of public corporations, too, would be subjected to pressure by organized interest-groups. The dairy farmers' coöperative would come to the municipal milk plant demanding higher prices for fluid milk, while the wagon-drivers' union would exert continuous pressure for increases in wage rates. The problem of fortifying the directors against such demands and securing adequate representation of the consumer interest would not be easily solved.

When these difficulties have been taken into account, public operation of monopolized industries still appears to have decisive advantages. Restriction of output in order to maximize profits could be largely eliminated, and industrial policy could be oriented toward the provision of capacity output at mininum cost. Public operation of certain key industries would also facilitate other lines of public policy. Control of milk and perhaps of bread would aid in providing the necessaries of life to those in need. Control of steel and cement would decrease the cost of public works, and would greatly assist the government in combatting depression. Control of nickel, chemicals and explosives would aid materially in problems of foreign policy and national defense.

ADDITIONAL PROPOSALS

The remaining suggestions may be discussed much more briefly. They contemplate (1) removal of the support now given to combines and monopolies by the tariff and patent laws, (2) provision of more adequate information to consumers, (3) repeal of part of the existing price-fixing legislation, (4) more careful regulation of new securities issues, and (5) amendment of the British North America Act.

It was pointed out in Chapter VII that tariff protection tends to increase the price which a combine can charge, and that patents have in some cases been used to exclude competitors and regulate production. A partial remedy for these abuses is already available. The Combines Investigation Act provides that if the operations of a combine have been facilitated by customs duties the Governor in Council may direct that the duties be reduced or eliminated, while if a patent has been misused the Minister of Justice may apply to the Exchequer Court for a judgment revoking the patent.[11] These provisions have

[11] Combines Investigation Act, Sections 29–30.

never been used, possibly because the Act has thus far been applied largely to industries which do not rely on patents or tariff protection. In future cases involving manufacturing industries, the applicability of these remedies should be seriously considered, and the Commissioner's report should contain recommendations on this point. The Tariff Board, too, might well give increased attention to the extent of domestic competition in framing its recommendations for tariff changes.

Imperfect knowledge of commodities by consumers renders the process of competition very haphazard. Superior products do not necessarily drive out inferior goods, and consumers do not necessarily derive the greatest satisfaction from their incomes. The Dominion already has in the National Research Council a well-equipped research staff with considerable experience in the testing of commodities. The gasoline grades recommended by the Council are now in effect in several provinces. This sort of work should be greatly expanded. Development of minimum standards for the more important consumer goods, award of the trade-mark "Canada Standard" to goods meeting these minimum requirements,[12] and education of consumers to the significance of this mark would do much to remove inferior goods from the market. A second and more difficult step would be the development and enforcement of grading systems for important products which are susceptible of being graded. Detailed analysis of the relative merits of particular brands is perhaps too capable of abuse to be entrusted to a government agency, but voluntary organizations of consumers for this purpose should be given every encouragement.

Price-fixing legislation should in general be avoided. The purpose of price-fixing schemes is usually to protect investments threatened by excess capacity and falling prices, though this

[12] This power is now possessed by the Dominion Trade and Industry Commission (i. e., the Tariff Board) and has been upheld by the Privy Council. No provision has been made for its administration, however, and it has remained a dead letter.

purpose is cloaked by attempting to identify the interests of producers with the public interest. The consumer interest, however, often requires that producers shall suffer losses and failure. It is not suggested that all of the existing control legislation should be repealed. Controlled marketing of perishable agricultural products seems desirable in order to prevent waste and to ensure fair treatment of growers by dealers. Care should be taken, however, to see that control is not used to restrict output and raise prices at the expense of consumers. The consumer interest is by no means adequately safeguarded in existing provincial marketing acts.[13] The attempt of British Columbia to enforce lower prices on coal and gasoline producers also seems a desirable experiment. At the least, much valuable statistical information will be accumulated by the Control Board. At best, the technique may prove useful in dealing with that difficult group of industries controlled by a few powerful producers.[14]

Some agency should be charged with ensuring that new security issues are supported by actual assets rather than by the

[13] It is unfortunately difficult if not impossible to protect consumers merely by inserting additional clauses into the law. An attempt was made in the United States under the N. R. A. to protect the consumer interest through a Consumer Advisory Board, and through consumer representatives on individual code authorities. These representatives were in most cases able and well-intentioned. They had no political pressure group behind them, however, and their opinions and complaints tended to be ignored. The basic difficulty thus appears to be the lack of consumer organization and education. Until much more progress has been made in this field, producer groups will probably continue to have their way before legislatures and administrative bodies.

[14] The argument that price fixing is usually bad should not be taken as meaning that competition is always desirable. It is quite possible that competition may lead to extravagantly high production costs, rapid depletion of natural resources, and other consequences harmful to consumers. Where this occurs, however, the proper remedy is not a private cartel with (usually nominal) government supervision, but rather, as suggested above, outright public operation.

optimism of promoters. This function might be performed either by an enlarged and revivified Companies Branch of the State Department or by a separate commission. It is possible that stricter scrutiny at Ottawa would lead more companies to seek provincial charters, but this might be offset by the added prestige which Dominion incorporation would carry. It must be realized, of course, that regulation of security issues at this time locks the stable door much too late. The corporate structure of the country has now settled down into relatively permanent form and it is unlikely that merger movements in future will attain the proportions of the twenties. But if the water cannot be squeezed from previous issues, at least additional inflation of capital accounts may be prevented.

Finally, it is possible that some of the measures proposed above may encounter judicial disapproval as invasions of "property and civil rights in the provinces." In this event, or even in anticipation of the event, the British North America Act should be amended in such a way as to enlarge and clarify the federal power of economic regulation. Whether this should be done by enlarging the language of the trade and commerce clause, or by inserting limitations into the property and civil rights clause, or by some other method is a matter for legal draftsmen to determine.[15]

[15] It will be seen that the writer agrees in general with the position taken by Professor V. W. Bladen in a paper read in 1932: "Where the combine is facilitated by legal privilege, e. g., the tariff or patent rights, abolish the privilege. Where the combine arises without such legal assistance accept it as inevitable, and probably advantageous, but be prepared to regulate and control it. . . . As to the nature of the control, I think it would probably have to be adapted to each special case." Four types of control were suggested: public ownership, special boards to control the prices of necessaries of life, excess profits taxation, and education of consumers. (Proceedings of the Canadian Political Science Association, 1932.) The writer would be rather more optimistic than Professor Bladen concerning the possibility of maintaining or restoring competition, rather more pessimistic concerning the feasibility of control by special boards.

THE PROBLEM OF POWER

The measures outlined above would appear to be in the public interest. They run strongly against the trend of recent legislation, however, and would undoubtedly encounter violent opposition in Parliament and elsewhere. The root of this dilemma lies in the domination of the processes of government by business groups whose interest, as Adam Smith acutely perceived, "is never exactly the same with that of the public, who have generally an interest to deceive and even to oppress the public, and who accordingly have, upon many occasions, both deceived and oppressed it." [16] While this domination continues, measures which strike at the sources of business profits cannot expect to succeed. Precisely because they are framed in the general interest they are bound to encounter the enmity of producer groups bent on stabilizing their individual positions though they shake the economy to pieces in the process.

The public is not only poorly organized to protect its interests, but is largely ignorant of those interests. Most people at present know little and can learn little about economic affairs. The influence of the controlled press is bent toward convincing the public that "what helps business helps Canada," and conversely that every attempt to control business is an attack on individual liberty and democratic government. Over against this skilful and pervasive propaganda can be set the small but growing efforts of independent educational forces. University and high school courses in the social sciences, adult education associations, and consumer organizations can all make a contribution in this field. Much may be expected also from the development of trade unions and independent political parties, which have played so great an educational rôle in other countries. On the growth of these forces in Canada the solution of these and other pressing problems may eventually depend.

[16] *The Wealth of Nations*, Book I, ch. XI.

APPENDIX

DOMINION STATUTES DEALING WITH COMBINATION

SECTIONS 496, 497 AND 498 OF THE CRIMINAL CODE OF CANADA

Conspiracy in Restraint of Trade

496. A conspiracy in restraint of trade is an agreement between two or more persons to do or procure to be done any unlawful act in restraint of trade.

497. The purposes of a trade union are not, by reason merely that they are in restraint of trade, unlawful within the meaning of the last preceding section.

498. Every one is guilty of an indictable offence and liable to a penalty not exceeding four thousand dollars and not less than two hundred dollars, or two years' imprisonment, or, if a corporation, is liable to a penalty not exceeding ten thousand dollars, and not less than one thousand dollars, who conspires, combines, agrees or arranges with any other person, or with any railway, steamship, steamboat or transportation company,

(*a*) to unduly limit the facilities for transporting, producing, manufacturing, supplying, storing or dealing in any article or commodity which may be a subject of trade or commerce; or

(*b*) to restrain or injure trade or commerce in relation to any such article or commodity; or

(*c*) to unduly prevent, limit, or lessen the manufacture or production of any such article or commodity, or to unreasonably enhance the price thereof; or

(*d*) to unduly prevent or lessen competition in the production, manufacture, purchase, barter, sale, transportation or supply of any such article or commodity, or in the price of insurance upon person or property.

2. Nothing in this section shall be construed to apply to combinations of workmen or employees for their own reasonable protection as such workmen or employees.

An Act to provide for the Investigation of Combines, Monopolies, Trusts and Mergers

Chapter 26 of the Revised Statutes of Canada, 1927

As amended by Chapter 54 of the Statutes of 1935 and by Chapter 23 of the Statutes of 1937

SHORT TITLE

1. This Act may be cited as the Combines Investigation Act.

INTERPRETATION

2. In this Act, unless the context otherwise requires,

(1) "Combine" means a combination having relation to any commodity which may be the subject of trade or commerce, of two or more persons by way of actual or tacit contract, agreement or arrangement having or designed to have the effect of

(*a*) limiting facilities for transporting, producing, manufacturing, supplying, storing or dealing, or

(*b*) preventing, limiting or lessening manufacture or production, or

(*c*) fixing a common price or a resale price, or a common rental, or a common cost of storage or transportation, or

(*d*) enhancing the price, rental or cost of article, rental, storage or transportation, or

(*e*) preventing or lessening competition in, or substantially controlling within any particular area or district or generally, production, manufacture, purchase, barter, sale, storage, transportation, insurance or supply, or

(*f*) otherwise restraining or injuring trade or commerce;

or a merger, trust or monopoly; which combination, merger, trust or monopoly has operated or is likely to operate to the detriment or against the interest of the public, whether consumers, producers or others.

(2) "Commissioner" means the Commissioner of the Combines Investigation Act appointed as hereinafter provided.

(3) "Corporation" includes "Company."

(4) "Merger, trust or monopoly" means one or more persons

(*a*) who has or have purchased, leased or otherwise acquired any control over or interest in the whole or part of the business of another; or (*b*) who either substantially or completely control, throughout any particular area or district in Canada or throughout Canada the class or species of business in which he is or they are engaged;

and extends and applies only to the business of manufacturing, producing, transporting, purchasing, supplying, storing or dealing in commodities which may be the subject of trade or commerce: Provided that this subsection shall not be construed or applied so as to limit or impair any right or interest derived under *The Patent Act, 1935*, or under any other statute of Canada.

(5) "Minister" means the Minister of Labour.

(6) "Special commissioner" means a temporary commissioner appointed as hereinafter provided for the purpose of conducting an investigation.

3. No proceedings under this Act shall be deemed invalid by reason of any defect of form or any technical irregularity.

4. Nothing in this Act shall be construed to apply to combinations of workmen or employees for their own reasonable protection as such workmen or employees.

ADMINISTRATION

5. (1) The Governor in Council may appoint an officer to be known as the Commissioner of the Combines Investigation Act.

(2) The Commissioner shall perform the duties and exercise the powers conferred upon him under this Act and shall report directly to the Minister as required by this Act.

(3) The Commissioner shall, before entering upon his duties, take and subscribe before the Clerk of the Privy Council, and shall file in the office of the said Clerk, an oath of office in the following form: —

> "I do solemnly swear that I will faithfully, truly and impartially, and to the best of my judgment, skill and ability, execute the powers and trusts reposed in me as Commissioner of the Combines Investigation Act. So help me God."

(4) The Commissioner shall be paid such salary as may be from time to time fixed and allowed by the Governor in Council.

6. (1) An Assistant Commissioner of the Combines Investigation Act may be appointed in the manner authorized by law.

(2) When the Commissioner is absent or unable to act, or when so authorized by the Commissioner with respect to any investigation

or matter, the Assistant Commissioner, or, if he also is at the same time absent or unable to act, another officer designated by the Minister, may and shall exercise the powers and perform the duties of the Commissioner.

7. (1) The Governor in Council may appoint, from time to time, one or more persons to be special commissioners under this Act.

(2) It shall be the duty of a special commissioner to conduct an investigation into and concerning any alleged combine indicated in the Order in Council signifying his appointment.

(3) Every special commissioner shall have, with respect to and for the duration of the investigation which he is appointed to conduct, the powers which are conferred on the Commissioner in sections fourteen to twenty-four, both inclusive, of this Act; and wherever the word "Commissioner" occurs in sections fourteen to twenty-four, both inclusive, and thirty-three to thirty-six, both inclusive, of this Act, it shall be deemed to include the words "special commissioner."

(4) The exercise of any of the powers herein conferred upon special commissioners shall not be held to limit or qualify the powers by this Act conferred upon the Commissioner.

8. (1) The Commissioner may, with the approval of the Governor in Council, employ such temporary, technical and special assistants as may be required to meet the special conditions that may arise in carrying out the provisions of this Act.

(2) Any technical or special assistant or other qualified person employed under this Act shall, when so authorized or deputed by the Commissioner, inquire into any matter within the scope of this Act as may be directed by the Commissioner.

9. (1) Any special commissioner and any temporary, technical and special assistants employed by the Commissioner shall be paid for their services and expenses as may be determined by the Governor in Council.

(2) The remuneration and expenses of the Commissioner and of any special commissioner and of the temporary, technical and special assistants employed by the Commissioner, and of any counsel instructed by the Minister of Justice under this Act, shall be paid out of such appropriations as are provided by Parliament to defray the cost of administering this Act.

(3) The *Civil Service Act* and other Acts relating to the Civil Service, insofar as applicable, shall, except as otherwise provided in

section five of this Act, apply to the Commissioner and to all other permanent employees under this Act.

10. It shall be the duty of the Commissioner

(*a*) to receive and register, and, subject to the provisions of this Act, to deal with applications for investigation of alleged combines;

(*b*) to bring at once to the Minister's attention every such application;

(*c*) to conduct such correspondence with the applicants and all other persons as may be necessary;

(*d*) to call for such returns and to make such inquiries as he may consider to be necessary in order that he may thoroughly examine into the matter brought to his attention by any application for an investigation;

(*e*) to make reports from time to time to the Minister;

(*f*) to keep a register in which shall be entered the particulars of all applications, inquiries, reports and recommendations, and safely to keep all applications, records of inquiries, correspondence, returns, reports, recommendations, evidence and documents relating to applications and proceedings conducted by the Commissioner and when so required to transmit all or any of such to the Minister;

(*g*) to supply to any persons on request information as to this Act or any regulations thereunder;

(*h*) generally to do all such things and take all such proceedings as may be required in the performance of his duties under this Act or under any regulations made hereunder.

APPLICATIONS

11. (1) Any six persons, British subjects, resident in Canada, of the full age of twenty-one years, who are of the opinion that a combine exists, may apply in writing to the Commissioner for an investigation of such alleged combine, and shall place before the Commissioner the evidence on which such opinion is based.

(2) The application shall be accompanied by a statement in the form of a solemn or statutory declaration showing

(*a*) the names and addresses of the applicants, and at their election the name and address of any one of their number, or of any attorney, solicitor or counsel, whom they may, for the purpose of receiving any communication to be made pursuant to this Act, have authorized to represent them;

(*b*) the nature of the alleged combine and the names of the persons believed to be concerned therein and privy thereto;

(*c*) the manner in which, and where possible the extent to which, the alleged combine is believed to operate or to be about to operate to the detriment or against the interest of the public whether consumers, producers or others.

INVESTIGATIONS

12. The Commissioner shall on application made under the last preceding section, or on direction by the Minister, cause an inquiry to be made into all such matters with respect to the said alleged combine as he shall consider necessary to enquire into with the view of determining whether a combine exists or is being formed.

13. (1) If, after such preliminary inquiry as the Commissioner deems the circumstances warrant, the Commissioner is of the opinion that the application is frivolous or vexatious, or does not justify further inquiry, the Commissioner may decide that no further inquiry is justified and shall inform the applicant of the decision giving the grounds therefor.

(2) The Commissioner shall thereupon make a report in writing to the Minister showing the inquiry made, the information obtained and his conclusions.

(3) On written request of the applicants or on his own motion, the Minister may review the decision of the Commissioner under this section, and may, if in his opinion the circumstances warrant, instruct the Commissioner to make further investigation.

14. The Commissioner may at any time in the course of an inquiry, by notice in writing, require any person, and in the case of a corporation any officer of such corporation, to make and render unto the Commissioner, within a time stated in such notice, or from time to time, a written return under oath or affirmation showing in detail such information with respect to the business of the person named in the notice as is by the notice required, and such person or officer shall make and render unto the Commissioner, precisely as required a written return under oath or affirmation showing in detail the information required; and, without restricting the generality of the foregoing, the Commissioner may require a full disclosure of all contracts or agreements which the person, named in the notice, may have at any time entered into with any other person, touching or concerning the business of the said person so named in the notice.

15. Repealed.

16. The Commissioner shall have authority to investigate the business, or any part thereof, of any person who is or is believed by the Commissioner to be a member of any combine or a party or privy thereto, and to authorize a representative on his behalf to enter and examine the premises, books, papers and records of such person.

17. Every person who is in possession or control of any such business, premises, books, papers or records as are referred to in the last preceding section shall give and afford to the Commissioner admission and access thereto whenever and as often as demanded.

18. All provisions of the *Inquiries Act* not repugnant to the provisions of this Act shall apply to any inquiry or investigation under this Act, and the Commissioner shall have all the powers of a commissioner appointed under the *Inquiries Act*, except in so far as any such powers may be inconsistent with the provisions of this Act.

19. No person shall in any manner impede or prevent or attempt to impede or prevent any investigation, examination or inquiry under this Act.

20. All books, papers, records or things produced before the Commissioner, whether voluntarily or in pursuance of an order, may be inspected by the Commissioner and also by such persons as the Commissioner directs, and copies thereof may be made by or at the instance of the Commissioner.

21. Repealed.

22. (1) The Commissioner may order that any person resident or present in Canada be examined upon oath before, or make production of books, papers, records or articles to, the Commissioner or before or to any other person named for the purpose by the order of the Commissioner and may make such orders as seem to the Commissioner to be proper for securing the attendance of such witness and his examination, and the production by him of books, papers, records or articles, and the use of evidence so obtained, and may otherwise exercise, for the enforcement of such orders or punishment for disobedience thereof, all powers that are exercised by any superior court in Canada for the enforcement of subpoenas to witnesses or punishment of disobedience thereof.

(2) Any person summoned before the Commissioner shall be competent and may be compelled to give evidence as a witness.

(3) Every person who is summoned and duly attends as a witness shall be entitled to an allowance for attendance and travelling expenses according to the scale in force with respect to witnesses in civil suits in the superior courts of the province in which the inquiry is being conducted.

(4) The Minister may issue commissions to take evidence in another country, and may make all proper orders for the purpose and for the return and use of the evidence so obtained.

(5) Orders to witnesses and all other orders, process or proceedings shall be signed by a commissioner.

23. (1) The Commissioner may accept or require evidence upon affidavit or written affirmation, in every case in which it seems to him proper to do so.

(2) The Commissioner and all persons authorized to administer oaths to be used in any of the superior courts of any province may administer oaths in such province to be used in applications, matters or proceedings before the Commissioner.

(3) All persons authorized to administer oaths within or out of Canada, in or concerning any proceedings had or to be had in the Supreme Court of Canada or in the Exchequer Court of Canada, may administer oaths in or concerning any application, matter or proceeding before the Commissioner.

24. No person shall be excused from attending and giving evidence and producing books, papers, or records, in obedience to the order of the Commissioner, on the ground that the oral evidence or documents required of him may tend to criminate him or subject him to any proceeding or penalty, but no such oral evidence so required shall be used or receivable against such person in any criminal proceedings thereafter instituted against him, other than a prosecution for perjury in giving evidence upon such investigation, inquiry, cause or proceeding; nor shall any such documents be used or receivable in any criminal proceedings except proceedings under this Act or under section four hundred and ninety-eight of the *Criminal Code.*

25. The proceedings before the Commissioner and any special commissioner shall be conducted in private, but the Commissioner may order that all or any portion of the proceedings shall be conducted in public. All preliminary investigations shall be conducted in private.

26. Whenever in the opinion of the Commissioner the public interest so requires, the Commissioner may apply to the Minister of Justice to instruct counsel to conduct the investigation before the Commissioner and upon such application the Minister of Justice may instruct counsel accordingly.

REPORTS

27. (1) The Commissioner at the conclusion of every investigation which he conducts shall make a report in writing and without delay transmit it to the Minister. Such report shall set out fully the conclusions reached, the action, if any, taken, and any other material which may be required by regulation under this Act.

(2) The Commissioner shall at the same time deliver into the custody from whence they came, if not already delivered, all books, papers, records and other documents in his possession as evidence relating to the investigation, but before doing so the Commissioner may extract from such documents and certify as true copies such relevant parts thereof as he may deem to be necessary for any purpose of this Act, whereafter such parts, so certified shall have and be accorded in all courts the same probative force as the equivalent parts of the originals of which they are copies.

(3) Every special commissioner at the conclusion of the investigation which he conducts shall make a report in writing which he shall sign and transmit to the Commissioner, together with the evidence taken at the investigation, certified by the special commissioner, and all documents and papers relating to the investigation remaining in his custody; and the Commissioner shall without delay transmit the report to the Minister.

(4) The Minister may call for an interim report at any time, and it shall be the duty of the Commissioner or special commissioner, as the case may be, whenever thereunto required by the Minister, to render an interim report setting out the action taken, the evidence obtained and any conclusions reached at the date thereof.

(5) Any report of the Commissioner or of a special commissioner, other than an interim report or a report of a preliminary inquiry under section thirteen of this Act, shall within fifteen days after its receipt by the Minister be made public, unless the Commissioner states in writing to the Minister that he believes the public interest would be better served by withholding publication, in which case the Minister

may decide whether the report, either in whole or in part, shall be made public.

28. The Minister may publish and supply copies of any report in such manner and upon such terms as he deems proper.

REMEDIES

29. Whenever, from or as a result of an investigation under the provisions of this Act, or from or as a result of a judgment of the Supreme Court or Exchequer Court of Canada or of any superior court, or circuit, district or county court in Canada, it appears to the satisfaction of the Governor in Council that with regard to any article of commerce, there exists any combine to promote unduly the advantage of manufacturers or dealers at the expense of the public, and if it appears to the Governor in Council that such disadvantage to the public is facilitated by the duties of custom imposed on the article, or on any like article, the Governor in Council may direct either that such article be admitted into Canada free of duty, or that the duty thereon be reduced to such amount or rate as will, in the opinion of the Governor in Council, give the public the benefit of reasonable competition.

30. Repealed.

31. (1) Whenever in the opinion of the Commissioner an offence has been committed against any of the provisions of this Act, the Commissioner may remit to the attorney general of any province within which such alleged offence shall have been committed, for such action as such attorney general may be pleased to institute because of the conditions appearing,

(*a*) any return or returns which may have been made or rendered pursuant to this Act and are in the possession of the Commissioner and relevant to such alleged offence; and

(*b*) the evidence taken on any investigation by the Commissioner or by any special commissioner and the report of the Commissioner or special commissioner.

(2) If within three months after remission aforesaid, or within such shorter period as the Governor in Council shall decide, no such action shall have been taken by or at the instance of the attorney general of the province as to the Governor in Council the case seems in the public interest to require, the Attorney General of Canada may on the relation of any person who is resident in Canada and of

the full age of twenty-one years permit an information to be laid against such person or persons as in the opinion of the Attorney General of Canada shall have been guilty of an offence against any of the provisions of this Act.

(3) The Minister of Justice may instruct counsel to attend on behalf of the Minister at all proceedings consequent on any information being so laid.

OFFENCES AND PENALTIES

32. (1) Every one is guilty of an indictable offence and liable to a penalty not exceeding ten thousand dollars or to two years imprisonment, or if a corporation to a penalty not exceeding twenty-five thousand dollars, who is a party or privy to or knowingly assists in the formation or operation of a combine within the meaning of this Act.

(2) No prosecution for any offence under this section shall be commenced, otherwise than at the instance of the Attorney General of Canada or of the attorney general of a province.

[The next six sections provide additional penalties for refusal to give evidence, refusal to make written returns, or impeding an investigation in any other way.]

PROCEDURE

39. When an indictment is found against any person for any offence against this Act the accused shall have the option to be tried before the judge presiding at the court at which the indictment is found, or the judge presiding at any subsequent sitting of such court, or at any court where the indictment comes on for trial, without the intervention of a jury; and in the event of such option being exercised the proceedings subsequent thereto shall be regulated in so far as may be applicable by Part XVIII of the *Criminal Code*, respecting speedy trials of indictable offences.

REGULATIONS

40. (1) The Governor in Council may make such regulations, not inconsistent with this Act, as to him seem necessary for carrying out the provisions of this Act and for the efficient administration thereof.

(2) Such regulations shall be published in the *Canada Gazette*, and upon being so published they shall have the same force as if they formed part of this Act.

(3) The regulations shall be laid before both Houses of Parliament within fifteen days after such publication, if Parliament be then

sitting, and if Parliament is not then sitting, then within fifteen days after the opening of the next session thereof.

41. The Commissioner shall, annually, report to the Minister his proceedings under this Act and he shall lay such report before Parliament if it be then sitting, and, if it be not then sitting, within the first fifteen days of its then next session.

42. (1) Notwithstanding anything in this Act, neither the Commissioner nor any special commissioner nor any other person shall have power to compel the attendance of any witness or the production of any book, paper, records or article, or the examination of any person under oath, or have power to exercise for the enforcement of any order made by such Commissioner, special commissioner or person or for punishment on account of disobedience of such order the powers that are exercised by superior courts for the enforcement of subpoenas to witnesses or punishment of disobedience thereof, unless and until on the application of the Minister (which shall be heard and determined *ex parte*) either the President of the Exchequer Court of Canada or the Chief Commissioner of the Dominion Trade and Industry Commission shall have certified, as either of them may, that it is fit and proper that the action mentioned in the application should be taken: Provided that when any investigation under this Act is proceeding in any province and the Commissioner or special commissioner is desirous of exercising power to commit to prison or otherwise penalize pursuant to this Act any person whether for contempt or otherwise, the application may be made by the Commissioner or special commissioner upon reasonable notice to the person concerned, to a judge of the Supreme or Superior Court of the Province, who shall for the purposes of the application have the powers which by this section are conferred upon the President of the Exchequer Court and the Chief Commissioner of the Dominion Trade and Industry Commission.

(2) The provisions of this section which relate to the Chief Commissioner of the Dominion Trade and Industry Commission shall apply only whilst such Chief Commissioner is a barrister of one of the provinces of Canada of at least ten years standing.

(3) Such President, Chief Commissioner and judge, respectively, may, before granting such certificate, require the applicant to secure and subsequently produce to him any further evidence or proof of relevant circumstances as he shall deem to be necessary.

The following section was enacted as section 28 of The Combines Investigation Act Amendment Act, 1935: —

No person shall be charged with, tried for or convicted of an offence against this Act, by the same information, upon the same evidence or at the same time as he is charged with, tried for or convicted of an offence against section four hundred and ninety-eight of the *Criminal Code*. 1935, c. 54, s. 28.

SECTION 498A OF THE CRIMINAL CODE OF CANADA

Price Discrimination

*498*A. Every person engaged in trade or commerce or industry is guilty of an indictable offence and liable to a penalty not exceeding one thousand dollars or to one month's imprisonment, or, if a corporation, to a penalty not exceeding five thousand dollars, who

(*a*) is a party or privy to, or assists in, any transaction of sale which discriminates, to his knowledge, against competitors of the purchaser in that any discount, rebate or allowance is granted to the purchaser over and above any discount, rebate or allowance available at the time of such transaction to the aforesaid competitors in respect of a sale of goods of like quality and quantity;

The provisions of this paragraph shall not, however, prevent a co-operative society returning to producers or consumers, or a co-operative wholesale society returning to its constituent retail members, the whole or any part of the net surplus made in its trading operations in proportion to purchases made from or sales to the society;

(*b*) engages in a policy of selling goods in any area of Canada at prices lower than those exacted by such seller elsewhere in Canada, for the purpose of destroying competition or eliminating a competitor in such part of Canada;

(*c*) engages in a policy of selling goods at prices unreasonably low for the purpose of destroying competition or eliminating a competitor.

An Act to establish a Dominion Trade and Industry Commission

1. This Act may be cited as *The Dominion Trade and Industry Commission Act, 1935.*

DOMINION TRADE AND INDUSTRY COMMISSION

3. (1) There shall be a Commission to be known as the Dominion Trade and Industry Commission consisting of three Commissioners, of whom one shall be the Chief Commissioner and another the Assistant Chief Commissioner.

(2) The members for the time being of the Tariff Board shall, by virtue of holding office as members of the said Board and by virtue of this Act, be the Commissioners, and the Chairman and the Vice-Chairman of the said Board shall be the Chief Commissioner and Assistant Chief Commissioner respectively.

(3) Each Commissioner shall hold office only during such time as he continues to hold office as a member of the Tariff Board.

. . . .

PRICE AND PRODUCTION AGREEMENTS

14. (1) In any case where the Commission, after full investigation under the *Combines Investigation Act*, is unanimously of opinion that wasteful or demoralizing competition exists in any specific industry, and that agreements between the persons engaged in the industry to modify such competition by controlling and regulating prices or production would not result in injury to or undue restraint of trade or be detrimental to or against the interest of the public, or where such agreements exist and in the unanimous opinion of the Commission but for their existence wasteful or demoralizing competition would exist in any specific industry, the Commission may so advise the Governor in Council and recommend that certain agreements be approved.

(2) The Governor in Council may, if of opinion that the conclusions of the Commission are well founded, approve of any such agreement, and shall make regulations requiring the Commission to determine from time to time whether the agreement is resulting in injury to or undue restraint of trade or is detrimental to the public interest.

(3) The Commission shall require persons engaged in the industry to furnish full information relating to operations within the industry under the agreement and may at any time, of its own motion and in its absolute discretion, advise the Governor in Council to rescind the approval of the agreement and the Governor in Council may rescind the approval accordingly.

(4) In any case where the Governor in Council has approved an agreement under this section, no prosecution of a party to such agreement shall be instituted under the *Combines Investigation Act* or

under sections four hundred and ninety-eight and four hundred and ninety-eight A or any other relevant section of the *Criminal Code* for an offence arising in the performance of such agreement, except with the consent of the Commission. [Held invalid by the Supreme Court of Canada, June, 1936.]

COMMODITY STANDARDS

15. (1) The Commission shall be charged with responsibility to recommend the prosecution of offences against acts of the Parliament of Canada and regulations thereunder, relating to commodity standards and the Attorney General of Canada may require the Director of Public Prosecutions to institute criminal proceedings for the punishment of any such offence.

(2) The Commission may,—

(*a*) study, investigate, report and advise upon any question relating to commodity standards, the grading of commodities and the protection of consumers generally;

(*b*) inquire and hear representatives of industry and trade and of consumers as to the desirability of establishing commodity standards and grades for any commodity and report thereon to the Minister.

National Research Council

16. In addition to its powers and duties under any other statute or law, the National Research Council shall, on the request of the Commission, from time to time,—

(*a*) study, investigate, report and advise upon all matters relating to commodity standards;

(*b*) prepare draft specifications of commodity standards for any commodity or grade, and recommend methods of designating such grade;

(*c*) analyze and report upon any commodity as to its quality, properties and content, and as to whether and to what extent it conforms to the requirements of any recognized or generally accepted standard.

17. (1) The National Research Council shall, in respect of any commodity forwarded to it by the Commission or the Director of Public Prosecutions, report

(*a*) the ingredients of such commodity, in so far as such information may be necessary to the proper use of the commodity;

(*b*) any adulterants and harmful, injurious or deleterious substances the commodity may be found to contain;

(*c*) its quality and probable performance and efficiency; and

(*d*) whether it conforms to any recognized or generally accepted standard and specification;

and if adequate information to answer the inquiry is not already available, the National Research Council shall analyze or test the commodity.

(2) The report of the National Research Council upon any analysis or test made under the provisions of this section shall not be used for advertising or commercial purposes in any way; and any person who contravenes the provisions of this subsection shall be guilty of an offence and liable upon summary conviction, for each such offense, to a penalty not exceeding one hundred dollars.

(3) No action or other proceedings may be instituted against the National Research Council or any officer or employee of the Council, in respect of any advice, information or report given or made in good faith under this Act or any other Act of the Parliament of Canada.

"Canada Standard"

18. (1) Notwithstanding anything contained in *The Unfair Competition Act, 1932*, or any other statute or law, the words "Canada Standard" or initials "C.S." shall be a national trademark and the exclusive property in and the right to the use of such trademark is hereby declared to be vested in His Majesty in the right of the Dominion of Canada, subject to the provisions of this Act.

(2) Such national trademark, as applied to any commodity pursuant to the provisions of this Act or any other Act of the Parliament of Canada, shall constitute a representation that such commodity conforms to the requirements of a specification of a commodity standard for such commodity or class of commodity established under the provisions of any Act of the Parliament of Canada.

19. (1) Any producer or manufacturer or dealer or merchant in Canada may apply the national trademark "Canada Standard" or initials "C.S.," to any commodity produced or manufactured or sold by him or to the covering thereof, in such manner as the Commission may by regulation prescribe, under and subject to the following conditions: —

(*a*) Such commodity shall conform to the requirements of a specification of a commodity standard for such commodity or class of commodity established under the provisions of any Act of the Parliament of Canada;

(*b*) Where grade designations, whether numerical or alphabetical or special, have been established under the provisions of any Act of the Parliament of Canada for various qualities of such commodity, the appropriate grade designation for each quality of such commodity shall be conspicuously applied to the commodity, or on the covering thereof, in association with the words "Canada Standard" or initials "C.S." in such form as the Commission may by regulation prescribe: Provided that the Commission may by regulation prescribe a list of specific commodities to which, in its opinion, it is impossible to apply this paragraph, and this paragraph shall not apply to any commodity appearing in such list.

(2) Every person who applies the national trademark "Canada Standard" or initials "C.S.," to any commodity in violation of the conditions hereinbefore provided shall be guilty of an offense and liable upon indictment, or upon summary conviction, to a penalty, for each and every such offence, not exceeding five thousand dollars in the case of a corporation, and not exceeding one thousand dollars in the case of an individual and in addition in the case of an individual to imprisonment for any term not exceeding six months.

UNFAIR TRADE PRACTICES

20. The Commission shall receive complaints respecting unfair trade practices and may investigate the same and, either before or after an investigation, if of opinion that the practice complained of constitutes an offence against any Dominion law prohibiting unfair trade practices, may communicate the complaint and such evidence, if any, in support thereof as is in the possession of the Commission to the Attorney General of Canada with a recommendation that all persons who are parties or privies to such offence be prosecuted for violation of the applicable Act. The Attorney General of Canada, if he concurs in such recommendation, may refer it with such complaint and such evidence, if any, either to the Director of Public Prosecutions or to the Attorney General of the province within which the offence is alleged to have been committed for such action as may seem to be appropriate in the circumstances.

DIRECTOR OF PROSECUTIONS

21. (1) The Governor in Council may appoint an officer to be called the Director of Public Prosecutions with a salary not exceeding twelve thousand dollars per annum.

(2) A person appointed as Director of Public Prosecutions shall be a barrister or advocate of at least ten years standing at the bar of any of the provinces of Canada.

(3) The Director of Public Prosecutions shall hold office during good behaviour for a period of ten years from the date of appointment but may be removed for cause at any time by the Governor in Council.

22. It shall be the duty of the Director of Public Prosecutions under the superintendence of the Minister of Justice

(*a*) to institute, at the instance of the Attorney General of Canada criminal proceedings for violation of any of the laws prohibiting unfair trade practices in cases which appear to be of importance or difficulty or in which special circumstances or the refusal or failure of any other person to institute, such proceedings appear to render the action of such Director necessary to secure the due prosecution of an offender;

(*b*) to give such advice or assistance to the Attorney General of any province in connection with the prosecution of offenders against laws prohibiting unfair trade practices as appears necessary to secure the prosecution of such offenders;

(*c*) to assist the Commission in the conduct of any investigation where it is alleged or complained that an offence against any of the laws prohibiting unfair trade practices has been or appears to be about to be committed.

FAIR TRADE CONFERENCES

23. (1) The Commission may from time to time at the instance of the Governor in Council or at the request of representative persons engaged in any industry, or of its own motion, invite persons engaged in such industry to a conference for the purpose of considering the commercial practices prevailing in such industry and determining what practices are unfair or undesirable in the interest of the industry and of any person engaged in such industry and of the general public.

(2) The Commission may make public the general opinion of the conference or the opinion of the Commission as to and trade practice considered to be unfair or undesirable.

CO-OPERATION WITH BOARDS OF TRADE

24. The Commission may co-operate with and assist in any manner in which it deems advisable any board of trade or chamber of commerce in connection with any commercial arbitration being conducted by or under the direction or authority of such board of trade or chamber of commerce.

ECONOMIC INVESTIGATION

25. The Commission shall, when so required by the Governor in Council, study, investigate, report and advise upon questions relating to the general trend of social or economic conditions or to any social or economic problem of Canada, and shall co-operate, when so required, with the Economic Council, established under *The Economic Council of Canada Act, 1935,* in connection with any economic investigation.

GENERAL

26. All the provisions of the *Inquiries Act*, the *Combines Investigation Act* and of the *Tariff Act*, and of any amendment thereto not repugnant to the provisions of this Act shall apply to any inquiry or investigation under this Act and the Commission shall have all the powers of a commissioner appointed under the *Inquiries Act*, except in so far as any such powers may be inconsistent with the provisions of this Act.

27. (1) The Commission shall within fifteen days after making any report, recommendation or finding under this Act make the same public in such manner as seems desirable unless the Commission is unanimously of the opinion that the public interest would not be served by publication or that the public interest would be better served by withholding publication.

(2) Wherever possible the Commission shall with the report, recommendation or finding make public the reasons and the facts upon which the decision is based.

(3) In the case of any agreement or proposed agreement for the control and regulation of prices or production, the Commission shall in such manner as seems desirable make the same public, and shall fix a date at least fifteen days from the date of publication aforesaid for hearing representations by any interested persons whether producers, consumers or others.

28. This Act shall come into force on the first day of October, 1935.

BIBLIOGRAPHY

SELECTED BIBLIOGRAPHY

A. BOOKS AND ARTICLES

Ball, J. A., *Canadian Anti-trust Legislation* (Baltimore, 1934).

Bladen, V. W., "Combines and Public Policy," in *Proceedings of the Canadian Political Science Association*, 1932.

Canadian Bar Review, May, 1935. (Issue devoted to questions of Canadian constitutional law.)

Curtis, C. A., "Resale Price Maintenance," in *Canadian Journal of Economics and Political Science*, August, 1938.

Donald, W. J., *The Canadian Iron and Steel Industry* (Boston and New York, 1915).

Drummond, W. M., "Price Raising in the Dairy Industry," in *Canadian Journal of Economics and Political Science*, November, 1935.

—— "The Marketing of Whole Milk," in *Canadian Journal of Economics and Political Science*, August, 1937.

Elliott, W. Y. (ed.), *International Control in the Non-Ferrous Metals* (New York, 1937).

Finkelman, J., "Combines and Public Policy," in *Proceedings of the Canadian Political Science Association*, 1932.

Forsey, E., *Economic and Social Aspects of the Nova Scotia Coal Industry*, McGill Studies in Economics, No. 5, Toronto, 1927.

Griffin, H. L., "Public Policy in Relation to the Wheat Market," in *Canadian Journal of Economics and Political Science*, August, 1935.

Guthrie, J., *The Newsprint Paper Industry* (Doctoral thesis, Harvard University, 1939, unpublished).

Innis, H. A., and Plumptre, A. F. W. (ed.), *The Canadian Economy and its Problems* (Toronto, 1934).

—— (ed.), *The Dairy Industry in Canada* (New Haven, 1937).

League for Social Reconstruction, *Social Planning for Canada* (Toronto, 1935).

McDougall, J. L., and Plumptre, A. F. W., "The Inflexibility of Canadian Wholesale Prices," in *Canadian Journal of Economics and Political Science*, November, 1938.

MacGibbon, D. A., *The Canadian Grain Trade* (Toronto, 1932).

Marsh, L. C., "The Areand Act," in *Canadian Journal of Economics and Political Science*, August, 1936.

Marshall, H., Southard, F. A., and Taylor, K. W., *Canadian American Industry* (New Haven, 1936).

Patton, H. S., "Canadian Wheat Policy since the World War," in *Canadian Journal of Economics and Political Science*, May, 1937.

Reynolds, L. G., "The Canadian Baking Industry," in *Quarterly Journal of Economics*, August, 1938.

Skelton, O. D., *General Economic History of the Dominion, 1867–1912* (Toronto, 1913).

Stapells, H. G., *The Recent Consolidation Movement in Canadian Industry* (Master's thesis, University of Toronto, 1922, unpublished).

B. PUBLIC DOCUMENTS

Advisory Board on Tariff and Taxation, Record of Public Hearings on Reference No. 2 (Iron and Steel Industry), 1929.

Board of Commerce of Canada, First Annual Report, 1920.

Department of Labour: Report of investigation into an alleged combine in the marketing of fruit and vegetables in western Canada, 1925.

—— Report of investigation into an alleged combine in the retailing of coal in Winnipeg, 1925.

—— Report of investigation into an alleged combine in the marketing of New Brunswick potatoes, 1926.

—— Report of investigation into an alleged combine in the manufacture of bread in Montreal, 1926.

—— Report of investigation into an alleged combine in the marketing of fruit and vegetables in Ontario, 1926.

—— Interim report of the investigation of the Proprietary Articles Trade Association, 1926; final report of the investigation of the P. A. T. A., 1927.

—— Report of investigation into the Amalgamated Builders' Council, 1929.

—— Report of investigation into the Electrical Estimators' Association, 1930.

—— Report of investigation into an alleged combine in the motion picture industry in Canada, 1931.

—— Report of investigation into an alleged combine in the bread baking industry in Canada, 1931.

—— Report of investigation into an alleged combine in the distribution of anthracite coal, 1933. (Published, 1936.)

—— Report of investigation into an alleged combine in the buying of tobacco in Ontario, 1933.

—— Report of investigation into an alleged combine in the distribution of tobacco products, 1938.

—— Report of investigation into an alleged combine in the manufacture of paperboard shipping containers, 1939.

Dominion Bureau of Statistics, Census of Merchandising and Service Establishments, Retail Trade, 1934; Distribution of Sales by Manufacturing Plants, 1934; Wholesale Trade, 1936.

Dominion Bureau of Statistics, A Decade of Retail Trade, 1923–33.

House of Commons, Report of the select committee appointed to investigate and report upon alleged combinations in manufacture, trade and insurance in Canada. Journals of the House of Commons, 1888, Vol. XXII, Appendix 3.

—— Proceedings of the select committee appointed to inquire into the prices charged for lumber in Manitoba, Alberta, and Saskatchewan. Journals of the House of Commons, 1906–07, Vol. XLII, Part II, Appendix 6.

—— Standing Committee on Banking and Commerce, Minutes of the investigation into the manufacture and sale of gasoline, 1932.

—— Standing Committee on Banking and Commerce, Minutes of the investigation into the newsprint industry, 1934.

—— Report of the Special Committee on Farm Implement Prices, 1937.

—— Debates, 1889, Vol. II, p. 1113 ff., p. 1438 ff.; 1891, Vol. II, p. 2553 ff.; 1909–10, Vol. II, p. 2057 ff., Vol. IV, p. 6823 ff.; 1923, Vol. I, p. 989 ff., Vol. III, p. 2520 ff.; 1934, p. 188 ff.; 1935, p. 3472 ff., p. 3506 ff.; 1937, p. 1432 ff.

Special commissioner appointed to investigate the alleged combination of paper mannufacturers and dealers, Report, Sessional Papers, 1902, No. 53.

Royal Commission on the tobacco trade of Canada, Report, Sessional Papers, 1903, No. 62.

Royal Commission on the Cost of Living, Report, 1919, 2 volumes.

Royal Commission on Price Spreads and Mass Buying, Minutes of Proceedings and Evidence, 6 volumes, 1935; Final Report, 1935.

Royal Commission on the Textile Industry, Report, 1936. (See also the brief of Mr. J. C. McRuer, Counsel to the Commission.)

Royal Grain Inquiry Commission, Report, 1938.

Province of Alberta, Royal Commission on the Coal Industry, Report, 1935.

Province of British Columbia, Royal Commission on Coal and Petroleum Products, Report, 1936, 2 volumes.

Province of Quebec, Report on the Dairy Industry in Quebec (prepared for the Quebec Provincial Dairy Commission by Dr. M. C. Bond, 1932).

Province of Saskatchewan, Royal Milk Inquiry Commission, 1933.

Tariff Board of Canada, Reports on Reference Numbers

17 (boiler tubes)
40 (brass, copper and nickel silver commodities)
84 (petroleum products)
91 (automotive industry).

INDEX

INDEX

Bei Fragen zur Produktsicherheit wenden Sie sich bitte an:
If you have any questions regarding product safety,
please contact:

Walter de Gruyter GmbH
Genthiner Straße 13
10785 Berlin
productsafety@degruyterbrill.com